Summer Bridge Middle School™

6th to 7th grade

Written by:

Frankie Long
Dr. Leland Graham

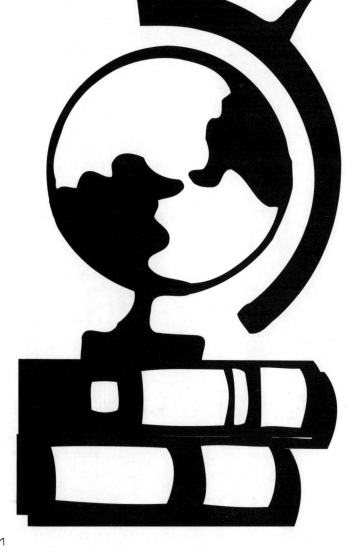

Format & Design by:	Michele D. Van Leeuwen
Cover by:	Nathan Pinnock
Student Entries	
Art:	Katie Fields
Literature:	Erin A. Camp
Product Development Director:	Dante J. Orazzi
Director of Marketing & Creative Development:	George Starks

Summer Bridge Middle School™
6th to 7th Grade

For information, write:
Rainbow Bridge Publishing
332 West Martin Lane, PO Box 571470
Salt Lake City, UT 84157-1470
801-268-8887
www.rainbowbridgepub.com

Many thanks to all involved in the development of this book, including:
Jeff Burk, Brook Call, Danielle Duckworth, Dayna Duckworth,
Dorothy Duckworth, Julie Moore, K'Lee Reynolds

and special thanks to the Van Leeuwen family:
Scott, Grayson, Denise and Tanner.

and to proofreaders:
Jennifer Moore and Marie Ann Bauer

and to typesetters:
John Spilane and Collin Surles

TIME & TECHNOLOGY SECTION DEVELOPMENT
Concept Director: George Starks
Product Development Director: Dante J. Orazzi
Illustrations & Layout: Amanda Sorensen

Printing History:
First Printing 1998
Second Printing 1999
Third Printing 2000

ISBN: 1-887923-09-8

Printed in the United States of America
10 9 8 7 6 5 4 3 2 1

Table of Contents

Creating Partnerships...iv

Summer Bridge Middle School Blueprint for Success..........................vi

Social Skills and Self Worth...viii

Fun & Educational Activities For Parents and Children to Do Together...............x

How to Encourage Children to Voluntarily Pick Up a Book and Read...........xii

Books You'll Love to Read..xiii

Language Arts..1
    6th grade in Review..3
    7th grade in Preview...33

Mathematics..43
    6th grade in Review..44
    7th grade in Preview...75

Social Studies..85
    6th grade in Review..86
    7th grade in Preview..117

Science..127
    6th grade in Review..128
    7th grade in Preview..159

Answer Section..168

Bonus Section
TIME & TECHNOLOGY...TT1-16

Creating Partnerships

Dear Parents,

You're creating a partnership because you've become involved in your child's education. Picking up this workbook clearly shows your child that education is important; something to value. Welcome to Summer Bridge Middle School™!

Let me tell you how this unique series of workbooks came to be. As a parent with school age children, and with the summer quickly approaching, I was concerned the skills they had worked so hard to develop would take a good licking if I didn't do something to support them. In addition, I was apprehensive about their adjustment to school in the fall after three months of playing.

I went to their teachers for help. In speaking with them, other school administrators, and parents, I found I wasn't alone with my concerns. In fact, I was told approximately 80 percent of what children are taught in school is lost within a month, unless that knowledge is reinforced quickly and continuously. I certainly didn't want that to happen to my children.

The search began. I looked all over for appropriate workbooks. Oh, yes…I'm sure you'll agree, if you've ever gone out looking, there are lots to choose from. But they're either too hard or too simple, or usually didn't match what my children learned in school. I wasn't looking for perfection, but it sure seemed that way. I simply wanted to buy something that correlated with the curriculum guidelines from the Department of Education.

I found myself back in front of my children's teachers, asking where I could find such materials. They knew of none. So…

With a team composed of award-winning teachers, informed educators, and concerned parents, we put our own books together. You have in your hands the results of literally thousands of hours of work. All of the activities—over 240 in each book—follow the curriculum guidelines I mentioned earlier. And we've taken it one step further—Summer Bridge Middle School™ has been successfully tested on thousands of children.

And what about my children—or better yet, what about <u>your children?</u>
If you'd like to <u>find them thinking while having fun,</u>
    <u>motivated by a desire to learn,</u>
        <u>confident and excited</u> when the new school year rolls around,
            use *Summer Bridge Middle School*™ as suggested.
Yes, we've got many testimonials to the workbooks' successes.

If you'd like to:

- <u>reach your goal of keeping your child active</u> the smart way,
- <u>successfully bridge the gap over the summer</u>
- with an <u>easy-to-use</u> daily program—
- <u>all without hassles</u>—
- yet, <u>produce</u> the results of <u>busy, happy, and learning children,</u>
  it can now be accomplished.

    It's terrific you're involved. Thank you for your purchase. We at Summer Bridge Publishing would love to hear about your success. Call 1-800-598-1441 with your story.

Best to you,

Michele Van Leeuwen

Michele D. Van Leeuwen
Creator of *Summer Bridge Middle School*™

P.S. Summer Bridge Activities™, preschool through 6th grade (a seven workbook series), and Summer Bridge Middle School™, 6th to 7th and 7th to 8th grades, also <u>work great</u> for those <u>students who are off-track</u> from year-round school, vacations, trips, illness, breaks from school, etc. Try it.

Summer Bridge Middle School™ Blueprint for Success

Books You'll Love to Read

- A suggested list of reading books (xiii).
- The recommended time for reading each day is 1to1-1/2 hours. This amount of time will help you maintain and increase your reading skills.
- It is suggested that you determine the amount of reading time that is best for you. By reading every day you will find success in future challenges.
- Set a goal to develop good reading habits.

Sections of Summer Bridge Middle School™

- There are four sections to Summer Bridge Middle School™.
- Each section is made up of one subject.
  1-Language Arts, 2-Mathematics, 3-Social Studies, 4-Science
- Each section includes 30 pages of Review and 8 pages of Preview.
- Each section becomes progressively more challenging.
- Summer Bridge Middle School prepares students for standardized achievement tests.
- This book is set up to meet your busy and active lifestyle. We recommend you complete one to two pages each day from any one of the four subjects.

Language Arts
6th grade in Review
- Grammar   • Spelling   • Vocabulary • Reading Comprehension   • Proofreading
- Dictionary Skills   • Writing   • Research

7th grade in Preview
- Grammar   • Spelling   • Vocabulary • Reading Comprehension   • Writing

Mathematics
6th grade in Review
- Estimation
- Integers
- Geometry
- Equations
- Graphing
- Statistics
- Probability

7th grade in Preview
- Symmetry
- Surface Area
- Congruency
- Statistics
- Integers
- Equations
- Pythagorean Theorem

Social Studies
6th grade in Review
- Geography
- History
- Economics
- Government
- Charts
- Graphs
- Maps
- Tables

7th grade in Preview
- Geography
- Charts
- Graphs
- Maps
- Tables

Science
6th grade in Review
- Life Science
- Earth Science
- Biological Science
- Physical Science

7th grade in Preview
- Life Science
- Earth Science
- Biological Science
- Physical Science

This section includes some fun experiments, but they could also be dangerous, so remember: **Safety First!** Be sure your work area is clean and safe. Use aprons to protect your clothing. Use safety glasses when necessary. Follow directions carefully. Label all containers. Even after all that, our attorney insisted that we stress the importance of safety by providing you with the following warning:

The science experiments presented in this book should only be performed under adult supervision. Failure to follow the precise instructions in the text may result in bodily injury, property damage or death. The author and publisher cannot be responsible for any injuries or property damage received as a result of deviation from the text or failure to provide adequate adult supervision.

Time and Technology Section
- This section is located in the back of the book after the answer pages.
- Encourage your child to think creatively as he/she completes the exercises and activities.
- Relate stories & examples from your own life to help your child understand the passage of time and how it relates to history and changes in our society.

Social Skills and Self Worth

Be Honest With Yourself And Other People - First, you should realize that this is the only way these social skills will work. Dishonesty may work for a little while, but it will catch up with you and soon be discovered. Your integrity is your self worth, value yourself and others will.

Have Pride In Yourself - There is no point in trying to be different from who you really are, others will find out what you are like anyway. There may be things you want to improve on to become a better person. Be proud of who you are, no one likes a phony.

Stay True To Your Principles - Don't give up what you believe in to to make friends. Think about what you believe in, be confident in yourself, and know why you believe this way. You do not have to change in order for anyone to like you.

Lend A Listening Ear - When you listen to someone it makes them feel good and important. Look them in the eyes. Give them your full attention. You are complimenting them and they will like you for that.

Seek Common Ground - Places you go determine the kind of people you will meet. Be sure to get out and mix with others. Introduce yourself, keep in mind most people are just as cautious as you are about meeting people. Generally they will be glad you spoke first.

Dress To Impress - When you go out, others will notice your general appearance before you have a chance to even speak. Take pride in yourself and how you look.

Remembering Names & Faces - Follow these three simple steps:
   a - Hear the name so you can remember it. If you were unable to catch their name the first time, ask again - that is a compliment. It shows that you are interested.
   b - In your conversation, call them by their name as soon as possible. This will help you remember.
   c - Picture their name spelled out in your mind, with their face in the background or relate their name with something you are familiar with to help you remember.

Talk With Confidence In Your Voice - When you use your voice be kind, clear and enthusiastic. Avoid being a loud mouth and include others in conversation. You will make friends by making them feel a part of the activity.

Have Personality - Smile, you will win friends. Have humor, everyone needs to laugh. Friendship is all about having fun!

Lend A Helping Hand - You'll be admired for your kindness. Politeness shows respect for others.

Initiate A Conversation - Talk about famous people, your favorite athletes, or current events.

Keep The Conversation Alive - Find out what the other person's interests are. Ask questions like: "What do you like doing after of school?", "Where were you born?", "What is your favorite movie?" These types of questions require more than just "yes" or "no" answers. Listen to the response . Look for things that both of you have a common interest in to keep the conversation alive.

Everybody Has An Opinion - Share your opinions , but at the same time respect other peoples' right to have their own opinion, which may be different than yours.

Don't Burden Others - When trying to develop a friendship keep your problems to yourself until a later time. Forcing your burdens on someone may only scare them away.

Respect Privacy - Talk about common interests, but do not pry into their personal life.

Don't Be A Gossiper - When you gossip you hurt others as well as yourself. People who gossip lose the trust of others and may even lose the chance of making new friends.

Confidence In Yourself - Share your accomplishments, but don't brag or boast (to praise yourself or possessions). Nothing will turn someone away faster than bragging.

Be Positive With Your Friends - Build your friends up by complimenting them on their strengths instead of tearing them down in front of others. Everybody has weaknesses, including you. But with a friend's support, all weaknesses can turn into strengths. People like to be around others who make them feel good about themselves and the company they keep.

Fun & Educational Activities
For Parents and Children to Do Together

1. Have a safety planning meeting with your children. Help them understand proper procedures in case of fire, earthquake, tornado, etc.

2. **Give your child a bearhug and a compliment today.**

3. Go through the calendar with your child and mark any special days—birthdays, family events, etc.

4. **Make plans to visit your local high school or college. Find a football or gymnastics practice to watch.**

5. Go through your closet together and carefully choose some items to be donated to charity,

6. **Bake cookies with your child. Wrap some and take them to a neighbor.**

7. Make a list of errands to run. Give the list to your child; let him/her decide the order in which to run the errands and the shortest and fastest way to get around town.

8. **Read a newspaper with your child. Cut out current articles and talk about them.**

9. Go to the library and check out books about your child's favorite interests.

10. **Ask your child to describe as many feelings as he/she can, completing sentences like "Happiness is..." or "Sadness is..."**

11. Work together with your child, listing ways to save electricity at home. Try to implement those ideas immediately.

12. **Ask specific questions about your child's day: "What was the most fun? What did you like the best?"**

13. Go on a penny hike. At each corner, flip a coin—tails go left, heads go right.

14. **Make plans to attend something musical with your child—a ballet, the symphony, a concert in the park.**

15. Take a nature walk to enjoy the season.

16. **Take some time to read with your child today.**

17. Encourage your child to develop a hobby—photography, rock or stamp collecting, model building, museum exploring.

18. **Put a special "I love you" note in your child's lunch or backpack.**

19. Plan a few minutes to play a game with your child—cards, board games, catch, hide-and-seek, etc.

20. **Both you and your child select something to read silently. After a period of time, summarize for each other what you read.**

21. Find out which science subjects interest your child—astronomy, sea life, the environment, etc. Check out books from the library and read together.

22. **Plan a picnic at a large park with trails, ponds, trees, and animals. Take a walk and look for signs and sounds of summer.**

23. See how many words you and your child can write in five minutes that end in "-all." Score one point for four-letter words, and three points for five-letter and six-letter words.

24. **Take your child somewhere to observe the clouds. Are they all the same? Can you find any shapes in the clouds?**

25. Let your child experiment with watercolors. Suggest a landscape or a still life.

How to Encourage Children to Voluntarily Pick Up a Book and Read

You can help your child develop good reading habits. Most experts agree reading with your child is the most important thing you can do. Start your child's reading off right with the books included in the Summer Middle School™ book list.

Set aside time each day. Stretch out with a book from the list which follows. Read some of the books you enjoyed when you were your child's age.

Visit the library to find books that meet your child's specific interests. Ask a librarian which books are popular among children of your child's grade. Ask the librarian about other resources, such as stories on cassettes, videotapes, records, and even computers.

Encourage a variety of reading materials. Help your child understand directions by reading house numbers and street signs.

But best of all, show your child you like to read. Sit down with a good book. After dinner, share stories and ideas that might interest your child from the newspapers and magazines you're reading.

Books You'll Love to Read
6th to 7th Grade

Adler, C.S.
Tuna Fish Thanksgiving
Willie, the Frog Prince

Aiken, Joan
The Wolves of Willoughby Chase

Alexander, Lloyd
The Black Cauldron
The High King
Remarkable Journey of Prince Jen

Alphin, Elaine
Ghost Cadet

Amoss, Berthe
Lost Magic

Armstrong, William H.
Sounder

Avi
Nothing but the Truth

Babbitt, Natalie
The Search for Delicious
Tuck Everlasting

Barron, T.A.
The Ancient One

Birdseye, Tom
Tucker

Bond, Nancy
A String in the Harp

Brittain, Bill
The Wish Giver

Brooks, Bruce
Everywhere

Burch, Robert
Queenie Peavy

Burnett, Frances
A Little Princess
The Secret Garden

Byars, Betsy
The Midnight Fox

Calvert, Patricia
The Snowbird

Choi, Sook Nyul
Year of Impossible Goodbyes

Christopher, Matt
Tight End

Cleary, Beverly
Ramona the Pest

Cleaver, Vera
Where the Lilies Bloom

Conrad, Pam
Prairie Songs

Cooper, Susan
The Grey King

Corcoran, Barbara
  The Sky is Falling

Cushman, Karen
  Catherine, Called Birdy

Dahl, Roald
  Charlie and the Chocolate Factory
  Danny, the Champion of the World
  James and the Giant Peach

DeAngeli, Maguerite
  The Door in the Wall

DeJong, Meindert
  The Wheel on the School

DeTrevino, Elizabeth
  I, Juan de Pareja

Eager, Edward
  Half Magic

Eckert, Allan W.
  Incident at Hawk's Hill

Edwards, Julie
  Last of the Really Great Whangdoodles
  Mandy

Enright, Elizabeth
  Gone-Away Lake
  Thimble Summer

Estes, Eleanor
  Ginger Pye
  The Hundred Dresses
  The Moffats

Field, Rachel
  Calico Bush

Fitzgerald, John D.
  The Great Brain at the Academy

Fleischman, Paul
  The Borning Room

Fleischman, Sid
  Mr. Mysterious & Company

Fox, Paula
  Monkey Island
  The Slave Dancer

Freedman, Russell
  The Wright Brothers . . .
  How They Invented the Airplane

Gannett, Ruth S.
  My Father's Dragon

Gates, Doris
  Blue Willow

George, Jean Craighead
  Julie of the Wolves
  My Side of the Mountain
  On the Far Side of the Mountain

Gilbreth, Frank B.
  Cheaper by the Dozen

Gray, Elizabeth
  Adam of the Road

Hahn, Mary Downing
  The Spanish Kidnapping Disaster

Heide, Florence
  Banana Twist

Henry, Marguerite
  Brighty of the Grand Canyon

Hermes, Patricia
Mama, Let's Dance

Holm, Anne
North to Freedom

Hudson, Jan
Sweetgrass

Jensen, Dorothea
The Riddle of Penncroft Farm

Juster, Norton
The Phantom Tollbooth

Keith, Harold
Rifles for Watie

Khedian, David
The Road from Home

Knight, Eric
Lassie Come Home

Krumgold, Joseph
And Now Miguel

L'Engle, Madeline
A Ring of Endless Light

Langton, Jane
The Fledgling

Lawson, Robert
Ben and Me
Rabbit Hill

LeGuin, Ursula K.
The Tombs of Atuan

Levoy, Myron
The Witch of Fourth Street

Lewis, C.S.
The Magician's Nephew
Prince Caspian
The Voyage of the Dawn Treader

London, Jack
The Call of the Wild

Lowry, Lois
Anastasia at Your Service
Taking Care of Terrific

MacDonald, Betty
Hello, Mrs. Piggle-Wiggle

McCloskey, Robert
Homer Price

McKinley, Robin
The Blue Sword

Mills, Claudia
Hannah on Her Way

Naylor, Phyllis Reynolds
The Agony of Alice

O'Dell, Scott
The Black Pearl
Island of the Blue Dolphins
Sing Down the Moon

Park, Barbara
My Mother Got Married

Paterson, Katherine Paton
Bridge to Terabithia
Great Gilly Hopkins

Paton Walsh, Jill
The Green Book

Paulsen, Gary
The Haymeadow
Tracker

Raskin, Ellen
The Westing Game

Roberts, Willo
Baby-sitting is a Dangerous Job
Jo and the Bandit

Ruckman, Ivy
Night of the Twisters

Sawyer, Ruth
Roller Skates

Seredy, Kate
The White Stag

Smith, Dodie
Hundred and One Dalmatians

Snyder, Zilpha Keatley
The Headless Cupid
The Witches of Worm

Speare, Elizabeth
The Witch of Blackbird Pond

Streatfeild, Noel
Ballet Shoes

Taylor, Mildred
Let the Circle Be Unbroken
Roll of Thunder, Hear My Cry

Temple, Frances
Taste of Salt

Thesman, Jean
When the Road Ends

Travers, P.L.
Mary Poppins

Ullman, James R.
Banner in the Sky

VanLeeuwen, Jean
Great Summer Camp Catastrophe

White, E.B.
Charlotte's Web

Wilder, Laura Ingalls
By the Shores of Silver Lake

Winthrop, Elizabeth
The Castle in the Attic

Yep, Laurence
Dragonwings

Zindel, Paul
The Pigman and Me

Happy Reading This Summer

Language Arts

6th Grade in Review

- Grammar • Spelling • Vocabulary
- Reading Comprehension • Proofreading
- Dictionary Skills • Writing • Research

Mastering Good Study Techniques

Throughout this review section, keep in mind all of the basic techniques that will help you study more effectively, not only during the summer months but also during your school year. In order to make the best use of these skills, follow these helpful study hints:

- *Find a proper study area in which to work.* The best place, of course, would be a quiet, well-lit study area that is away from interruptions, distractions and conversations. Make sure you have a comfortable chair and a good writing surface.

- *Designate a regular time to study.* Set aside a certain time each day to study. During this time, all other activities should stop: no television, visits, phone calls, or other interruptions from your parents or any other family members.

- *Keep a daily, weekly or monthly planner.* You will find it helpful to keep a planner or calendar which is a good way to keep track of all of your assignments, upcoming tests, after-school activities, family outings, and household chores.

- *Acquire all of the proper materials for your study area.* Be sure to have all of the proper school supplies that you need in order to study. Your study area should include the following items: pencils, colored pencils, pencil sharpener, erasers, pens, three-holed lined paper, paper clips, three-ring binder, ruler, highlighter, glue stick, index cards, student planner or calendar (daily, weekly, or monthly), dictionary, and a thesaurus.

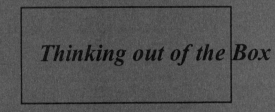

Thinking out of the Box

The nurses at St. Mary's Hospital were working overtime. None of them had slept for five days. Yet all of them were still alert and energetic. How could that be?

Write an S (sentence) in the blank if the sentence expresses a complete thought. Write an F (sentence fragment) in the blank if the words do not express a complete thought.

_____ 1. Write your name at the top of your test and turn it in when you have finished.

_____ 2. The quiet author in the gray suit, who was standing in the hallway.

_____ 3. "Shut your eyes and hold out your arms," Jackie said jokingly.

_____ 4. Will you please help the sixth graders in their canned goods drive?

_____ 5. Not too long after the movie _Titanic_ ended.

_____ 6. When the new teacher opened the door to her classroom.

_____ 7. Matthew told Mrs. Wages that his homework was in _cyberspace_.

_____ 8. Because their unusual sounds were so disgusting.

_____ 9. Carrie and Marcia attended last Saturday's basketball game.

_____10. Dr. Harrison told his nurse, "Please give Jonathan his flu shot."

Find the word in each list that is spelled incorrectly. Cross it out and write it correctly above the list of words.

11. _____
courageous
advertisment
invitation
argument

12. _____
employer
busest
admitting
bedding

13. _____
liesure
friendly
irregular
singing

14. _____
terminate
apreciate
disastrous
curious

15. _____
changable
peaceable
approval
celebration

16. _____
innocent
misspell
athaletic
succeed

17. _____
nodding
protien
adequate
insecure

18. _____
necessary
prohibit
ocassion
physician

19. _____
truly
famous
statment
noticeable

20. _____
drugist
receipt
padding
buyers

21. _____
examination
progress
classicial
fascinate

22. _____
ocupation
generosity
sensitive
opportunity

Read the phrase below. Then look for the word that has the same or almost the same meaning (*synonym*) as the underlined word. Fill in the bubble for the word that means the same.

1. A significant detection
   - O A. surprising
   - O B. fruitful
   - O C. important
   - O D. extend

2. A quick response
   - O A. bargain
   - O B. answer
   - O C. calmness
   - O D. detail

3. The vacant building
   - O A. empty
   - O B. involved
   - O C. crowded
   - O D. noisy

4. To irritate your sister
   - O A. interview
   - O B. annoy
   - O C. pursue
   - O D. enjoy

5. To champion a cause
   - O A. overcome
   - O B. maintain
   - O C. confront
   - O D. defend

6. To complete my work
   - O A. finish
   - O B. fake
   - O C. lose
   - O D. promise

7. A miserable cold
   - O A. tired
   - O B. cheerful
   - O C. terrible
   - O D. agreeable

8. A thorough report
   - O A. incomplete
   - O B. complete
   - O C. average
   - O D. typical

9. To reside in New Jersey
   - O A. search
   - O B. visit
   - O C. enter
   - O D. live

Read each sentence and punctuate it correctly. Write what kind of sentence it is on the line: declarative, interrogative, imperative, or exclamatory.

10. I would like to invite you to speak at the Spanish Club meeting _____

11. Can you arrive at the school by 3:00 _____

12. Give me your introduction or fact sheet before the meeting _____

13. Will you need a microphone and a podium _____

14. We feel that your message is important to our club members _____

15. Our meetings usually last about one hour _____

16. Watch out for the mud puddles in the parking lot _____

17. Give me any receipts for handouts or any other expenses _____

18. We look forward to your appearance at our school _____

A Character Sketch

A character sketch is a description of a real or imaginary character. Select one of your friends to write about. Describe your friend's appearance. Include some of your friend's favorite things. What are some interesting facts about your friend? What are some things that your friend does not like. When you finish, check your spelling, punctuation and capitalization.

_____
_____
_____
_____
_____
_____
_____
_____
_____
_____
_____

The subject and verb in a sentence must agree in number. Read the sentences below and then underline the <u>subject</u> and circle the verb. Write _S_ in the blank if the subject is _singular_. Write _P_ if it is _plural_. Write _C_ if it is collective (team, crowd).

_____ 1. The boys (run, runs) around the track every day during P.E.

_____ 2. The girls' basketball team (play, plays) hard every Thursday night.

_____ 3. Toni and her sister (rides, ride) the school bus every day except Friday.

_____ 4. Our school band (practices, practice) after school three times a week.

_____ 5. You (was, were) really lucky to have seen the last hockey game of the season.

_____ 6. They have decided to (jog, jogs) around the track after school each day.

_____ 7. The ten girls (is, are) going to the neighborhood swimming party next Sunday.

_____ 8. The Science Fair judging (was, were) held on Thursday in the gymnasium.

_____ 9. Who can guess how many pennies (is, are) in this fish bowl?

_____10. The football crowd always (stand, stands) for the national anthem.

A hyphen is used to link words so that they will fit at the ends of lines. Broken words should only be divided between syllables, and one syllable words, even a long one such as *through,* are never divided. Use your own dictionary to help you. Show where you should divide the words below by drawing lines between the syllables.

1. q u a n t i t y

2. h a m b u r g e r

3. p a r a t r o o p e r

4. l a u g h t e r

5. d i s a p p o i n t

6. i m m e d i a t e

7. y e a r n

8. s u s p i c i o n

9. r e c e s s

10. n e g a t i v e

11. i r r e g u l a r

12. e s t a b l i s h

13. b r a n c h

14. f r e q u e n c y

15. o r i g i n a l

Rewrite the paragraphs below. They contain sentence fragments and run-on sentences. Decide where the sentences should be separated. Add punctuation marks and capitals.

Music and Dancing

In the past. People in Europe and America danced their traditional folk dances at fairs, festivals, weddings and celebrations, folk dances are very old, and the steps have been passed down from parents to children for hundreds of years. Today they are mostly performed by dance groups. In national costumes.

In other parts of the world. People have traditional dances. Which they perform at festivals or use to tell stories. Of their gods and heroes.

_____
_____
_____
_____
_____
_____
_____
_____
_____
_____

A *proper noun* names a *particular* person, place, or thing and begins with a capital letter. Aunt Marie, Atlanta, and *The Outsiders* are *proper nouns*. A *common noun* does not name a particular person, place or thing and does not begin with a capital letter (unless it appears at the beginning of a sentence). Aunt, city, and book are *common nouns*. Match the proper noun to the common noun.

_____ 1. movie
_____ 2. song
_____ 3. school
_____ 4. store
_____ 5. book title
_____ 6. sacred book
_____ 7. country
_____ 8. language
_____ 9. monument
_____ 10. church
_____ 11. religion
_____ 12. painting
_____ 13. mountain range
_____ 14. title
_____ 15. government body
_____ 16. sea
_____ 17. city

A. *Cracker Jackson*
B. Statue of Liberty
C. *Titanic*
D. Caspian
E. J.C. Penny
F. Hindu
G. Quran
H. Washington Middle School
I. Holy Cross
J. House of Representatives
K. the *Mona Lisa*
L. Seattle
M. Egypt
N. "Yellow Submarine"
O. Doctor
P. French
Q. Ural

The word search below contains all of the words from the common noun word list above.

```
Y S C F Y R T N U O C T H E
B D C I T U A V K F I C G L
O P O H T T I B K T R N V A
O A K B O Y L M L U A X N N
K I E T T O M E H R M Y O G
T N S V P N L C N Q P L I U
I T C W Q S E I Q T Z F G A
T I X M O M A M S F C Y I G
L N S N O T D K N T N B L E
E G G V N M F P J R O C E C
J Q I U F W W R F W E R R Y
L E O T T T Z B A E S V E G
U M D D T N E M U N O M O J
S A C R E D B O O K B D X G
```

Of the words that *sound alike* (or are homonyms), fill in the blank with the word that best completes the meaning of the sentence. If there are two blanks in a sentence, write the correct one in its corresponding blank.

1. My little sister was totally _____ with the baseball game.   **board/bored**

2. Mrs. Cook told our class that we sounded like a _____ of buffaloes.   **heard/herd**

3. _____ completing the questions to the test now.   **They're/Their**

4. Visitors to the school are not _____ in this area.   **allowed/aloud**

5. My best friend and I _____ the mathematics test.   **passed/past**

6. Our family stayed in the luxury hotel _____ where all the guests were provided _____ chocolates at night.   **sweet/suite**

7. I don't know _____ we should go to the picnic because of the approaching _____ conditions.   **weather/whether**

8. When the _____ toured our part of the building, he stated his main _____ or rule of conduct.   **principal/principle**

9. _____ your name at the top of your paper when you finish.   **Write/Right**

10. The cheerleaders printed the sign in all _____ letters.   **capital/capitol**

A *prepositional phrase* is a group of words that begins with a preposition and ends with a noun or pronoun. Underline the *prepositional phrases* in the following sentences.

11. My older sister received a love letter from her new boyfriend.

12. Mrs. Powell's sixth grade class enjoyed learning about the Oregon Trail.

13. Last summer my family and I went on vacation to the Grand Canyon.

14. Students, you may use your calculator for the problems on this test.

15. The impatient driver behind us continued to honk his horn.

16. I believe I saw your science book underneath your coat.

17. My mother always eats a banana in the morning with breakfast and an apple with lunch.

18. The new clothing store is around the corner and across the street from the dry cleaners.

Finding the correctly spelled word. Fill in the bubble for the word that is spelled correctly and best completes the sentence.

1. Nancy studied all weekend for her _____.
   - ○ a. examenation
   - ○ b. exumination
   - ○ c. examination
   - ○ d. esamanation

2. My mother uses a brown _____ rug in the den.
   - ○ a. reverseible
   - ○ b. reversible
   - ○ c. reversable
   - ○ d. reversaible

3. The monthly PTA meeting will be held in the _____.
   - ○ a. cafitiria
   - ○ b. cafetiria
   - ○ c. caffeteria
   - ○ d. cafeteria

4. An _____ is an account of a person's life written by himself.
   - ○ a. autobiography
   - ○ b. autabiography
   - ○ c. autobiogrephy

5. Give the police officer the _____ he needs.
   - ○ a. infermation
   - ○ b. information
   - ○ c. infirmation
   - ○ d. infurmation

6. The principal said that this has been a daily _____.
   - ○ a. ocurence
   - ○ b. occurence
   - ○ c. occurrence
   - ○ d. occurrance

7. My grandparents celebrated their fiftieth_____.
   - ○ a. anniversy
   - ○ b. anniversery
   - ○ c. anniversary
   - ○ d. aniverssary

8. George _____ the chocolate milk.
   - ○ a. perfered
   - ○ b. prefferred
   - ○ c. perferred
   - ○ d. preferred

9. How would you _____ with the Spanish student?
   - ○ a. communicate
   - ○ b. comunicate
   - ○ c. communicat
   - ○ d. comunnicate

Capitalization and Punctuation. Read the following sentences. Choose the correct sentence in each group by filling in the bubble next to it.

10. ○ a. Virginia's dog mondale is a sheltie.
    ○ b. sharon's cat Millie is missing
    ○ c. I dont like cats or dogs!
    ○ d. My mother's dog died last week.

11. ○ a. tonight I have to study for my tests.
    ○ b. I have to really study for my tests.
    ○ c. Have you studied for your tests
    ○ d. does Wanda ever study for tests?

12. ○ a. Do you like syrup on your pancakes?
    ○ b. ask mother to serve you pancakes?
    ○ c. Why don't you like pancakes.
    ○ d. i could not eat all the pancakes

13. ○ a. Did Roger say he wanted to go!
    ○ b. do you think she will tell Mr. Wade
    ○ c. Have you ever visited Vermont?
    ○ d. i am returning your test papers today

14. ○ a. The Chef stormed out of the Kitchen.
    ○ b. the store manager ordered the bicycle
    ○ c. Can you park the car in the garage.
    ○ d. Thomas, please take out the garbage.

15. ○ a. Our favorite neighbors moved today.
    ○ b. your library book is due Friday?
    ○ c. Aren't you glad today is a Holiday?
    ○ d. our family stayed at the Ritz hotel

The Compound Sentence. A *compound sentence* is a sentence that has two or more simple sentences, usually joined by a connecting word. The words *and, but, or, nor, for,* or *yet* connect the simple sentences. If a sentence is simple, write *S.* If a sentence is compound, write *C.*

___ 1. My little sister is only five years old, and she loves to play with her dolls all day.

___ 2. It is very important to always listen to what is being said in class.

___ 3. I do not like cats, but my mother and sister love them.

___ 4. My two shelties always wait for me to walk them in the afternoon.

___ 5. The students had worked hard on the science projects, but they did not win any prizes.

___ 6. Mrs. Walker told our class to complete the research papers by Friday.

___ 7. Mr. Thomas and Ms. Edwards volunteered to help serve the refreshments at the meeting.

___ 8. Please board the ship as soon as possible, and present your ticket to the attendant.

___ 9. My dad and I built a dog house, but our dog would not stay in it.

___10. My cousins and their parents plan to visit us this summer.

Choosing *who* and *whom*. *Who* generally is used as a subject. *Whom* is used as an object. Complete each sentence below with *who* or *whom.*

11. From _____ have you received invitations to the Christmas parties?

12. There are a lot of students _____ really like our new math teacher, Mr. Watkins.

13. _____ do you students know in San Diego, California?

14. Everyone in the courtroom wondered _____ the mysterious witness would be.

15. If I had known _____ he was, I would have been more friendly.

16. The two men _____ the police arrested for a parking ticket were wanted for robbery.

17. I do not remember to _____ I lent my science book.

18. Philip Anderson is a student _____, I think, is really qualified for president of our class.

19. No one has figured out to _____ the teacher was referring.

20. I wonder _____ sent me this wonderful birthday card.

Transitive and Intransitive Verbs. A *transitive verb* is a verb that has a direct object. An *intransitive verb* is a verb that does not have a direct object. Underline the verbs or verb phrases. Circle the direct object if there is one. Identify the verb by writing *transitive* or *intransitive* in the blank to the right of each sentence.

1. Jennifer and Carl love their new bicycles. _____

2. Jennifer and Carl took a tour of Idaho last summer. _____

3. They rode quite far every day. _____

4. Carl climbed long hills so easily. _____

5. The science fair judges explained the contest rules. _____

6. The contestants still misunderstood. _____

7. The new waiter ignored the impatient customers. _____

8. The butler is the main suspect in the murder. _____

9. Our art teacher assigned several projects for the week. _____

10. The scared girls followed a trail into the deep woods. _____

Today, people move every few years. Of course, by moving often, people can experience different places, friends and climates. However, some people just prefer to stay in one place all their lives and never move far from home. Write a paragraph stating whether you think it is better to stay in one place or to move often and live in different places.

_____

_____

_____

_____

_____

_____

_____

_____

_____

_____

_____

_____

_____

An *adverb* is a word that modifies a verb, an adjective, or another adverb. Underline the adverb in each sentence. At the end of the sentence, write the word it modifies.

1. Tommy really likes his new part-time job. _____

2. Willie always goes to basketball practice after school. _____

3. Mrs. Campbell never gives tests on Fridays. _____

4. The old house at the end of the street burned quickly. _____

5. Since Bryan was very tired, he decided to go to bed. _____

6. Sherry studied hard for her mathematics test. _____

7. Monica and her news staff work quickly to gather the daily news. _____

8. Heather was too tired to write her research report last night. _____

9. Suddenly, he heard a loud noise from the garage. _____

10. Roger worked all the math problems easily. _____

Commas are used to separate three or more words or phrases that are used in a series. Read the following sentences. Then separate the items in a series by inserting commas in the right places.

11. We learned that the Alps are located in France Italy Switzerland Austria and Yugoslavia.

12. Cynthia plays the piano the organ the violin and the harp.

13. For lunch we were served hamburgers french fries salad ice cream and milk.

14. Omar ran out the door down the block through the gate and into the park.

15. When asked by the visitors, Mark could not give clear exact and correct directions.

16. Mrs. Walker Ms. Grant and Mr. Thomas planned the sixth grade school dance.

17. Mr. Clinton campaigned in Nevada Utah Colorado and New Mexico.

18. After dinner, grandmother washed the dishes told ghost stories and watched the stars.

19. Rob's father barbecued chicken ribs and corn for the family reunion.

20. At summer camp, you can choose from swimming tennis hiking bicycling or crafts.

Pronoun and Antecedent. The *antecedent* of a pronoun is the word or group of words to which the pronoun refers. A pronoun must agree with its *antecedent* in number and gender. Write the *antecedent* for each underlined pronoun.

1. Carla did research for the report that <u>she</u> wrote. _____

2. Her report was about Sweden, and <u>it</u> was for school. _____

3. Carla used two libraries, and <u>they</u> had great information. _____

4. Sweden's wealth of natural resources has made <u>it</u> a prosperous country. _____

5. All of the sixth grade students brought <u>their</u> lunches to the school picnic. _____

6. Would you please lend me <u>one</u> of your coats? _____

7. The students turned in <u>their</u> research papers on time. _____

8. Dr. Harrison measured Keith's heartbeat. <u>It</u> was normal. _____

9. George won first place in the competition. <u>He</u> is a great athlete. _____

10. Sara and Juanita have made up their minds to do all <u>their</u> homework. _____

An *adjective* is a word that modifies, or describes, a noun or a pronoun. Remember: An *adjective* tells what kind, which one, or how many about something. Circle the adjective or adjectives in each sentence. Do not circle *a, an,* or *the.*

11. We stayed at Lake Hotel in Yellowstone National Park for several days.

12. Red, yellow and blue balloons decorated the ballroom.

13. Kelly saw those priceless paintings in the museum in New York.

14. Providence is a historical city in Rhode Island.

15. The contest rules are on the back of the green folder.

16. Tony's sculptures, bright and unusual, are on display in the auditorium.

17. These science projects are the best I have seen in years.

18. Alice, quiet and studious, is always on time for class.

19. Ginger is a beautiful, clever, Spanish dancer.

20. We have endured five days of hard, steady rain.

A *conjunction* is a word that connects words or groups of words. Circle the coordinating, correlative, or subordinating conjunction in each sentence.

1. I really enjoy watching television, but I cannot watch it too often.

2. Because my parents do not like to watch television, I often read or study.

3. Do you like to play football or basketball?

4. Either you do this report or you will not pass this course.

5. When my sister returned from the mall, she had spent over two hundred dollars.

6. Neither movies nor television can compare to a great book.

7. Susan opened her locker, and she found a note from her boyfriend.

8. Although Tony had finished all of his homework, he was not prepared for the quiz.

9. Angela finished writing the letter, but she did not mail it.

10. Yvonne has loved to dance since she was three.

***Subjects* and *Verbs* Agree. Write the correct form of the verb for each sentence in the blank provided. Be sure to check your answer by reading the completed sentence to yourself.**

_____ 11. At the state science fair, the winner (receives, receive) a trophy and a plaque.

_____ 12. The assistant principal (makes, make) the afternoon announcements each day.

_____ 13. To earn money, Denise and Donna (does, do) baby-sitting after school.

_____ 14. The principal said either pants or a skirt (is, are) appropriate at school.

_____ 15. You (was, were) the only one to finish the research paper on time.

_____ 16. The singer in the photographs (has, have) performed well all week long.

_____ 17. The dogs in the pet shop (looks, look) so cute and adorable.

_____ 18. In that closet (is, are) my old clothes, shoes, and coats.

_____ 19. The football players and their coach (practices, practice) every day.

_____ 20. California and Nevada (shares, share) a border.

An *interjection* is a word or phrase used to show strong surprise or strong feelings. An *interjection* is independent of the other words in a sentence. Fill in the blanks with the appropriate *interjection*. Then complete the word search.

Oh	Whew	Hurrah	Goodness
Alas	Ouch	Gosh	Ugh
Gracious	My	Well	Wow

1. _ _ _ _ expressing astonishment, dismay or relief
2. _ _ _ _ _ _ _ _ exclamation of surprise or alarm
3. _ _ _ _ an exclamation of surprise, wonder, pleasure or joy
4. _ _ _ _ _ _ _ an exclamation of joy, applause or approval
5. _ _ an expression of surprise or pain
6. _ _ _ _ _ an exclamation or a mild oath
7. _ _ _ _ expressing sorrow, grief, pity or concern
8. _ _ _ expressing disgust or horror
9. _ _ _ _ _ used to express surprise or agreement
10. _ _ an exclamation of surprise
11. _ _ _ _ an exclamation expressing sudden pain
12. _ _ _ _ _ _ _ _ _ an exclamation of surprise

```
G S R R H L Y M W A
C O U O R Q A H L O
G O S O I K E A G O
T H J H I W S O G U
H S I H E C O P V P
A W Q N O D A N Y M
R O M U N N W R Z H
R Q C E B Y H E G G
U H S B P C N O L U
H S W O W J X Z T L
```

Whew!

Possessive pronouns show who or what owns something. Choose the *possessive pronoun* in each sentence below.

13. (Your, Yours) research topic sounds great.
14. Casey's topic is the heart, but (her, hers) is not.
15. Your topic is very easy, but (my, mine) is quite difficult.
16. My little brother wants (my, mine) help.
17. Look at (it's, its) topic and information.
18. The new computer is (our, ours).
19. (They're, Their) decisions are always final.
20. Where is (your, you're) science book?

Punctuating Direct Quotations. **Remember these rules about using quotation marks: Use** *quotation marks* **before and after the words of a direct quotation; a direct quotation begins with a capital letter; when a quoted sentence is divided into two parts by an interruping expression, the second part begins with a small letter. Punctuate the following sentences.**

1. Chuck answered I really like studying about Russia.

2. My parents were very impressed with my report on Russia Tyler remarked.

3. Can you think of any Russian foods that you would like asked Mrs. Slaton.

4. Oh, no groaned Isaac I don't want to eat Russian food for lunch.

5. I know the Russians make great chocolates said Margaret.

6. Could you take care of my two cats asked Mrs. Thomas while I'm on vacation?

7. I will be on vacation for two weeks said Mrs. Thomas.

8. Mrs. Thomas asked will you also water my plants about every three days.

9. Is there anything you would like me to bring you while I am in Mexico said Mrs. Thomas.

10. John said jokingly could you bring me a real taco.

An *appositive* **is a word or group of words that follows a noun. An** *appositive* **identifies or explains more about the noun it follows.** <u>Underline</u> **the appositive in each sentence. Add a comma or commas to set off the** *appositive* **from the rest of the sentence. Then write the noun it identifies in the blank provided.**

11. Dr. Marshall the principal announced the winners of the contest. _____

12. My friend Jessica won first place in the science fair. _____

13. Our English teacher Mrs. Kelly has written a book about Salt Lake City. _____

14. Two sixth graders Marshall and Tony were sent to the principal's office. _____

15. Basketball a team sport is our school's most popular sport. _____

16. The best basketball players Leon and Jose were too ill to play. _____

17. This department store the largest in the mall has sales all the time. _____

18. Our home computer a new model was on sale at the store. _____

19. Robert Carrell the special guest speaker is from Billings, Montana. _____

20. Ward my father's brother will join us for the family reunion this year. _____

Some words can be used both as *adjectives* and as *adverbs*. These words can be easily confused. Remember that an *adjective* modifies a noun or a pronoun. An *adverb* modifies a verb, an adjective or another adverb. Choose the word in the parentheses that correctly completes each sentence.

1. Corey Stanford is a (good, well) car salesperson.

2. He is always (polite, politely) to all of his automobile customers.

3. A good salesperson must relate to others (easy, easily).

4. All car salespeople have (interesting, interestingly) careers.

5. (Sure, Surely) you can understand why salespeople work so hard to earn commissions.

6. The new senator worked (hard, hardly) to implement his programs.

7. Sarah crawled (slow, slowly) to the end of the field.

8. Suddenly, Janis saw some of her (beautiful, beautifully) sculptures on display.

9. The bomb experts checked the site (thorough, thoroughly) before the President arrived.

10. Colin cut his knee (bad, badly) during football practice.

A *prefix* is a word part added to the beginning of a base word. A prefix changes the meaning of the base word to which it is added. Underline the prefix in each word. Then write the meaning of the word in the space next to it.

11.	inexpensive	21.	impolite
12.	cooperate	22.	unemployed
13.	disapprove	23.	recover
14.	immortal	24.	irregular
15.	disregard	25.	unoccupied
16.	impossible	26.	imprison
17.	insincere	27.	refresh
18.	dissatisfy	28.	disobey
19.	invisible	29.	discredit
20.	unstressed	30.	transplant

Comparative or *Superlative Degrees of Adjectives:* The *comparative* degree of an adjective is used when showing a comparison between two persons or things. Almost every adjective of one syllable forms its comparative degree by adding *-er*. An adjective with two or more syllables forms its comparative degree by adding *more* or *less* in front of the adjective. The *superlative* degree of an adjective is used when more than two persons or things are being compared. Adjectives of one syllable usually form the *superlative* degree by adding *-est.* An adjective of two or more syllables forms the superlative degree by adding *most* or *least* in front of the adjective. Write the correct *comparative* or *superlative* form of the adjective on the line provided.

1. young   Who is the _____ member in your family?
2. clear   We understood Sally was the _____ of all the presenters.
3. late   Have you heard the _____ weather forecast?
4. fast   Tommy has the _____ bicycle of all the professional racers.
5. great   *Titanic* was the _____ movie I have ever seen.
6. frequently   It rains _____ in April than in May here.
7. dark   The _____ clouds mean more rain is on the way.
8. hard   Mrs. Walker gave us the _____ math test that we have ever had.
9. silly   Sammy told the _____ joke possible in class today.
10. tall   Mark is the _____ player on the basketball team.
11. pretty   Jessica is considered the _____ girl in our sixth grade class.
12. wisely   Of the five finalists in the pageant, the last contestant answered the question _____ .
13. high   Our team climbed the _____ mountain in the Tetons.
14. close   In my dream, the man with a gun was coming _____ to me.
15. happy   I think Jose is _____ this year than last year.

Problem Verbs: *Lie/Lay; Sit/Set; Rise/Raise.* **If necessary, review these problem verbs before completing this exercise. Circle the correct verb in each of the following sentences.**

16. The old yellow cat (lie, lay) on the front porch all morning.
17. The little boy (set, sat) very still while his hair was being cut.
18. My grandfather had (lain, laid) on the sofa watching his favorite program.
19. The sun (rises, raises) in the east.
20. Has the curtain (risen, raised) on the second act yet?
21. Why don't you come in and (set, sit) down for a while?
22. Martha said that she had (lain, laid) the scissors on the art table.
23. Mrs. Goodson asked each of us to (set, sat) the correct date and time on our computers.
24. George has (lain, laid) tile as a part-time job since he started college.
25. Cary and Julian (risen, raised) the school flag every morning before class.

Direct and *Indirect Objects*. A *direct object* is a noun or pronoun in the predicate that receives the action of the verb. To find the *direct* object, ask *who* or *what* after the action verb. An *indirect object* is a noun or pronoun in the predicate that answers the question *to whom?*, *for whom?*, *to what?*, or *for what?* after an action verb. Circle the verb in each sentence. Correctly label each *direct object* and *indirect object* on the line provided.

1. On the Fourth of July we ate barbecued <u>chicken</u>. _____

2. Sarah's mother offered the guests a <u>piece</u> of pie. _____

3. Mrs. Baker wrote the <u>assignment</u> on the blackboard. _____

4. Michele bought her pet a new <u>toy</u>. _____

5. Farmer John fed his horses all the <u>corn</u>. _____

6. The speaker gave that <u>question</u> some thought before answering. _____

7. My uncle told my little brother a ghost <u>story</u>. _____

8. The front desk clerk gave my mother and me <u>directions</u>. _____

9. Mr. Powell feeds his <u>birds</u> food once a day. _____

10. The salesperson sold us the last school <u>sweatshirt.</u> _____

Identifying Parts of Speech—Review. In each of the following sentences, identify the part of speech by placing a number in the blank provided. Use: 1-*noun*; 2-*pronoun*; 3-*verb*; 4-*adjective*; 5-*adverb*; 6-*preposition*; 7-*conjunction*; 8-*interjection*.

____ 11. <u>We</u> have looked everywhere for Mother's rings.
____ 12. <u>Look out</u>! You are too close to the edge of the cliff.
____ 13. Aunt Bessie <u>gathered</u> all the ingredients before baking the cake.
____ 14. The bomb exploded so <u>quickly</u> that we could not believe it.
____ 15. My father said that the chocolate <u>cake</u> was delicious.
____ 16. We visited Denver <u>because</u> my mother has relatives there.
____ 17. Orlando, Florida is a very <u>popular</u> tourist attraction.
____ 18. Franklin poured a bucket of water <u>over</u> the smoldering campfire.
____ 19. The last number on the <u>program</u> was an overture by Wagner.
____ 20. <u>Without</u> a word of protest the teacher sealed the letter.
____ 21. The lemonade <u>tasted</u> very sour.
____ 22. From that corner <u>she</u> could see my face with the car light upon it.
____ 23. On her pantry shelves were spread jars of canned apples, pears, <u>and</u> peaches.
____ 24. My grandfather noticed <u>an</u> old ladder standing against the stone wall.

Double Negatives. A *negative* **is a word that means "no." Using** *double negatives* **means using two negative words instead of one.** *Negatives* **are words such as** *no, not, none, never, no one, nothing* **and** *hardly.* **Rewrite each sentence. On the line provided, correct each** *double negative*

1. Angela didn't tell no one about her failing grade on the math test.

_____

2. Walter hadn't gone hardly ten steps when his name was called.

_____

3. Nobody never had a more interesting job of interviewing television guests.

_____

4. Cynthia said that she hadn't read nothing about Ms. Jane Pittman.

_____

5. My grandfather doesn't do nothing all day long.

_____

Professional baseball players earn large salaries. Of course, they earn more than our police officers, fire fighters, or even office workers. Naturally, they work shorter hours and for only part of a year. Many people think that baseball players earn too much for just playing ball. Others think that baseball players should earn as much as television and movie stars. Write a paragraph in which you state whether baseball players are paid too much or not. Explain your point of view. If you need additional space, use another sheet of paper.

_____
_____
_____
_____
_____
_____
_____
_____
_____
_____
_____
_____

Antonyms are words that have opposite meanings. For example: *east* and *west; accepted* and *rejected.* Match the *antonyms* by writing words from the Word Bank in the blanks.

1. forward _____

2. knowledge _____

3. abundant _____

4. cautious _____

5. fiction _____

6. logical _____

7. frugal _____

8. punish _____

9. encourage _____

10. permanent _____

11. fail _____

12. preserve _____

Word Bank
illogical
scarce
extravagant
temporary
waste
ignorance
pardon
succeed
nonfiction
backward
discourage
careful

Proofread the following friendly letter. Correct any errors in spelling, capitalization, punctuation or language usage.

aug 10 2000

Dear aunt Emily and uncle Bob;

Thank you so much for my Twelfieth birthday party. All of my friends really enjoyed the pizza and skating Party at Sals skating Palace.

Mom and dad must have tell you that i wanted a pizza and Skating party, i have hear from almost everyone who attended. What a great time?

As soon as the pictures is developed, me and Mom will send you some of the prints. I cant waite to see them!

Thanks again for such a wunderful birthday party.

Love,
Marsha

Spelling Demons: Don't let these spelling demons trick you. Find the 16 frequently misspelled words in the puzzle and circle them. The words may read from left to right, right to left, top to bottom, or bottom to top.

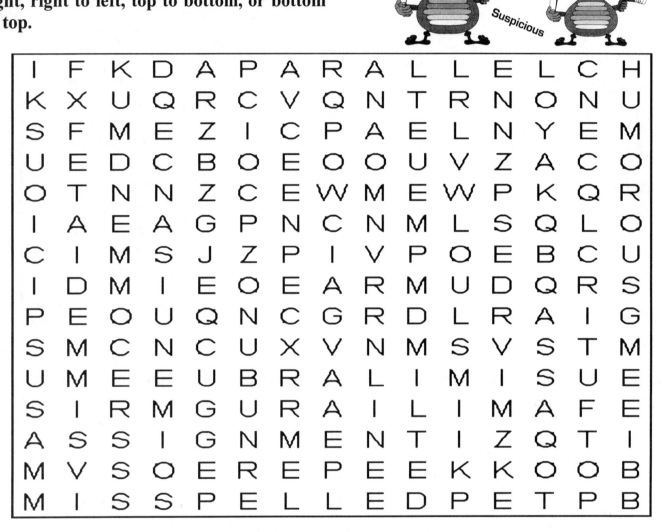

Vacuum
Humorous
Pursue
Weird
Suspicious

```
I  F  K  D  A  P  A  R  A  L  L  E  L  C  H
K  X  U  Q  R  C  V  Q  N  T  R  N  O  N  U
S  F  M  E  Z  I  C  P  A  E  L  N  Y  E  M
U  E  D  C  B  O  E  O  O  U  V  Z  A  C  O
O  T  N  N  Z  C  E  W  M  E  W  P  K  Q  R
I  A  E  A  G  P  N  C  N  M  L  S  Q  L  O
C  I  M  S  J  Z  P  I  V  P  O  E  B  C  U
I  D  M  I  E  O  E  A  R  M  U  D  Q  R  S
P  E  O  U  Q  N  C  G  R  D  L  R  A  I  G
S  M  C  N  C  U  X  V  N  M  S  V  S  T  M
U  M  E  E  U  B  R  A  L  I  M  I  S  U  E
S  I  R  M  G  U  R  A  I  L  I  M  A  F  E
A  S  S  I  G  N  M  E  N  T  I  Z  Q  T  I
M  V  S  O  E  R  E  P  E  E  K  K  O  O  B
M  I  S  S  P  E  L  L  E  D  P  E  T  P  B
```

Word Bank

accommodate
assignment
bookkeeper
convenience
familiar
humorous

immediate
misspelled
nuisance
parallel
pursue
recommend

similar
suspicious
vacuum
weird

Using End Marks, Commas, Semicolons, and Colons Correctly. Punctuate the following sentences by using end marks, commas, semicolons and colons.

1. Haley when is the last day of school

2. Well I think school ends on Tuesday June 6

3. I need to read my library book study my vocabulary words and finish my report.

4. Johnny completed his research report I have to finish writing mine.

5. Mrs. Roberts our substitute teacher has control over the students.

6. Diana Princess of Wales died in a car accident in Paris France on August 31 1997

7. The following students are absent today Steven Cook Chris Holbrook and Tim Sims.

8. Don't touch that wet paint

9. Dear Senator Starks

10. Sincerely

    Thomas Watson

11. My parents are very pleased with my grades I made all A's this semester.

12. If you ask me I think we should study for our math test.

13. Does your report include the following a table of contents the body several illustrations and a list of sources

Reference Materials. Match each reference source with its description.

____ 14. encyclopedia

____ 15. dictionary

____ 16. thesaurus

____ 17. almanac

____ 18. atlas

____ 19. telephone book

____ 20. newspaper

A. A book with names, telephone numbers and addresses of homes and businesses

B. A collection of maps

C. Books that contain information in alphabetical order about people, places, events, ideas as well as things

D. Statistical information on a variety of subjects, such as weather and population

E. Up-to-date information about events and people around the world

F. A book of synonyms and antonyms

G. A book that contains spellings, pronunciations and definitions of words

Combining Sentences. Good writers usually use some short sentences; however, they do not use them all the time. Combine each group of short, related sentences into one sentence by inserting adjectives, adverbs or prepositional phrases. There may be more than one correct way to combine the sentences. Add commas where they are necessary.

1. Jennifer wrote her letter.
   She wrote it on Friday.
   It was a letter to the President.

   _____

2. Joan finished the short story.
   Joan finally finished it.
   It was terribly boring.

   _____

3. The football players have arrived.
   They are ready to play.
   They are the varsity team.

   _____

4. During the summer I had a part-time job.
   I taught swimming at the club.
   The job was enjoyable.

   _____

5. We visited the zoo near my house.
   We went to see the elephants.
   We saw the giraffes.

   _____

6. We played softball in our backyard.
   We had a picnic.
   It was a beautiful day.

   _____

7. Rob did his assignment in class.
   The assignment was written.
   The class was math.

   _____

Diagramming Sentences. Diagram the following sentences.

1. My mother is a teacher.

   Example:

   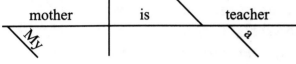

2. The custodian swept, washed, and waxed the floors.

3. Dad prepared them some spaghetti.

4. Our new school has a large, bright gym.

5. The new girl with blonde hair plays in our school band.

6. Finally, the small blue plane radioed the tower.

7. Wanda opened her locker, and she found a frog inside.

8. Sue printed her project on a large poster.

9. Dr. Jones, the principal, announced the winners.

10. He gave me this book, but I gave him nothing.

Reviewing *Comparative* and *Superlative*: Use the *comparative* form of an adjective or adverb to describe a comparison between two things, persons, places, or actions. The *superlative* form compares more than two things, persons, places or actions. When you add *er* or *est* to form the *comparative* or *superlative*, the spelling of an adjective may change. Add *er* or *est* to all adverbs with one syllable and to some adverbs with two syllables. Use *more* or *most* with most adjectives and adverbs with two syllables and with all adverbs with more than one syllable. Do *not* combine *more* or *most* with *er* or *est*.

Complete the chart below with each form of an adjective or adverb.

Positive	Comparative	Superlative	Positive	Comparative	Superlative
1. happy			6. slowly		
2. beautiful			7. far		
3. weak			8. quietly		
4. talented			9. politely		
5. loud			10. high		

Circle the correct form of the adjective or adverb from the two given in parentheses.

11. "Friends" is the (funnier, funniest) show of this television season.
12. The movie credits were (extreme, extremely) long.
13. Cindy read the story (more carefully, most carefully) than her younger sister did.
14. Martha was (sure, surely) she could finish her report on time.
15. She had done a (good, well) job of writing the paper.
16. Karen had prepared her speech (better, more better) than Philip.
17. Mrs. Clark listened to Karen (more attentively, most attentively) than I.
18. Tomorrow will be (warmer, more warmer) than today.
19. A new swimsuit will be (expensiver, more expensive) than I expected.
20. Between Alicia and Marcia, Marcia is the (taller, tallest).
21. ***Bridge to Teribithia*** is the (greater, greatest) book I have ever read.
22. Which state is (bigger, biggest), California or Florida?
23. Marshall is the (faster, fastest) runner on the track team.
24. Who is the (most old, oldest) member in your family?
25. George is the (less, least) noisy person in this classroom.
26. Jennifer knew she had done her (badly, best) work on the science project.
27. This crossword puzzle is (harder, more hard) than the last one we did.

Demonstrative Adjectives. Four adjectives that tell which one, or which ones, are *this, that, these,* and *those.* When they modify nouns or pronouns, they point out specific things. *This, that, these,* and *those* are called *demonstrative adjectives.* We use *this* and *that* with singular nouns. We use *these* and *those* with plural nouns. *Them* is always an objective pronoun. It is never used as an adjective. Circle the *demonstrative adjective* that correctly completes each sentence below.

1. (Those, That) colorful costumes will be used in the second act only.
2. Chuck needs (that, those) kind of picture to finish his collection.
3. (These, Those) tennis lessons last summer taught me a great deal.
4. My uncle reluctantly gave me (them, those) stamps from his collection.
5. Do you like (this, these) kind of cookie?
6. Mother thinks (those, them) sugar cookies are the best.
7. My uncle added (those, them) to his stamp collection.
8. Where did you get all of (those, them) old recordings?
9. Virginia often buys (them, these) sorts of antiques.
10. Greg likes (this, these) kind of cheese pizza.

A *contraction* is a word made by combining two words and omitting one or more letters. The apostrophe shows where a letter or letters have been omitted. Here are few examples: can not = can't   could not = couldn't   they are = they're   he would = he'd Underline the contractions in the sentences below. Write the contractions and the words the contractions stand for on the lines.

11. Denise and James said they're coming home tomorrow.
_____

12. Kelly can't come tomorrow night to baby-sit for you.
_____

13. You're going to answer her letter, aren't you?
_____

14. If they haven't arrived by noon, we'll start looking for them.
_____

15. We're still waiting for the girls to arrive.
_____

16. You won't see any drugs in this neighborhood.
_____

17. The singer couldn't see anything because of the bright lights.
_____

18. I'm going to perform in the next talent show.
_____

Reading Comprehension: Read the following original work, "Mission: Catastrophe!" by Erin Camp. Then answer the questions that follow on the next page.

Mission: Catastrophe!

At five o'clock in the morning, when most people are dead to the world, especially a bunch of kids on spring break, there was a great deal of activity at the dorms of the Space and Rocket Center in Huntsville, Alabama. Space Academy had been in session for two days, and today would be the BBF Team's simulator mission. The twenty kids filed onto the simulator floor and took their places. It was impossible for everyone to have their first choice of positions, but everyone seemed pleased with their assignment. The shuttle simulator was called Atlantis after the real space shuttle, and the commander for this mission was a student named Wayne. As the mission control and space station teams set up, the shuttle crew climbed into their seats. With the completion of the checklist and lift off, the mission was under way. After becoming situated in orbit, the crew began to prepare to dock with the space station Mir.

"Shuttle, you are go for OMS burn," the capcom (capsule communication), who was the only communication link to the shuttle crew, crackled over the radio.

"Copy, Houston," Wayne said, flipping some switches. The pilot to his right did the same.

"See the station yet?"

"Yeah," replied Wayne. "It's a strange looking thing, isn't it?"

"Maybe, but at least it works," the capcom replied.

"Isn't technology really wonderful? It's amazing what you can do with a few rolls of tacky foil, junk and a bad makeover."

"You ought to know, Wayne," the capcom said. Wayne could feel the grin on the other end.

"Funny. Anyway, we've got two minutes till we dock."

"Copy, Shuttle."

Wayne licked his lips. They were terribly chapped from the wind. Fortunately, he had stuffed some lip balm in his pocket as he left his bunk. He reached into his pocket to get the lip balm. His hands felt nothing that even remotely resembled lip balm. He dug deeper. It had to be there.

"Wayne . . . .," the radio crackled.

"One minute," Wayne said. He checked his shirt pocket again. Nothing.

"Wayne?" the capcom's voice was more annoyed now.

"I said hold on a minute!" Wayne growled. Where was that darn lip balm?

"Wayne, look out!" the pilot yelled, pointing to the screens.

"What?" he said, annoyed at the capcom, the pilot, and the world in general.

At that moment, the TV screen, which represented the shuttle windshield, displayed a scene that would reflect horror in everyone's eyes. The shuttle was crashing into the side of Mir. Wayne heard many noises and voices: the pilot's groan, the simulator counselor's laughter from the control center, and general pandemonium from mission control. Wayne buried his face in his hands and groaned. The screens turned red and the words **"NO SURVIVORS!"** filed across the screen in big white letters.

"I've seen some rather crazy things, but this takes the cake! That was sad, Wayne," he heard the capcom say as she tried unsuccessfully to keep the laughter from her voice.

"Hey, Wayne," one of the simulator counselors called over the radio. Wayne gritted his teeth. He knew what was coming. The counselor continued, "Now we can all guess what your team initials stand for . . . The **B**ig **B**rain **F**reeze. And you froze up!"

QUESTIONS ON "MISSION: CATASTROPHE!"

1. In the story "Mission: Catastrophe!" the kids were on
   - O A. summer vacation.
   - O B. a class field trip.
   - O C. spring break.
   - O D. a class assignment.

2. For two days, the kids had been at the
   - O A. Space Academy.
   - O B. Dental Academy.
   - O C. Police Academy.
   - O D. Summer Freedom Academy.

3. In the story, the shuttle simulator was called
   - O A. Challenger.
   - O B. Atlantis.
   - O C. Apollo.
   - O D. Endeavor.

4. The commander for this mission was a student named
   - O A. Mir.
   - O B. Walter.
   - O C. Capcom.
   - O D. Wayne.

5. How many kids filed on the simulator floor and took their places?
   - O A. twelve
   - O B. two
   - O C. twenty
   - O D. thirteen

6. According to the simulator counselor, the letters **BBF** really mean
   - O A. Big Brain Freeze   .
   - O B. Boys Bull Frogs.
   - O C. Big Bold Fighters.
   - O D. Bacon Burgers Forever.

7. What really caused Atlantis' crash with Mir?
   - O A. the pilot's groan
   - O B. a missing lip balm
   - O C. the tacky foil
   - O D. a cracked windshield

8. A correct sequence for this mission would be
   - O A. completion of checklist, shuttle crew boarding, liftoff, and crash.
   - O B. liftoff, orbit, checklist completion, and crash.
   - O C. liftoff, OMS burn, achieve orbit, and crash.
   - O D. complete checklist, liftoff, OMS burn, and crash.

9. What message appeared on the screen in big white letters?
   - O A. Big Brain Freeze
   - O B. Go For OMS burn
   - O C. Crazy things
   - O D. No Survivors

Outlining: One of the best ways to list information on a subject is to use an outline. A formal outline uses a standard pattern of indents, numbers and letters. Main topics are listed with Roman numerals (I, II, etc.) and subtopics are indented and listed with capital letters. Details that give further support are indented further and listed with Arabic numerals (1, 2, etc.). Details that support those details are indented further and listed with small letters. You have decided to write a research paper on *Pioneer Life in America.* Rearrange the items in the right column below into a formal outline in the left column. A few of the details and subtopics are filled in for you.

Pioneer Life In America

I. The pioneers

    A. _____

    B. _____

II. _____

    A. Crossing the Appalachians

    B. _____

III. _____

    A. _____

    B. _____

    C. _____

    D. _____

    E. Indian attacks

IV. Crossing the plains

    A. _____

    B. _____

Education and religion
Life on the trail
Establishing the frontier
Social activities
Moving westward
The wagon trail
A pioneer home
Conquering the wilderness
How the pioneers traveled
Law and order
A pioneer settlement

Vocabulary: It is important for your vocabulary to grow. To begin with, you must learn to be aware of words you do not know. Here are a few rules for improving your vocabulary: 1) Try to learn the meaning of a new word from the context, and then check your dictionary for accuracy; 2) Learn word parts and families; 3) Learn roots, prefixes, and suffixes; 4) Use your dictionary as often as possible; 5) Try to use new words in speaking and writing. From the list of four choices under each phrase, bubble in the one that is closest in meaning to the word appearing in italics.

1. a *trivial* argument
   - ○ a. friendly
   - ○ b. very important
   - ○ c. brutal
   - ○ d. not important

2. a *conceited* person
   - ○ a. vain
   - ○ b. considerate
   - ○ c. quick-witted
   - ○ d. happy

3. to *derive* the answer
   - ○ a. jot down
   - ○ b. recall
   - ○ c. figure out
   - ○ d. guess

4. to *penetrate* the wall
   - ○ a. cover
   - ○ b. pass through
   - ○ c. tear down
   - ○ d. hold up

5. a *disgraceful* act
   - ○ a. shameful
   - ○ b. unconcerned
   - ○ c. confused
   - ○ d. disgust

6. to *simplify* matters
   - ○ a. harder
   - ○ b. difficult
   - ○ c. make easier
   - ○ d. discover

7. *delirious* with joy
   - ○ a. greeted
   - ○ b. wildly excited
   - ○ c. weeping
   - ○ d. giggling

8. a very *agile* student
   - ○ a. lazy
   - ○ b. smart
   - ○ c. drowsy
   - ○ d. quick moving

9. a *somber* mood
   - ○ a. serious
   - ○ b. playful
   - ○ c. cheerful
   - ○ d. friendly

10. a serious *blunder*
    - ○ a. retreat
    - ○ b. mistake
    - ○ c. aptitude
    - ○ d. happening often

11. a *columnist*
    - ○ a. accountant
    - ○ b. secretary
    - ○ c. doctor
    - ○ d. newspaper writer

12. to *disregard*
    - ○ a. connect
    - ○ b. pay no attention
    - ○ c. omit
    - ○ d. bring together

13. to *compliment* her
    - ○ a. insult
    - ○ b. support
    - ○ c. delay
    - ○ d. praise

14. to *loathe* her
    - ○ a. hate
    - ○ b. love
    - ○ c. appreciate
    - ○ d. admire

15. an *avid* reader
    - ○ a. distressed
    - ○ b. fearful
    - ○ c. eager
    - ○ d. shy

16. a true *nuisance*
    - ○ a. association
    - ○ b. annoyance
    - ○ c. fellowship
    - ○ d. tribute

17. to *corrupt* someone
    - ○ a. to spoil
    - ○ b. to support
    - ○ c. to punish
    - ○ d. to fear

18. a *legible* note
    - ○ a. cannot spell
    - ○ b. cannot write
    - ○ c. cannot read
    - ○ d. easy to read

Vocabulary: **Choose the word that is closest in meaning to the word appearing in italics.**

20. an *option*
    - ○ a. choice
    - ○ b. restriction
    - ○ c. obstacle
    - ○ d. understanding

21. to *swindle* someone
    - ○ a. combat
    - ○ b. make friend with
    - ○ c. cheat
    - ○ d. scream at

22. a feeling of *anxiety*
    - ○ a. delight
    - ○ b. isolation
    - ○ c. blame
    - ○ d. great concern

23. to *reprimand* someone
    - ○ a. injury
    - ○ b. scold
    - ○ c. dislike
    - ○ d. lock up

24. a *reliable* person
    - ○ a. dependable
    - ○ b. thankful
    - ○ c. demanding
    - ○ d. interesting

25. *ethical* behavior
    - ○ a. inappropriate
    - ○ b. quite laughable
    - ○ c. correct
    - ○ d. peculiar

26. *objectionable* remark
    - ○ a. disagreeable
    - ○ b. administrative
    - ○ c. familiar
    - ○ d. authorized

27. a weekend of *tranquillity*
    - ○ a. calmness
    - ○ b. excitement
    - ○ c. peace
    - ○ d. confusion

28. the *ambiguous* meaning
    - ○ a. disgusting
    - ○ b. easily composed
    - ○ c. separate
    - ○ d. unclear

29. to *dissipate*
    - ○ a. proceed
    - ○ b. spread or scatter
    - ○ c. restrain
    - ○ d. control

30. a *petty* task
    - ○ a. unimportant
    - ○ b. very trying
    - ○ c. troublesome
    - ○ d. lengthy

31. an *obsolete* computer
    - ○ a. rebuilt
    - ○ b. out-of-date
    - ○ c. late model
    - ○ d. new model

32. to *surmise* the answer
    - ○ a. to guess
    - ○ b. to misunderstand
    - ○ c. to correct
    - ○ d. to write

33. the *ineligible* candidate
    - ○ a. qualified
    - ○ b. accomplished
    - ○ c. not qualified
    - ○ d. knowing

34. to *prohibit* swimming
    - ○ a. instruct
    - ○ b. permit
    - ○ c. discover
    - ○ d. not allow

35. the *insistent* old woman
    - ○ a. offensive
    - ○ b. demanding
    - ○ c. remarkable
    - ○ d. complicated

36. an *insolent* person
    - ○ a. unimportant
    - ○ b. rude and insulting
    - ○ c. not intelligent
    - ○ d. dishonest

37. to *acknowledge* his presence
    - ○ a. cooperate
    - ○ b. contradict
    - ○ c. admit
    - ○ d. refuse

38. to *grapple* with a problem
    - ○ a. to solve
    - ○ b. to struggle over
    - ○ c. to argue over
    - ○ d. to change

39. an *absurd* remark
    - ○ a. ridiculous
    - ○ b. good-hearted
    - ○ c. unkind
    - ○ d. unimportant

40. the *monotonous* sound
    - ○ a. noisy
    - ○ b. unhappy
    - ○ c. demanding
    - ○ d. unchanging

41. to *detect* a crime
    - ○ a. discover
    - ○ b. cover up
    - ○ c. scheme
    - ○ d. commit

Doodling:

TO DRAW OR SCRIBBLE AIMLESSLY

Language Arts

7th Grade Preview

- **Grammar** • **Spelling** • **Vocabulary**
- **Reading Comprehension** • **Writing**

Creating a Vocabulary Crossword Puzzle

From the list of vocabulary words below, create your own crossword puzzle. Of course, you will need to look up the definitions in order to create your own clues.

WORD LIST

admonish	candid	eerie	harass	obnoxious
agitate	component	enthrall	impede	perceive
arduous	conjure	fluctuate	inevitable	pretentious
blatant	desolate	formidable	lethargic	repudiate
buoyant	dissuade	grievous	menial	stringent

Capitalization: Capitalize the names and abbreviations of particular places, such as streets, cities, states, countries, continents, planets, bodies of water, mountains, buildings, and monuments.

Correct the mistakes in the following sentences. Cross out the small letters and write the capital letters above them.

1. The city bus stops at the corner of west palm street and houston mill road.

2. My mother and father always enjoy skiing in salt lake city, utah every winter.

3. Scott and Michele visited rome and venice when they were on vacation in italy.

4. In social studies class, we learned that the nile river flows into the mediterranean sea.

5. When our class visited washington, d.c., our favorite monument was the lincoln memorial.

6. My older brother George climbed mount logan in canada last summer.

7. asia is not only the largest continent but also it is one of the most diverse.

Finding the Misspelled Word. Many of the word groups in this exercise contain spelling mistakes. Some do not have any mistakes. Fill in the circle next to the word that contains a mistake. If you do not find a mistake, mark your answer *No Mistakes*.

8. ○ A. boundary
   ○ B. surprise
   ○ C. awfull
   ○ D. No Mistakes

9. ○ A. acidentally
   ○ B. recognize
   ○ C. perspiration
   ○ D. No Mistakes

10. ○ A. bracelet
    ○ B. government
    ○ C. disastrous
    ○ D. No Mistakes

11. ○ A. minature
    ○ B. library
    ○ C. celery
    ○ D. No Mistakes

12. ○ A. humorous
    ○ B. enthusastic
    ○ C. immediate
    ○ D. No Mistakes

13. ○ A. possibility
    ○ B. chocolate
    ○ C. temperiture
    ○ D. No Mistakes

14. ○ A. absolutely
    ○ B. celebration
    ○ C. admirable
    ○ D. No Mistakes

15. ○ A. confidentialy
    ○ B. dissatisfied
    ○ C. irrelevant
    ○ D. No Mistakes

16. ○ A. admitting
    ○ B. liesure
    ○ C. persuade
    ○ D. No Mistakes

Write an _S_ (sentence) in the blank if the sentence expresses a complete thought. Write an _F_ (sentence fragment) in the blank if the words do not express a complete thought.

_____ 1. Saw beautiful furniture and accessories in the new furniture store yesterday.

_____ 2. Two of my best friends spent the entire summer in Glacier National Park.

_____ 3. On the basketball court Sean was an efficient basketball player.

_____ 4. After spending several months on the coast of South Carolina.

_____ 5. Our hotel room located on the fifteenth floor was comfortable and clean.

_____ 6. Many wrecks occur on the four-lane highway which runs in front of my house.

_____ 7. Mainly because so many drivers fall asleep at the wheel.

_____ 8. To get away from the dullness of such a small town.

_____ 9. The automatic opening doors at the supermarket.

_____10. The loud thunder and lightning kept all of us awake all night.

Correcting Sentences by Adding Apostrophes. The _apostrophe_ is used to indicate possession of nouns (Mark's book). If the noun ends in _-s_ (whether singular or plural) add the apostrophe to indicate possession (teachers' assignments). If, however, the noun does _not_ end in _s_ (whether singular or plural) add the apostrophe and _s_ to indicate possession (fisherman's boat). Fill in the blanks with the correct possessive forms of the words enclosed in parentheses after each sentence.

11. Margaret has read twelve of _____ novels this school year. (Dickens)
12. Wanda admired the _____ uniforms at Buckingham Palace. (guardsmen)
13. The _____ accounts of the expressway accident were incorrect. (newspapers)
14. In a _____ time, Jonathan completed all of his college work. (year)
15. Have you decided to come to see _____ performance? (Margaret)
16. Dr. _____ house was built like an old Tudor house. (Harrison)
17. Please pack your _____ clothes and shoes before we leave today. (sister)
18. Can you tell me the _____ names in the short story? (characters)
19. Classes were dismissed on the day of the _____ reading convention. (teachers)
20. Both of the _____ ambassadors had refused to make an official statement. (nations)
21. The roses in Mr. _____ garden are blooming so well this season. (Harris)
22. _____ mother is an attractive, gracious woman. (Vincent)
23. The _____ birthday presents are in the attic behind the old clothes. (children)
24. Suddenly, the _____ whistle stopped the game. (referee)
25. The _____ mansion was lit by floodlights. (governor)

Agreement of Subject and Verb. In the blank provided, write the correct form of the verb for each sentence. Be sure to check your answer by reading the completed sentence to yourself.

_____ 1. Several of those new colors (appeals, appeal) to me.

_____ 2. The weather forecast (don't, doesn't) look that bad today.

_____ 3. Some of American history (fascinate, fascinates) me and my classmates.

_____ 4. The boy, together with his mother, (was, were) left standing there.

_____ 5. Neither the students nor their teacher (is, are) quite prepared today.

_____ 6. Many of the students in my class (walk, walks) to school.

_____ 7. All of these American writers (is, are) wonderful.

_____ 8. Everyone in my class (likes, like) a good short story.

_____ 9. Fifty dollars (was, were) just too much for me to pay.

_____ 10. Neither Allen nor Walt (wish, wishes) to play in this game.

Writing a Personal Narrative. Now you can write your own personal narrative. On a separate sheet of paper, jot down your first thoughts (i.e., *brainstorming*). Then make a *cluster* to explore your topic. Finally, add more details to your cluster of ideas.

Write a narrative paragraph about a trip or journey you have taken. You may want to write about one of the interesting places you and your parents or grandparents have visited. Ask your parents if they have any *pictures* of any trips that would help you in gaining ideas for your narrative.

Identifying Parts of Speech. Review the parts of speech before you begin this exercise.

Noun – names a person, place, thing or idea
Pronoun – takes the place of a noun
Verb – shows action or state of being
Adverb – modifies a verb, adjective or
     another adverb.
Adjective – modifies a noun or pronoun
	Preposition – relates a noun or pronoun to
	     to another word
	Conjunction – links words or groups of
	     words
	Interjection – expresses strong emotion
	     or surprise

In each of the following sentences, identify the part of speech of the underlined word.

_____ 1. My father's work schedule often takes <u>him</u> out of town.

_____ 2. <u>Oops!</u> I completely ruined my science poster.

_____ 3. Clark walked on the ice <u>very</u> carefully.

_____ 4. Huge crowds of <u>people</u> attended the Summer Olympics.

_____ 5. <u>Some</u> students really enjoyed the dance last Saturday night.

_____ 6. My father will examine the used car, <u>though</u> my aunt will buy it.

_____ 7. Michele <u>played</u> with her little sister while her mother cooked dinner.

_____ 8. My step father is a <u>plant</u> foreman.

_____ 9. Mrs. Walker is a neighbor <u>with</u> many responsibilities.

_____ 10. The beautiful bride <u>walked</u> slowly down the aisle.

_____ 11. The hikers sang folksongs as <u>they</u> walked the trails.

_____ 12. Our staff is <u>especially</u> busy at this time of the year.

Proofreading — Punctuation and Capitalization. The story of Elvis Presley really needs your help. This story is in need of a proofreader, which is you! Make the necessary corrections in capitalization and punctuation on the copy below.

   although elvis Aron presley did not invent rock 'n roll he did more than anyone to popularize it he was rock's most powerful performer From the mid-50's, the "King's" vocal mannerism, sideburns, and attitude made him an International Hero of the young

   During his lifetime, Elvis sold more than four hundred million records   he had forty-five golden hit records Elvis also appeared in thirty-two movies.

   when Presley died on august 16 1977 at the age of forty-two, many mourners journeyed to memphis, tennessee, Presley's home, to pay their last respects! Elvis left behind an almost immeasurable influence on popular music.

Possessive Pronouns. A possessive pronoun is one which shows ownership. A possessive pronoun takes the place of a possessive noun. Possessive pronouns never have apostrophes.

Examples: my, mine, your, yours, his, her, hers, its, our, ours, their, theirs

Circle the possessive pronouns in the following sentences.

1. Who is your favorite character in American History?
2. His name is Thomas Jefferson who was a Renaissance man.
3. He was the third president of our country.
4. Her vacation has been planned for a long time.
5. The antique furniture in my grandmother's house is theirs.
6. The azalea bush is dying; its leaves are covered with a fungus.
7. That brown leather glove must be mine.
8. Thomas, you know this is my locker.
9. Do you know their plans for the trip?
10. Is that blue suitcase hers?

Using Commas Correctly.
- **A comma is used after words of a direct address at the beginning of the sentence.**
    Phyllis, please call me Thursday morning.
- **A comma is used to set off an introductory phrase or dependent clause.**
    When I finish my homework, I need to study for a science test.
- **Use two commas to set off interrupting words or expressions.**
    What, in his opinion, is the best book on this list?

Add commas in the following sentences.

11. Social studies I believe is my favorite subject.
12. Can you tell me Ralph why you did not finish your homework?
13. When the students returned from lunch Mrs. Bates played a geography game.
14. Mrs. Bouie said off the record that she was very disappointed in our behavior.
15. Dr. Harrison what should I take for this skin rash?
16. Having listened to his story Donald's mother restricted him for a week.
17. When Mr. Noland gives us a test he leaves the room.
18. This I suppose is the easiest way to learn the states and capitals.
19. Blake are you hungry yet?
20. President Jimmy Carter was born in Plains which is a small town in Georgia.

TIME OUT: Can you think of a sentence where every word begins with the letter *w*? You can make your sentence as long as you like, but be sensible.

Homophones. Some words sound alike but are spelled differently and have different meanings. Words like these are called *homophones*.

its	belonging to it	stair	a step
it's	contraction for **it is**	stare	to look at intently
one	a single unit	their	belonging to them
won	gained a victory	there	a place; word that begins a sentence
whose	belonging to whom	they're	contraction for **they are**
who's	contraction for **who is**		
		to	part of infinitive; toward
your	belonging to you	too	also; more than enough
you're	contraction for **you are**	two	the number **2**

Complete each sentence below by writing the correct word on the line.

1. _____ purpose was to honor President Ronald Reagan.   (Its, It's)
2. _____ were many introductions and speeches at the conference.   (Their, There)
3. If _____ late to class, you must secure a pass from the office.   (your, you're)
4. _____ lives were influenced by Martin Luther King, Jr.?   (Who's, Whose)
5. At first there was some opposition _____ Tony's height.   (to, too, two)
6. After the Braves _____ the World Series, there was chaos in the streets.   (one, won)
7. Which topic does _____ social studies report cover?   (your, you're)
8. _____ performing in the second act of the play tonight.   (They're, There)
9. Which _____ of the pair of shoes do you prefer?   (one, won)
10. The science teacher offered us _____ choices for our research paper.   (to, two)

Descriptive Paragraph. A descriptive paragraph creates a word picture of a person, an animal, a place or a thing. The details are usually arranged in space order to help the readers picture the topic in their minds. Write a descriptive paragraph in which you describe a street or road outside your home in the late afternoon.

_____
_____
_____
_____
_____
_____
_____
_____

Writing a Business Letter. The style of a business letter is a little different from the style of a friendly letter. A business letter is somewhat more direct and more formal. Your letter will be a written record of your business transaction.

Write a business letter in which you had ordered a necklace for your mother's birthday from Coco's Designer Jewelry, 1727 Monroe Street, Chicago, Illinois 60625. In your order you had enclosed a check from your father in the amount of $31.98 including shipping charges. Your mother's birthday is only 10 days away. The necklace has not arrived. Be sure to indent at the beginning of each paragraph.

(your return address) _____

(your city, state, zip) _____

(today's date) _____

Coco's Designer Jewelry
1727 Monroe Street
Chicago, Illinois 60625

Attention: Mail Order Department

_____

_____

_____

_____

_____

_____

_____

_____

_____

_____

_____

(closing) _____

(signature) _____

TIME OUT: Find an envelope and address the envelope for this letter. Be sure to write the addresses in the proper places. Place capitals and punctuation marks where necessary.

Identifying Dependent Clauses.

> An *adjective clause* is a dependent clause that functions as an adjective modifying nouns or pronouns. An adjective clause usually begins with a relative pronoun, *who, whom, whose, whoever, which, what,* or *that.* An *adverb clause* is a dependent clause that functions as an adverb modifying verbs, adjectives, or other adverbs. An adverb clause usually begins with a *subordinating conjunction,* such as *until, when, as, although,* or *if.* A *noun clause* is a dependent clause that functions as a noun. Some of the words that can introduce noun clauses are *that, why, what, which, whichever, who, whom, whoever, whomever,* and *whose.*

In each of the following sentences, underline the dependent clause and then indicate if it is an adjective clause (**ADJ**), an adverb clause (**ADV**), or a noun clause (**N**).

_____ 1. Joseph has a brown sweater that his grandmother knitted.

_____ 2. If you listen carefully to the directions, you should do well on this assignment.

_____ 3. I practiced my music lesson daily until I could play the selection perfectly.

_____ 4. The computer teacher already knows what the problem is.

_____ 5. The jewelry that my mother lost was worth a great deal of money.

_____ 6. George always eats hot dogs when he attends a basketball game.

_____ 7. Mr. Sanders read the announcement of the winners to whoever would listen.

_____ 8. Mr. Sanders' voice cracked as he read the winners.

Irregular Verbs. In order to form the past and past participle for *regular verbs*, add *-ed* or *-d.* The past and past participle of *irregular verbs* are formed in a variety of ways. The chart below shows the forms for some commonly used irregular verbs. Past participle forms are used with helping verbs, such as *has, have, had, am, is, are, was,* and *were.*

PRESENT	PAST	PAST PARTICIPLE	PRESENT	PAST	PAST PARTICIPLE
begin	began	begun	leave	left	left
bring	brought	brought	lend	lent	lent
catch	caught	caught	throw	threw	thrown
drink	drank	drunk	know	knew	known
grow	grew	grown	draw	drew	drawn
show	showed	shown	swim	swam	swum

9. Ted Turner (threw, thrown) the first ball which started the baseball season.

10. Mrs. Parker said, "You may (begin, begun) the first part of the achievement test."

11. Have you (drank, drunk) all of the pink lemonade?

12. New students are (showed, shown) around the school by Mrs. Wright, our counselor.

13. My mother has (knew, known) our neighbors for about twelve years.

14. Several of my father's friends had (lend, lent) money to Melissa's family.

Mathematics

6th Grade in Review
• Estimation • Integers •Geometry
• Equations• Graphing • Statistics•Probability

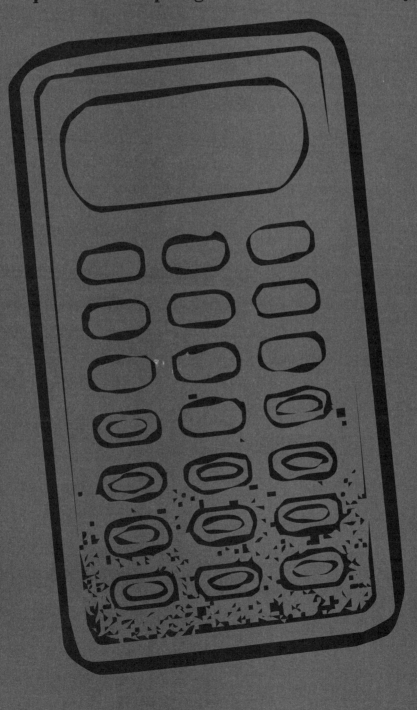

TOOTHPICK TRICKS

1. Use 13 toothpicks to create a toothpick creature like the one below. The creature is looking to the left. Move 2 toothpicks and make the creature look to the right.

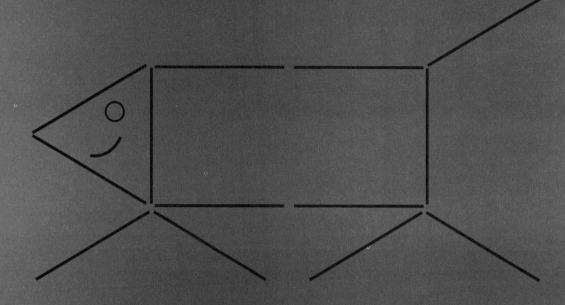

2. Use 12 toothpicks to create a 4-unit square then...
   a. Remove 2 toothpicks leaving 2 squares of different sizes.
   b. Move 3 toothpicks to form 3 identical squares.
   c. Move 4 toothpicks to form 3 identical squares.
   d. Move 2 toothpicks to form 7 squares which are not all identical.
   e. Move 4 toothpicks to form 10 squares which are not all identical.

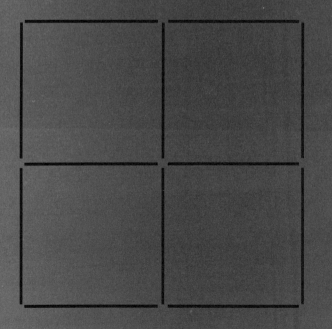

Expanded notation: Write each of the following numbers in its expanded form.

5,439   = 5,000 + 400 + 30 + 9

1.   37,057   = _____

2.   12,345 689   = _____

3.   187,042   = _____

4.   6,000,862   = _____

5.   51,008   = _____

6.   9,999,996   = _____

7.   5,412   = _____

8.   68,888,222   = _____

9.   805,603   = _____

10.   7,007   = _____

Party Time

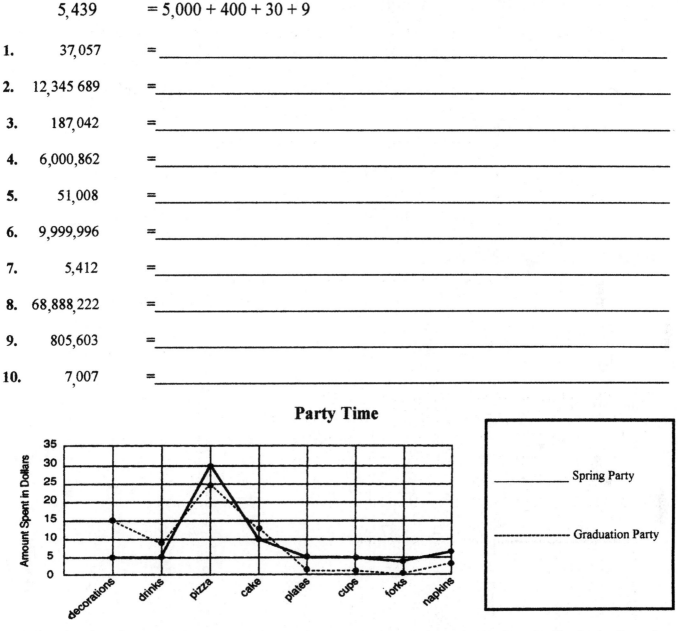

1. Approximately how much money was spent for paper plates, cups, forks and napkins for the Spring Party?

2. For which of the two parties was the bill greater for decorations and pizza?

3. Based on the budgets for each party which party had the most guests?

4. What was the total cost for each party? Spring _____   Graduation _____

5. What was the approximate difference in the amount spent on the two parties?

Rounding the Numbers.

Round to the nearest 100. **Example: 61** __100__

1. 187 _____

2. 732 _____

3. 1,957 _____

4. 6,848 _____

5. 153 _____

6. 9,072 _____

Round to the nearest 1,000

7. 601 _____

8. 8,765 _____

9. 14,531 _____

10. 58,444 _____

11. 131,032 _____

12. 772,277 _____

Round to the nearest 1,000,000

13. 8,922,067

_____

14. 9,638,013

_____

15. 6,362,161

_____

Estimate by rounding

16. 508 + 489 = _____

17.   87 + 187 = _____

18. 165 − 44 = _____

19. 1 481 − 392 = _____

20.   31 x 87 = _____

21. 29.34 x 5.37 = _____

22. 12.4 + 8.543 = _____

23. 32.78 - 18.29 = _____

24. 1.87 x .84 = _____

25.   47 ÷ 11 = _____

26. 409.4 ÷ 48.4 = _____

27. 14.948 ÷ 5.1 = _____

28. 1987.4 x 7.9 = _____

29. 648.09 - .987 = _____

30. .9871 x .87 = _____

Word Problem Using Estimation. Look at the chart below and choose the best estimate of the total number of students at Turner Middle School. Bubble in the best answer.

6th Grade	273
7th Grade	225
8th Grade	309

31. O   A. 200 + 200 + 300   O   C. 300 + 300 + 300
     O   B. 300 + 200 + 300   O   D. 300 + 200 + 400

Write the following using correct word form.

1. 187,653 _____

2. 87,460,030 _____

3. 222,333,189 _____

4. 1,234,567,890 _____

5. 543,201,065,483 _____

Reviewing Whole Number Operations.

6.   361,950
       27,075
 +   8,408

7.   100,239
      67,843
 + 341,795

8.   528,693
      17,012
 +   4,206

9.   238,679
 - 139,742

10.   31,700
 - 23,050

11.   401,061
 -   98,765

12.   876
   x 952

13.   401
   x 270

14.   275
   x 907

15. 90$\overline{)29,786}$

16. 143$\overline{)770,971}$

17. 64$\overline{)4,281}$

Multiples and Least Common Multiples.

1. Coco's Bake Shop sells pastries in groups of 4 and cookies by the half dozen (6). What is the least number of each you would need to buy in order to have an equal number of pastries and cookies? _____

List the next five multiples of each number.

2. 2 _____   3. 11 _____   4.   25 _____

5. 7 _____   6. 16 _____   7. 200 _____

8. 10 _____   9. 40 _____   10. 150 _____

Write the LCM (Least Common Multiple) of the numbers.

11. 2 and 5 _____   12. 4 and 12 _____   13. 3, 6, and 9 _____

14. 5 and 7 _____   15. 6 and 8 _____   16. 2, 3, and 5 _____

17. 3 and 6 _____   18. 8 and 12 _____   19. 3, 10, and 15 _____

A year whose number is divisible by 4 is a leap year. A number is divisible by 4 if the number formed by its last two digits is divisible by 4. The only exception is that a century year is a leap year only when its number is divisible by 400. Is the year a leap year? Write *Yes* or *No*.

20. 1812 ____   21. 1992 ____   22. 2100 ____   23. 1882 ____   24. 1900 ____

Challenge

If you were to live to be eighty years old, how many leap years will you see?

Factors and Greatest Common Factors. When one number is divisible by a second, the second number is called a factor of the first. Two numbers may have some factors that are the same. These numbers are called common factors. The greatest of the common factors of two numbers is called their greatest common factor (GCF). Complete the following:

1. factors of 4: __ __ __

   factors of 8: __ __ __ __

   common factors of 4 and 8: __ __ __

   GCF of 4 and 8: __

2. factors of 16: __ __ __ __ __

   factors of 20: __ __ __ __ __ __

   common factors of 16 and 20: __ __ __

   GCF of 16 and 20: __

Write the GCF of the numbers.

3. 5 and 15 ___

4. 12 and 24 ___

5. 4 and 6 ___

6. 18 and 21 ___

7. 7 and 15 ___

8. 12 and 44 ___

9. 15 and 18 ___

10. 15 and 40 ___

11. 13 and 21 ___

Challenge

12. There are 12 teachers and 42 students competing in the Student-Faculty Meet. What is the greatest number of players per team if the teacher teams and the student teams must have the same number of players?

Calculators Please

13. The number **496** has nine factors besides 496. The sum of these nine factors is 496. What are the nine factors?

Prime Factors. Prime numbers are numbers that have exactly 2 factors; 1 and itself. For example: the number *11* is prime. Its factors are *11* and *1*.

Composite numbers are numbers that have more than two factors. The number *18* is a composite number. Its factors are *1, 2, 3, 6, 9,* and *18*. The numbers *0* and *1* are neither prime nor composite. Every composite number can be written as a product of prime factors.

A factor tree will help identify the prime factors of a given number. To create a factor, tree factor the numbers until the end of each branch is a prime number.

2 x 3 x 3 x 5 is the prime factorization of 90. The order of the factors may vary. Complete the factor tree then write the prime factorization for each.

```
1.      36          2.  60          3.   54          4.   24
       / \              / \              / \              / \
     2 x 18            x                x                x
        / \              / \           / \  / \            / \
      2 x 9            x              x    x              x
         / \             / \                                / \
       3 x 3           x                                   x
 2 x 2 x 3 x 3      __ x __ x __ x __   __ x __ x __ x __  __ x __ x __ x __
```

On a separate sheet of paper, create a factor tree and prime factorization for each number.

  5. 72   6. 55   7. 44   8. 54   9. 95   10. 200

Twins and Triplets. Twin primes are pairs of prime numbers that differ by 2, such as 11 and 13. Three prime numbers that differ by 2 form a prime triplet.

11. Name the twin prime of 7. _____

12. Name the twin prime of 19. _____

13. Name the pairs of twin primes between 20 and 50. _____

14. Name a prime triplet less than 50. _____

15. Write the prime factorization of 175. _____

Fractions Review.
Ye Old Book Shop is open 8 hours per day, 6 days per week. Johnnie's off day is Monday. She works at the shop 4 hours each day that the shop is open. Using this information, solve the word problems below. Remember to reduce to the lowest terms.

1. What fraction of the hours in a day is the shop open?

2. What fraction of the hours in a week is the shop open?

3. What fraction of the hours in a week does Johnnie work?

4. What fraction of the days in a week is the shop open?

5. What fraction of the hours in a day does Johnnie work?

6. What fraction of the hours that the shop is open does Johnnie work?

Logically Speaking. One summer evening our family was sitting in the backyard watching lightning bugs. Suddenly five of the lightning bugs came straight toward us. As they approached, they began to increase in size. These were not your average lightning bugs! They were actually visitors from a far away world, Tryion. Each creature identified itself by name, Toto, Tondo, Toosh, Tibbitt, and Tutu. They asked to be introduced to our leader. Could you correctly introduce each of the aliens to our leader?

7. Toto stands between Tibbitt and Toosh.

8. Tibbitt's emblem is the △

9. Toosh is their leader and always stands at the front.

10. Tutu refuses to have anyone on her left.

_____ _____ _____ _____ _____

Fraction Review. The fraction 2/3 is read two-thirds. Remember: Write a fraction for the shaded part

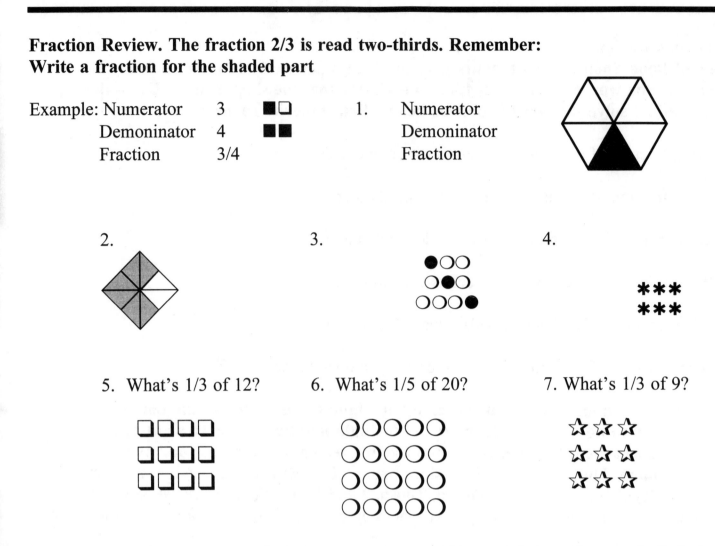

Example: Numerator   3
Demoninator   4
Fraction   3/4

1.   Numerator
Demoninator
Fraction

2.

3.

4.

5. What's 1/3 of 12?

6. What's 1/5 of 20?

7. What's 1/3 of 9?

All of the people in the graphic below are represented by a point on the graph. Label each point on the graph with the name of the person it represents.

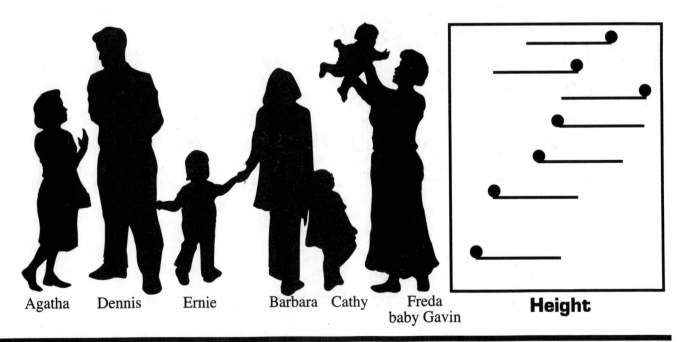

Agatha   Dennis   Ernie   Barbara Cathy   Freda
baby Gavin

Height

Equivalent Fractions. All fractions that name the same number are called *equivalent fractions* ($\frac{1}{5} \approx \frac{2}{10} \approx \frac{10}{50}$). Equivalent fractions are written by multiplying or dividing both the numerator and denominator by the same number.

Examples: $\frac{1}{5} = \frac{1 \times 2}{5 \times 2} = \frac{2}{10}$ $\frac{10}{50} = \frac{10 \div 10}{50 \div 10} = \frac{1}{5}$

1. $\frac{1}{12} = \frac{1 \times 3}{12 \times 3} = $

2. $\frac{3}{9} = \frac{3 \div 3}{9 \div 3} = $

3. $\frac{3}{4} = \frac{3 \times 3}{4 \times 3} = $

4. $\frac{1}{9} = \frac{1 \times}{9 \times} = \frac{4}{36}$

5. $\frac{20}{24} = \frac{20 \div}{24 \div} = \frac{5}{6}$

6. $\frac{2}{9} = \frac{8}{\quad}$

7. $\frac{1}{2} = \frac{\quad}{14}$

8. $\frac{8}{72} = \frac{\quad}{9}$

9. $\frac{7}{12} = \frac{14}{\quad}$

10. $\frac{13}{15} = \frac{\quad}{45}$

11. $\frac{1}{8} = \frac{\quad}{32}$

12. $\frac{1}{5} = \frac{4}{\quad}$

13. $\frac{8}{\quad} = \frac{24}{36}$

14. $\frac{\quad}{3} = \frac{18}{27}$

15. $\frac{7}{21} = \frac{\quad}{105}$

Name the two equivalent fractions by circling them.

16. $\frac{6}{10}, \frac{6}{8}, \frac{3}{5}, \frac{4}{10}$

17. $\frac{3}{12}, \frac{1}{12}, \frac{1}{3}, \frac{1}{4}$

18. $\frac{7}{8}, \frac{14}{17}, \frac{28}{32}, \frac{36}{40}$

19. $\frac{13}{26}, \frac{13}{39}, \frac{1}{13}, \frac{1}{2}$

20. $\frac{6}{10}, \frac{11}{20}, \frac{22}{40}, \frac{26}{40}$

21. $\frac{1}{2}, \frac{3}{8}, \frac{5}{12}, \frac{18}{48}$

22. $\frac{2}{9}, \frac{1}{6}, \frac{6}{54}, \frac{4}{18}$

23. $\frac{13}{14}, \frac{16}{28}, \frac{6}{7}, \frac{26}{28}$

24. $\frac{5}{7}, \frac{11}{15}, \frac{30}{35}, \frac{33}{45}$

Cross Products. Cross Products may be used to check if two fractions are equivalent. When cross products are equal, the fractions are equivalent.

Example: $\dfrac{2}{9}$, $\dfrac{4}{18}$ 2 x 18   4 x 9   ←   cross products

36   =   36

Check the cross products for equivalent fractions.

1. $\dfrac{3}{4}$, $\dfrac{9}{12}$

2. $\dfrac{2}{5}$, $\dfrac{21}{30}$

3. $\dfrac{1}{6}$, $\dfrac{2}{18}$

4. $\dfrac{5}{9}$, $\dfrac{20}{36}$

5. $\dfrac{7}{9}$, $\dfrac{35}{40}$

6. $\dfrac{8}{15}$, $\dfrac{24}{45}$

Comparing Fractions. To compare fractions with like denominators, compare their numerators.

To compare fractions with unlike denominators, rewrite fractions as equivalent fractions with a common denominator.

A common denominator is a common multiple of the denominators.

The least common denominator (LCD) is the least common multiple (LCM) of the denominators.

Examples:
Write equivalent fractions
with a denominator of 12.   Compare the fractions.

$\dfrac{2}{3} = \dfrac{8}{12}$ $\dfrac{3}{4} = \dfrac{9}{12}$ $\dfrac{8}{12} \langle \dfrac{9}{12}$, so $\dfrac{2}{3} \langle \dfrac{3}{4}$

What is the LCM of the denominators?

7. $\dfrac{1}{6}$, $\dfrac{1}{3}$ _____

8. $\dfrac{3}{4}$, $\dfrac{2}{3}$ _____

9. $\dfrac{1}{8}$, $\dfrac{1}{6}$ _____

10. $\dfrac{2}{5}$, $\dfrac{3}{8}$ _____

11. $\dfrac{3}{8}$, $\dfrac{5}{12}$ _____

12. $\dfrac{1}{2}$, $\dfrac{4}{5}$ _____

Rewrite the fractions. Use the LCD for each pair.

As an example:

1. $\dfrac{5}{6}, \dfrac{11}{12}$

2. $\dfrac{1}{3}, \dfrac{2}{5}$

3. $\dfrac{1}{4}, \dfrac{3}{10}$

4. $\dfrac{4}{11}, \dfrac{3}{33}$

Answer $\dfrac{10}{12}, \dfrac{11}{12}$

5. $\dfrac{1}{10}, \dfrac{4}{15}$

6. $\dfrac{1}{3}, \dfrac{2}{9}$

7. $\dfrac{3}{5}, \dfrac{4}{9}$

8. $\dfrac{1}{7}, \dfrac{5}{9}$

Write < or > to compare the fractions.

9. $\dfrac{1}{7} \quad \dfrac{4}{7}$

10. $\dfrac{3}{8} \quad \dfrac{3}{4}$

11. $\dfrac{1}{3} \quad \dfrac{1}{12}$

12. $\dfrac{1}{2} \quad \dfrac{1}{8}$

$\dfrac{2}{7} \quad \dfrac{4}{7}$

$\dfrac{5}{8} \quad \dfrac{3}{4}$

$\dfrac{1}{3} \quad \dfrac{5}{12}$

$\dfrac{1}{2} \quad \dfrac{3}{8}$

$\dfrac{3}{7} \quad \dfrac{4}{7}$

$\dfrac{7}{8} \quad \dfrac{3}{4}$

$\dfrac{1}{3} \quad \dfrac{7}{12}$

$\dfrac{1}{2} \quad \dfrac{5}{8}$

13. Tony spent $\dfrac{2}{3}$ of an hour on the Internet and $\dfrac{7}{8}$ of an hour watching television. On which activity did he spend more time?

14. Margaret completed $\dfrac{1}{4}$ of her project on Wednesday and another $\dfrac{1}{3}$ of the project on Friday. On which day did she complete more of her project?

15. Angela cooked $\dfrac{2}{5}$ of a pound of rice on Friday and $\dfrac{3}{7}$ of a pound on Saturday. On which day did she cook the most rice?

16. Madison and Ashton shared a pizza. Madison ate $\dfrac{3}{8}$ of the pizza and Ashton ate $\dfrac{1}{2}$. Who ate the most pizza?

Fractions - Simplify - Lowest Term. To simplify $\frac{6}{12}$, you can divide the numerator and denominator by the same non-zero number.

For example: $\frac{6}{12} = \frac{6 \div 3}{12 \div 3} = \frac{2}{4}$

To write $\frac{6}{12}$ in lowest terms, you can divide the numerator and denominator by 6, their Greatest Common Factor (GCF).

1. $\frac{4}{6} = \frac{4 \div 2}{6 \div 2} =$

2. $\frac{24}{32} = \frac{24 \div 8}{32 \div 8} =$

3. $\frac{3}{15} = \frac{3 \div 3}{15 \div 3} =$

4. $\frac{6}{24} = \frac{6 \div 6}{24 \div 6} =$

5. $\frac{20}{36} = \frac{20 \div 4}{36 \div 4} =$

6. $\frac{28}{36} = \frac{28 \div 4}{36 \div 4} =$

7. $\frac{6}{9} = \frac{6 \div}{9 \div} = \frac{2}{3}$

8. $\frac{12}{16} = \frac{12 \div}{16 \div} = \frac{3}{4}$

9. $\frac{9}{15} = \frac{9 \div}{15 \div} = \frac{3}{5}$

Write in lowest terms.

10. $\frac{2}{6}$

11. $\frac{8}{40}$

12. $\frac{7}{28}$

13. $\frac{9}{36}$

14. $\frac{14}{28}$

15. $\frac{14}{21}$

16. $\frac{26}{39}$

17. $\frac{8}{24}$

18. $\frac{12}{36}$

19. $\frac{35}{50}$

20. $\frac{15}{24}$

21. $\frac{16}{40}$

These are facts that a news reporter learned while reporting on a story down on the water front. Write the fraction in lowest terms.

22. The ice in the harbor is able to float because it is almost $\frac{900}{1,000}$ as heavy as water.

23. On an average fishing boat, $\frac{580}{720}$ of the day's catch was unusable.

24. On one of the larger cruise ships, $\frac{126}{2,394}$ passengers were from a foreign country.

Rewrite each mixed number as a fraction.

Step 1 Multiply the denominator by the whole number. $2\frac{3}{4}$ (4 x 2) = 8

Step 2 Add the numerator to the product.   8 + 3 = 11

Step 3 Write the sum over the denominator. $\frac{11}{4}$

1. $2\frac{1}{2}$

2. $4\frac{4}{5}$

3. $2\frac{3}{8}$

4. $4\frac{1}{5}$

5. $3\frac{2}{5}$

6. $2\frac{2}{3}$

7. $6\frac{1}{3}$

8. $6\frac{7}{9}$

9. $7\frac{5}{8}$

10. $7\frac{2}{3}$

11. $8\frac{1}{2}$

12. $1\frac{3}{4}$

13. $1\frac{1}{3}$

14. $1\frac{5}{8}$

15. $2\frac{2}{7}$

16. $6\frac{1}{15}$

Rewrite each fraction as a mixed or whole number. Use division to change fractions to a whole or mixed number (Round off to the whole number as in the following example).

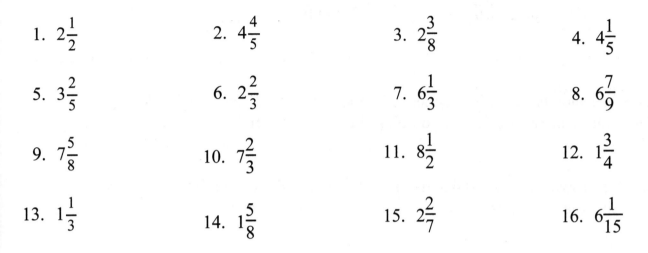

Example: $\frac{9}{3} \leftarrow 3\overline{)9}^{\,3} \rightarrow 3$

$\frac{11}{4} \leftarrow 4\overline{)11}^{\,2} \rightarrow 2\dfrac{3-remainder}{4-divisor} \rightarrow 3$

$\dfrac{-8}{\ \ 3}$

17. $\frac{11}{6}$

18. $\frac{17}{11}$

19. $\frac{15}{7}$

20. $\frac{33}{8}$

21. $\frac{26}{5}$

22. $\frac{40}{8}$

23. $\frac{25}{3}$

24. $\frac{80}{9}$

25. $\frac{32}{4}$

26. $\frac{41}{7}$

27. $\frac{31}{2}$

28. $\frac{88}{9}$

Write the quotient as a mixed number. Write the fraction in lowest terms.

1. $4\overline{)63}$

2. $6\overline{)26}$

3. $15\overline{)36}$

4. $9\overline{)84}$

5. $9\overline{)39}$

6. $15\overline{)50}$

7. $8\overline{)38}$

8. $12\overline{)78}$

9. The school's snack bar is selling popcorn by the bag or box. Each bag will fill half of a box. How many boxes are needed to hold 6 bags of popcorn?

10. A recipe for brownies calls for 4 squares of chocolate. How many recipes can be made using 48 chocolate squares?

11. If 16 students are going on a field trip and the school cafeteria provides 30 sandwiches for the group. How many sandwiches did each student receive?

12. The average serving of potatoes is 6 ozs. How many servings are there in 2 lbs. of potatoes?

TIME OUT: Faces and Shapes
Each of the figures is created by combining a series of shapes. Draw the faces for each figure. Then count how many of each face does the figure have.

a.　　　　　b.　　　　　c.　　　　　d.

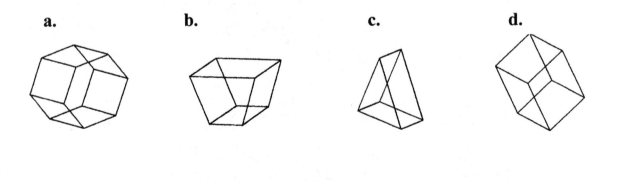

_____ _____　　_____ _____　　_____ _____　　_____ _____

_____ _____

Fractions to Decimals. To convert a fraction to a decimal, divide the numerator by the denominator. Zeros can be added after the decimal point in the dividend as often as needed until the digits in the quotient begin to repeat (repeating decimal). A repeating decimal may be shown by drawing a bar over the digit or digits that repeat. When the answer is a repeating decimal, it is often rounded off. Mixed numbers may be written as decimals. Divide the fractional part of the mixed number. Add the whole number and the decimal.

Example: $2\frac{4}{5} \rightarrow \frac{4}{5} \rightarrow 5\overline{)4.0}^{\,0.8} \rightarrow 2 + 0.8 = 2.8$

Write as a decimal.

1. $\frac{2}{5}$

2. $\frac{9}{40}$

3. $\frac{7}{80}$

4. $\frac{5}{9}$

5. $\frac{7}{22}$

6. $4\frac{7}{100}$

7. $9\frac{1}{8}$

8. $4\frac{5}{8}$

9. $\frac{9}{50}$

10. $\frac{1}{40}$

11. $\frac{1}{3}$

12. $\frac{7}{12}$

13. $\frac{1}{11}$

14. $8\frac{67}{100}$

15. $1\frac{3}{8}$

16. $5\frac{17}{25}$

17. $\frac{1}{50}$

18. $\frac{3}{8}$

19. $\frac{5}{11}$

20. $\frac{1}{15}$

21. $\frac{568}{1,000}$

22. $7\frac{87}{100}$

23. $7\frac{2}{5}$

24. $3\frac{10}{16}$

25. $\frac{3}{4}$

26. $\frac{16}{25}$

27. $\frac{37}{45}$

28. $\frac{5}{6}$

29. $5\frac{3}{10}$

30. $7\frac{201}{1,000}$

31. $8\frac{4}{5}$

32. $9\frac{3}{5}$

TIME OUT: Which costs more per pound, a prime rib that costs $31.35 and weighs 5 lbs. or a small car that costs $6,492 and weighs 1,200 lbs.? Write the steps you would take to answer this question.

Addition and Subtraction of fractions. To add or subtract fractions with like denominators, write the sum or difference of the numerator over the common denominator. Then write the answer in lowest terms.

Examples: $\dfrac{1}{8} + \dfrac{3}{8} = \dfrac{4}{8} = \dfrac{1}{2}$ $\qquad\qquad$ $\dfrac{3}{8} - \dfrac{1}{8} = \dfrac{2}{8} = \dfrac{1}{4}$

1. $\dfrac{1}{4} + \dfrac{2}{4} =$ $\qquad$ 6. $\dfrac{3}{8} + \dfrac{3}{8} =$ $\qquad$ 11. $\dfrac{4}{11} + \dfrac{5}{11} =$

2. $\dfrac{8}{9} + \dfrac{2}{9} =$ $\qquad$ 7. $\dfrac{13}{15} + \dfrac{4}{15} =$ $\qquad$ 12. $\dfrac{7}{12} + \dfrac{5}{12} =$

3. $\dfrac{3}{4} - \dfrac{1}{4} =$ $\qquad$ 8. $\dfrac{4}{5} - \dfrac{2}{5} =$ $\qquad$ 13. $\dfrac{9}{15} - \dfrac{4}{15} =$

4. $\dfrac{9}{20} - \dfrac{3}{20} =$ $\qquad$ 9. $\dfrac{10}{27} - \dfrac{4}{27} =$ $\qquad$ 14. $\dfrac{33}{48} - \dfrac{27}{48} =$

5. $\dfrac{3}{16} + \dfrac{1}{16} + \dfrac{5}{16} =$ $\qquad$ 10. $\dfrac{7}{19} + \dfrac{1}{19} + \dfrac{7}{19} =$ $\qquad$ 15. $\dfrac{11}{15} + \dfrac{2}{15} + \dfrac{8}{15} =$

Adding and subtracting fractions with unlike denominators. Rewrite each fraction as an equivalent fraction with the least common denominator. Problems will be easier to solve if the LCD is used but any common multiple of the denominators can be used as a common denominator.

16. Example $\dfrac{1}{2} + \dfrac{1}{4} + \dfrac{1}{6} =$ $\qquad$ 19. $\dfrac{1}{2} + \dfrac{2}{3} + \dfrac{1}{4} =$ $\qquad$ 22. $\dfrac{1}{2} + \dfrac{1}{3} + \dfrac{1}{5} =$

$\qquad$ Answer $\dfrac{6}{12} + \dfrac{3}{12} + \dfrac{2}{12} = \dfrac{11}{12}$

17. $\dfrac{1}{2} - \dfrac{1}{5} =$ $\qquad$ 20. $\dfrac{8}{9} - \dfrac{5}{6} =$ $\qquad$ 23. $\dfrac{3}{4} - \dfrac{5}{12} =$

18. $\dfrac{3}{4} + \dfrac{5}{7} =$ $\qquad$ 21. $\dfrac{3}{8} + \dfrac{1}{4} =$ $\qquad$ 24. $\dfrac{3}{10} - \dfrac{1}{4} =$

Addition and Subtraction of mixed numbers. To add a mixed number, first rewrite all of the fractions with a common denominator. Then add the fractions. Add the whole numbers and regroup the answers.

Example:

$$5\frac{2}{3} = 5\frac{8}{12}$$
$$+\,4\frac{3}{4} = +\,4\frac{9}{12}$$
$$9\frac{17}{12} = 9 + 1\frac{5}{12} = 10\frac{5}{12}$$

To subtract fractions or mixed numbers with unlike denominators, rewrite fractions as equivalent fractions with a common denominator. Subtract the fractions. Subtract the whole numbers.

Example:

$$6\frac{5}{6} = 6\frac{5}{6}$$
$$-\,4\frac{1}{3} = -\,4\frac{2}{6}$$
$$2\frac{3}{6} = 2\frac{1}{2}$$

1.
$$3\frac{9}{10}$$
$$+\,4\frac{1}{4}$$

2.
$$6\frac{7}{8}$$
$$+\,4\frac{1}{4}$$

3.
$$11\frac{2}{3}$$
$$-\,7\frac{3}{5}$$

4.
$$12\frac{3}{4}$$
$$-\,4\frac{7}{20}$$

5.
$$3\frac{9}{10}$$
$$+\,4\frac{7}{10}$$

6.
$$8\frac{1}{2}$$
$$+\,7\frac{3}{5}$$

Multiplying fractions and whole numbers.

$$\frac{1}{5} \times 3 = \frac{1 \times 3}{5} = \frac{3}{5} \quad \textbf{and} \quad 3 \times \frac{1}{5} = \frac{3 \times 1}{5} = \frac{3}{5}$$

Multiplying fractions.

$$\frac{3}{4} \times \frac{1}{2} = \frac{3 \times 1}{4 \times 2} = \frac{\text{(multiply the numerators)}}{\text{(multiply the denominators)}} = \frac{3}{8}$$

A fractional answer is usually expressed in lowest terms. It may be necessary to divide the numerator and the denominator of the product by a common factor.

$$\frac{1}{4} \times \frac{2}{3} = \frac{1 \times 2}{4 \times 3} = \frac{2}{12} \frac{\text{(divide the numerator by 2)}}{\text{(divide the denominator by 2)}} = \frac{1}{6}$$

Or divide one of the numerators and one of the denominators by a common factor before multiplying.

$$\frac{1}{4} \times \frac{2}{3} = \frac{1}{4} \times \frac{2}{3} = \frac{\text{(divide numerator by 2)}}{\text{(divide denominator by 2)}} = \frac{1 \times 1}{2 \times 3} = \frac{1}{6}$$

Solve the problems below.

1. $\frac{3}{8} \times \frac{7}{9}$

2. $\frac{3}{4} \times \frac{8}{16}$

3. $\frac{2}{9} \times \frac{5}{4}$

4. $\frac{5}{6} \times \frac{2}{5}$

5. $\frac{7}{12} \times \frac{6}{7}$

6. $\frac{8}{15} \times \frac{5}{15}$

7. $\frac{4}{7} \times \frac{5}{16}$

8. $\frac{4}{5} \times \frac{10}{12}$

9. $\frac{7}{8} \times \frac{3}{14}$

10. $\frac{3}{6} \times \frac{2}{5}$

11. $\frac{9}{12} \times \frac{6}{15}$

12. $\frac{2}{6} \times \frac{5}{8}$

13. $\frac{1}{8} \times \frac{4}{6}$

14. $\frac{3}{4} \times \frac{12}{18}$

15. $\frac{4}{3} \times \frac{7}{11}$

16. $\frac{5}{6} \times \frac{6}{13}$

17. $\frac{8}{13} \times \frac{7}{24}$

18. $\frac{9}{16} \times \frac{2}{13}$

Multiplying mixed numbers. First write the mixed number as an improper fraction. Whole numbers may be written with a denominator of one (1).

$$5\frac{2}{3} \times 12 = \frac{17}{3} \times \frac{12}{1} \times = \frac{68}{1} = 68$$

To multiply two mixed numbers, first write both mixed numbers as improper fractions.

$$2\frac{2}{7} \times 4\frac{1}{4} = \frac{16}{7} \times \frac{17}{4} = \frac{68}{7} = 9\frac{5}{7}$$

Solve the problems below.

1. $4\frac{2}{3} \times 2\frac{5}{8}$ 4. $3\frac{1}{7} \times 5\frac{1}{12}$

2. $3\frac{7}{8} \times 4$ 5. $6\frac{4}{12} \times 3$

3. $7\frac{5}{8} \times 2\frac{1}{3}$ 6. $2\frac{3}{5} \times 4$

Reciprocals are a pair of numbers whose product is one (1).

$$\frac{5}{6} \times \frac{6}{5} = 1 \qquad\qquad \frac{8}{7} \times \frac{7}{8} = 1 \qquad\qquad \frac{3}{1} \times \frac{1}{3} = 1$$

The product of zero (0) and any number is always zero (0) , never one (1). Zero (0) has no reciprocal.

Write the reciprocal.

7. $\frac{3}{5}$ 11. $\frac{5}{9}$ 15. $\frac{18}{21}$ 19. $\frac{13}{14}$

8. $\frac{4}{8}$ 12. $\frac{3}{4}$ 16. 25   20. $\frac{6}{25}$

9. $\frac{7}{11}$ 13. 8   17. 142   21. 32

10. $\frac{6}{12}$ 14. $\frac{8}{11}$ 18. $\frac{4}{7}$ 22. 16

Dividing fractions and whole numbers. To divide a fraction by a whole number, convert the whole number to an improper fraction and multiply by the reciprocal of the divisor.

$$\frac{3}{4} \div 3 = \frac{3}{4} \times \frac{1}{3} = \frac{1}{4}$$

Division of fractions. To divide by a fraction, multiply by the reciprocal of the divisor. To divide by $\frac{3}{8}$, multiply by its reciprocal $\frac{8}{3}$.

$$\frac{3}{4} \div \frac{3}{8} = \frac{3}{4} \times \frac{8}{3} = \frac{1 \times 2}{1 \times 1} = \frac{2}{1} = 2$$

Dividing mixed numbers. First convert mixed numbers to improper fractions, then multiply by the reciprocal.

$$10 \div 1\frac{1}{4} = 10 \div \frac{5}{4} = 10 \times \frac{4}{5} = \frac{10}{1} \times \frac{4}{5} = \frac{8}{1} = 8$$

Solve the problems below.

1. $\frac{3}{4} \div \frac{1}{2}$

2. $\frac{5}{6} \div \frac{7}{12}$

3. $7 \div 1\frac{1}{8}$

4. $\frac{3}{4} \div \frac{2}{3}$

5. $6 \div 9\frac{1}{2}$

6. $11 \div 6\frac{7}{8}$

7. $\frac{5}{8} \div \frac{2}{3}$

8. $\frac{4}{11} \div \frac{12}{22}$

9. $8\frac{2}{3} \div 6\frac{1}{4}$

10. $17\frac{1}{8} \div 16\frac{1}{3}$

11. $\frac{1}{8} \div \frac{5}{6}$

12. $\frac{3}{10} \div \frac{2}{5}$

Write $<$, $>$, or $=$ to compare the numbers.

13. $4\frac{1}{8} \div 2\frac{1}{3} \ \square \ 6\frac{1}{5} \div 1\frac{1}{2}$

14. $3\frac{1}{2} + 2\frac{1}{8} \ \square \ 4\frac{2}{3} - 1\frac{7}{8}$

15. $5\frac{1}{4} \times 2\frac{3}{8} \ \square \ 7\frac{1}{3} + 2\frac{1}{4}$

16. $15\frac{1}{2} \div 2\frac{3}{7} \ \square \ 14\frac{2}{3} \times 3\frac{1}{2}$

Problem Solving — Fractions

1. Tanner has a picture that is 15 inches square. He wants to frame it using wood trim that is sold by the yard. How much trim will he need?

First, find the perimeter of the picture.	(p = 60)
Then, change inches to yards.	(y = 36")
Finally, reduce to the lowest terms.	(p ÷ 36)

2. Denise is making a bead necklace. The project calls for 72 white beads and 36 red beads. Beads are sold at a cost of 25¢ per dozen. What will the beads cost?

3. Deborah has created a wall hanging 22" x 38". What will it cost for edging to trim the picture if the cost of the edging is 39¢ per foot?

4. Grayson has a 12 gallon gasoline tank in his car. The gauge is registering $\frac{1}{8}$ full. Grayson knows he will burn $3\frac{1}{2}$ gallons of gas going to and from school.

   A. How much gas does he now have?
   B. Can Grayson make it to school and back today without buying gas?
   C. What is the least amount of gas Grayson can buy and not run out of gas before he gets home?
   D. How many gallons of gas would Grayson need to buy if he were able to fill up now?

5. At Washington Middle School, $\frac{2}{3}$ of the sixth grade students like pizza. Of these students, $\frac{5}{8}$ also enjoy nachos. What fraction of the sixth graders will eat both pizza and nachos?

6. About $\frac{1}{6}$ of the sixth graders study French. Of these, $\frac{3}{4}$ are first year students. What part of the students in the sixth grade are first year French students?

7. For a social studies project, $\frac{5}{6}$ of the students wrote about Africa. Of these students, $\frac{3}{10}$ wrote about North African countries. What part of the students wrote about North African countries?

Ratios: A ratio is a quotient of two numbers that is used to compare one quantity to another. Ratios are used to compare numbers or quantities. Ratios can be written in several ways but are usually read the same way. When a ratio is written as a fraction, it may be reduced to the lowest terms.

✧ ✧ ✧   🔔 🔔 🔔
✧ ✧ ✧   🔔 🔔 🔔 $\dfrac{6 \text{ stars}}{9 \text{ bells}}$ $\dfrac{2}{3}$ or 2 : 3
        🔔 🔔 🔔

Ratio Problems: Write a ratio as a fraction in the lowest terms to compare numbers in a table.

Results of Student Survey About Cafeteria Food

Excellent to good 37 : 167 or $\dfrac{37}{167}$

1. fair to good

2. poor to excellent

3. good to fair

4. poor to fair

5. excellent to total

6. poor to total

Opinion	No. of Responses
Excellent	37
Good	167
Fair	154
Poor	58
TOTAL	**416**

Towers Middle School has 825 students and 43 teachers. Write the ratio as a fraction in lowest terms.

     7. What is the ratio of students to teachers?

     8. What is the ratio of teachers to students?

Sometimes ratios compare measurements. When they do, be certain the measurements are written in the same units. Rewrite the ratio so that both terms are expressed in the same unit. If possible, write the ratio in the lowest terms.

     Example: $\dfrac{3\ cm}{1\ m} = \dfrac{3\ cm}{100\ cm} = \dfrac{3}{100}$

9. $\dfrac{12\ minutes}{1\ hour}$

10. $\dfrac{5\ days}{6\ weeks}$

11. $\dfrac{35\ mm}{50\ cm}$

12. $\dfrac{3\ kg}{150\ g}$

When a ratio is used to compare quantities of different kinds, the ratio is called a **rate**. The **cost per each** is known as the **unit rate**. The unit rate is found by dividing the amount of money by the number of items.

$$\$360 \text{ for } 20 \text{ lessons} = \$18 \text{ per lesson}$$

Complete the following:

A. $\dfrac{24}{8} = \dfrac{}{1}$ B. $\dfrac{40}{10} = \dfrac{}{1}$ C. $\dfrac{300}{15} = \dfrac{}{1}$ D. $\dfrac{962}{26} = \dfrac{}{1}$

Find the unit rate for the following:

1. Brad receives $126.75 for selling 169 show tickets.

2. Speedy Delivery charges $173.30 for 1733 packages.

3. Flowers from Posey's Boutique cost $187.50 for 25 bouquets.

4. There are 1000 nails in 25 boxes.

5. Crown Camera charged $1600 for 5 cameras.

6. Speedy Printing Press prints 3000 pages in 60 minutes.

7. At Tower Theater, there are 1200 people in 50 rows.

8. Carnegie Library has reserved 478 books for 239 students.

9. Juanita has 20 tokens for 5 bus rides.

10. Perfect Photo Shop charges $20.88 for 72 color prints.

Complete the table.

Grayson's Part-time Earnings

Dollars Earned	$48.50	?	?	?
Number of Days	1	2	5	10

TIME OUT: The students in Mrs. Brady's class have $\dfrac{1}{2}$ hour to complete 3 sections of a math quiz. They have the same amount of time to do each section. How much time do they have for each section of the quiz?

Proportions: An equation which states that two ratios are equal is called a proportion. There are two ways to write a proportion.

$$\frac{40}{5} = \frac{48}{6} \qquad\qquad 40 : 5 = 48 : 6$$

This proportion is read as *40 is to 5 as 48 is to 6.*

Write as ratios. Are they equal? Write *Yes* or *No*.

1. 1 out of 2 votes
   5 out of 10 votes

2. 3 absent out of 25
   4 absent out of 30

3. 85 correct out of 100
   165 correct out of 200

4. 6 out of 7 days
   7 out of 8 days

5. 15 wins out of 21 games
   10 wins out of 14 games

6. 120 sold out of 125
   360 sold out of 370

Write as an equal ratio. Then write the proportion in two ways.

7. 21 to 36 students

8. 12 out of 20 scouts

9. 30 chores in 1 hour

10. 4 boys per team

11. 300 feet in 45 seconds

12. 26 weeks in 6 months

To solve a proportion, complete two equal ratios. In the problem $\frac{3}{2} = \frac{n}{8}$ find a fraction equivalent to $\frac{3}{2}$ with a denominator of 8.

$$\frac{3}{2} = \frac{3 \times 4}{2 \times 4} = \frac{12}{8} \quad \text{So, } n = 12.$$

Write the proportion using equal ratios.

13. 1 is to 5 as p is to 10

14. 4 is to 12 as 20 is to a

15. 5 adults is to 15 children as x adults
    is to 30 children

16. 1 is to 3 as 2 is to x

17. 2 is to k as 4 is to 9

18. 5 wins is to 7 games as 10 wins
    is to x games

Complete the proportions.

1. $\dfrac{3}{10} = \dfrac{6}{n}$

2. $\dfrac{16}{8} = \dfrac{4}{a}$

3. $\dfrac{3}{6} = \dfrac{n}{36}$

4. $\dfrac{8}{5} = \dfrac{24}{a}$

5. $\dfrac{9}{2} = \dfrac{a}{20}$

6. $\dfrac{30}{45} = \dfrac{6}{a}$

7. $\dfrac{56}{64} = \dfrac{7}{x}$

8. $\dfrac{11}{15} = \dfrac{22}{x}$

9. $\dfrac{17}{3} = \dfrac{x}{9}$

10. $\dfrac{27}{33} = \dfrac{n}{11}$

11. $\dfrac{46}{20} = \dfrac{y}{10}$

12. $\dfrac{13}{4} = \dfrac{p}{16}$

Solve.

13. If a new game requires 3 players, then how many players will be needed to play 6 games?

14. Emma bought 3 pens for $.89. She also bought a dozen clips for $1.06. How much did she spend?

Cross Multiplying. Cross multiplying is another way to solve a proportion. The symbol ? is used when checking to see if a proportion is true.

$$\dfrac{4}{5} \; ? \; \dfrac{8}{10}$$
$$4 \times 10 \; ? \; 5 \times 8$$
$$40 = 40$$

The proportion is **true.**

In order to solve an equation with a missing number find the missing number in the proportion by following these steps:

$$\dfrac{10}{6} = \dfrac{n}{36}$$
$$6 \times n = 10 \times 36$$
$$6 \times n = 360$$
$$n = 360 \div 6$$
$$n = 60$$

Complete. Is the proportion true? Write *Yes* **or** *No.*

15. $\dfrac{5}{6} \; ? \; \dfrac{4}{7}$

   $5 \times 7 =$

   $4 \times 6 =$

16. $\dfrac{6}{4} \; ? \; \dfrac{15}{10}$

   $6 \times 10 =$

   $4 \times 15 =$

17. $\dfrac{3}{12} \; ? \; \dfrac{2}{8}$

   $3 \times 8 =$

   $12 \times 2 =$

Percent: A percent compares a number to 100. The symbol **%** means *per hundred.* You can think of a percent as the ratio of a number to 100.

50% is the ratio of 50 to 100.

These examples show how to write a percent as a fraction in lowest terms.

$$31\% = \frac{31}{100} \qquad 80\% = \frac{80}{100} = \frac{4}{5}$$

These examples show how to write a fraction as a percent.

- When the denominator is 100, just write the numerator with a percent symbol.

$$\frac{7}{100} = 7\% \qquad \frac{42}{100} = 42$$

- When the denominator is not 100, first write an equivalent fraction with a denominator of 100.

$$\frac{1}{4} = \frac{25}{100} = 25\%$$

Exercises. Complete by writing the percent as a fraction in lowest terms.

1. $13\% = \frac{\quad}{100}$

2. $27\% = \frac{\quad}{100}$

3. $9\% = \frac{\quad}{100}$

4. $40\% = \frac{\quad}{100} = \frac{\quad}{\quad}$

5. $50\% = \frac{\quad}{100} = \frac{\quad}{\quad}$

6. $90\% = \frac{\quad}{100} = \frac{\quad}{\quad}$

7. $85\% = \frac{\quad}{100} = \frac{\quad}{\quad}$

8. $12\% = \frac{\quad}{100} = \frac{\quad}{\quad}$

9. $4\% = \frac{\quad}{100} = \frac{\quad}{\quad}$

Complete by writing the fraction as percent.

10. $\frac{67}{100} = \boxed{}\%$

11. $\frac{7}{100} = \boxed{}\%$

12. $\frac{9}{10} = \frac{\quad}{100} = \boxed{}\%$

Decimals and Percent

In a survey, 43 out of 100 people said they owned a home computer.

You can write the decimal, 0.43, as a percent.

$$0.43 = \frac{43}{100} = 43\%$$

Sometimes a fraction can not be written with a denominator of 100. When this happens, first divide, then write the fraction as a decimal.

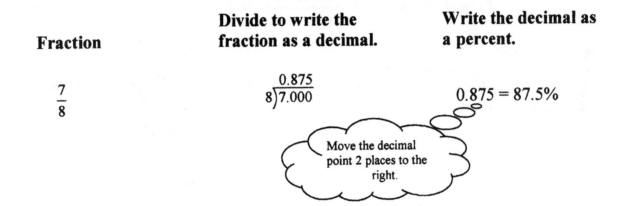

Fraction	Divide to write the fraction as a decimal.	Write the decimal as a percent.
$\frac{7}{8}$	$8\overline{)7.000}$ 0.875	$0.875 = 87.5\%$

Move the decimal point 2 places to the right.

Exercises. Complete by writing the decimal as a percent.

1. $0.65 = \frac{}{100} = \boxed{}\%$

2. $0.07 = \frac{}{100} = \boxed{}\%$

3. $0.03 = \frac{}{100} = \boxed{}\%$

4. $0.12 = \frac{}{100} = \boxed{}\%$

5. $0.72 = \frac{}{100} = \boxed{}\%$

6. $0.41 = \frac{}{100} = \boxed{}\%$

7. $0.29 = \frac{}{100} = \boxed{}\%$

8. $0.50 = \frac{}{100} = \boxed{}\%$

9. $0.84 = \frac{}{100} = \boxed{}\%$

Complete by writing the percent as a decimal.

10. $34\% = \frac{}{100} = 0.\_\_$

11. $58\% = \frac{}{100} = 0.\_\_$

12. $13\% = \frac{}{100} = 0.\_\_$

13. $91\% = \frac{}{100} = 0.\_\_$

14. $8\% = \frac{}{100} = 0.\_\_$

15. $16\% = \frac{}{100} = 0.\_\_$

Probability: To choose the day to clean your room, you would close your eyes and mark an x on a weekly calendar. There are seven possible outcomes, the days from Monday through Sunday. Since Thursday is obviously one of the seven outcomes, the probability of choosing Thursday is 1 out of 7, or $\frac{1}{7}$.

This can be written as follows P (Thursday) = $\frac{1}{7}$.

There are two weekend days, Saturday and Sunday.

P (weekend day) = $\frac{2}{7}$ P (weekday) = $\frac{5}{7}$

If all the outcomes are equally likely, we use a formula to find probabilities.

$$Probability = \frac{no.\ of\ favorable\ outcomes}{total\ number\ of\ outcomes}$$

Complete:

A. A box containing letter tiles has 2 A's, 4 B's, 6 T's, and 12 M's. What is the probability of picking the following at random?

    1. an A   2. a B   3. a T   4. an M

B. A letter from the word *Engineer* is chosen without looking. Write the probability of the outcome.

    5. the letter **E**   6. the letter **N**   7. a vowel   8. a consonant

C. Carla invited 18 people to a party. The guests included 4 cousins, 2 aunts, 10 friends, and 2 uncles. Write the probability that the first guest arriving at the party is the following:

    9. a cousin   10. a friend   11. an uncle   12. a nephew

D. There are 3 green, 7 red, and 2 yellow marbles in a jar. They are all the same size and shape. You choose a marble without looking. Write the probability of the outcome.

    13. a green marble   14. a red marble   15. a yellow marble   16. a purple marble

TIME OUT: Here's a quick review of some of the pages in the mathematics section. Try any of the review problems where you feel you may need additional practice.

Write the number in expanded notation.

1. 46,876 = _____

Round to the nearest thousand.

2. 1304 _____   3. 6503 _____   4. 5978 _____   5. 9399 _____

Write the LCM (Least Common Multiple) of the numbers.

6. 3 and 15 _____   7. 12 and 18 _____   8. 20 and 25 _____   9. 8 and 12 _____

Name the two equivalent fractions by circling them.

10. $\frac{13}{14}, \frac{16}{28}, \frac{6}{7}, \frac{26}{28}$ 11. $\frac{6}{10}, \frac{11}{20}, \frac{22}{40}, \frac{26}{40}$ 12. $\frac{7}{8}, \frac{14}{17}, \frac{28}{32}, \frac{36}{40}$ 13. $\frac{2}{9}, \frac{1}{6}, \frac{6}{54}, \frac{4}{18}$

Write in the lowest terms.

14. $\frac{4}{6}$ 15. $\frac{10}{20}$ 16. $\frac{21}{49}$ 17. $\frac{10}{15}$ 18. $\frac{16}{36}$

Adding and Subtracting Fractions.

19. $\frac{3}{11} + \frac{5}{11}$ 20. $\frac{5}{9} - \frac{2}{9}$ 21. $\frac{15}{16} - \frac{5}{16}$ 22. $\frac{5}{18} + \frac{3}{18}$

Multiply. Write the product in the lowest terms.

23. $\frac{2}{3} \times \frac{5}{8}$ 24. $3\frac{1}{3} \times 4\frac{1}{4}$ 25. $28 \times \frac{4}{7}$ 26. $2\frac{2}{7} \times 1\frac{2}{5}$ 27. $5 \times \frac{3}{7}$

Divide. Write the quotient in the lowest terms.

28. $\frac{2}{3} \div 8$ 29. $2\frac{1}{7} \div \frac{3}{7}$ 30. $13 \div \frac{2}{10}$ 31. $6\frac{3}{4} \div 2\frac{1}{8}$ 32. $\frac{4}{9} \div 9$

Write as a percent.

33. $\frac{79}{100}$ 34. 0.83   35. $\frac{3}{20}$ 36. 0.05   37. $\frac{13}{25}$

Doodling: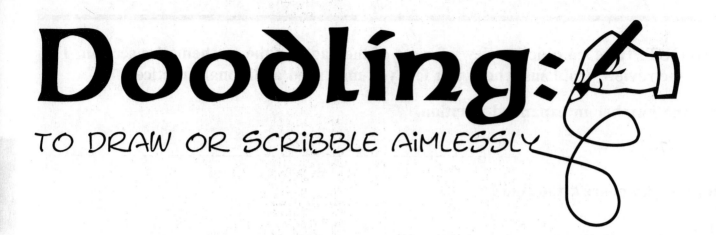

TO DRAW OR SCRIBBLE AiMLESSLY

Doodling:
TO DRAW OR SCRIBBLE AiMLESSLY

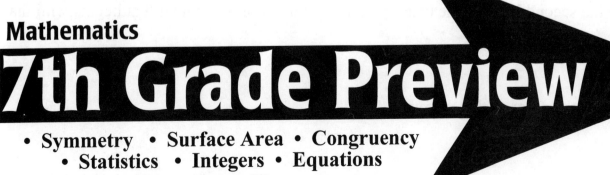

Mathematics
7th Grade Preview

- Symmetry • Surface Area • Congruency
- Statistics • Integers • Equations
- Pythagorean Theorem

TRY OUT YOUR MATH SKILLS. Do not skip ahead. Read each message one line at a time and do exactly what the message says.

1. Pick a number from 1 to 9.

2. Subtract 5.

3. Multiply by 3.

4. Square the number (multiply by the same number, not square root).

5. Add the digits until you get only one digit (e.g. 64=6+4=10=1+0+1).

6. If the number is less than 5, add five, otherwise, subtract 4.

7. Multiply by 2.

8. Subtract 6.

9. Match the digit to a letter in the alphabet: 1=A; 2=B; 3=C, etc.

10. Pick the name of a country that begins with that letter.

11. Take the second letter in the country name and think of a mammal that begins with that letter.

12. Think of the color of that mammal.

Symmetry – a figure that can be folded so that both halves fit exactly on one another is said to be **symmetrical**. The fold line is called a <u>line of symmetry</u>.

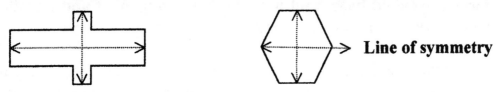 **Line of symmetry**

Is there a fold line of symmetry for each figure? Write *yes* or *no* by each one. If *yes* draw it.

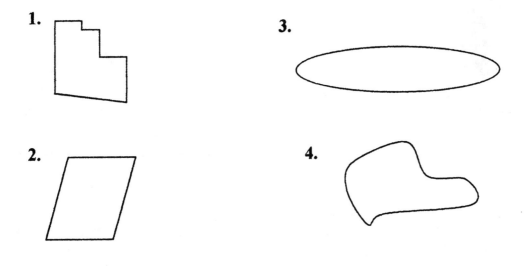

1.

3.

2.

4.

Is the dashed line a line of symmetry? Write *yes* or *no*.

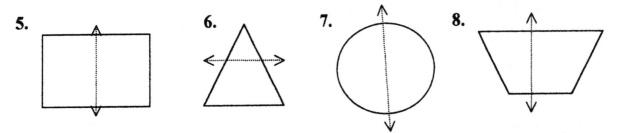

5.

6.

7.

8.

Is the dot a point of symmetry? Write *yes* or *no*.

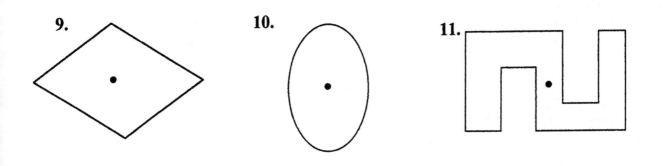

9.

10.

11.

Surface Area: Prisms and Pyramids – the surface area of a prism or pyramid is the sum of the areas of all its faces and bases. A prism is a figure with 5 or more sides or faces. Two of the faces are called bases and must be both congruent and parallel. A pyramid has 4 or more faces. Only one face is called the base.

The prism below has 6 vertexes and 5 faces.

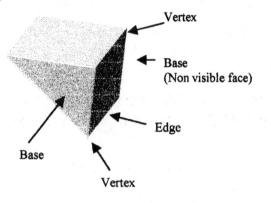

A pyramid has 4 or more faces. Only one face is a base. The pyramid below has 4 vertexes and 4 faces.

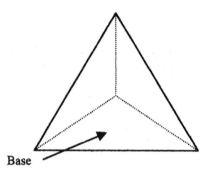

Volume of a Rectangular Prism. The volume of a figure is the amount of space it contains; volume is measured in cubic units. Formula to find volume of a rectangular prism:

Volume = Length x Width x Height

$$V = L \times W \times H$$

What is the volume if the edges have the given lengths?

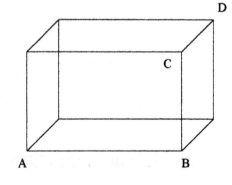

1. AB = 18 cm
    BC = 9 cm
    CD = 7 cm

2. AB = 15 cm
    BC = 8 cm
    CD = 6 cm

3. AB = 11 m
    BC = 6 m
    CD = 4 m

4. AB = 4 cm
    BC = 18 cm
    CD = 0.7 cm

5. AB = 9 m
    BC = 5 m
    CD = 4 m

6. AB = 5.2 cm
    BC = 5.2 cm
    CD = 7.3 cm

Congruency – figures that have the exact same size and shape are congruent figures. Corresponding or matching parts of congruent figures are also congruent.

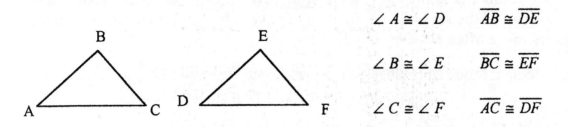

$$\angle A \cong \angle D \qquad \overline{AB} \cong \overline{DE}$$

$$\angle B \cong \angle E \qquad \overline{BC} \cong \overline{EF}$$

$$\angle C \cong \angle F \qquad \overline{AC} \cong \overline{DF}$$

When referring to two congruent polygons, it is customary to list their corresponding vertexes in the same order. Diagonal $\overline{BD}$ divides parallelogram ABCD into two congruent triangles.

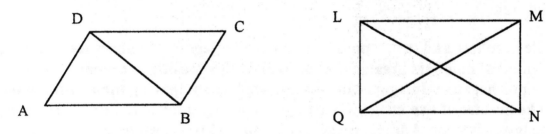

$\nabla ABD \cong \nabla CDB.$ Complete the statement.

1. $\angle A \cong \angle$ ____

2. $\angle ADB \cong \angle$ ____

3. $\angle DBA \cong \angle$ ____

4. $\overline{AB} \cong$ ____

Hidden Triangles

In parallelogram $LQNM$ (found above), $\nabla LNQ \cong MQN.$ Complete the statement.

5. $\overline{LN} \cong$ ____

6. $\overline{NQ} \cong$ ____

7. $\overline{LQ} \cong$ ____

8. $\angle LNQ \cong \angle$ ____

9. $\angle QLN \cong \angle$ ____

10. $\angle LQN \cong \angle$ ____

Statistics and Integers

Mean, Median, Mode and Range. Given a series of numbers the difference between the greatest and least number is the _range_. The _median_ is the middle number in an ordered set of data. The _mean_ of the series of numbers is the average. _Mode_ is a number in a set of data that appears more often than other numbers.

Give the Mean, Median, Mode and Range for each series of numbers.

Series of numbers.

	Median	Mean	Mode	Range
1. 21, 19, 17, 11, 24, 16				
2. 78, 45, 39, 62, 70				
3. 28, 56, 44, 32, 52, 27,				
4. 130, 128, 180, 149				

Integers – whole numbers and their opposites are called integers. Numbers less than zero are negative numbers; numbers greater than zero are called positive numbers. Zero is neither positive nor negative. Integers can be compared by comparing their position on a number line. The greater of two integers is always the one greater to the right. The integer to the left is the lesser integer. Adding integers – the sum of two positive integers is a positive integer. The sum of two negative integers is a negative integer. The sum of a positive integer and a negative integer may be a positive integer, a negative integer or zero.

Is the number an integer? Write *Yes* or *No*.

5. 8   6. .07   7. $\frac{1}{4}$ 8. $^-14$ 9. π 10. 0   11. 5

Write the opposite of the integer.

12. $^-1$	22. 6	32. 160	42. 199
13. 3	23. $^-7$	33. 240	43. 467
14. $^-5$	24. $^-8$	34. 9999	44. 81
15. $^-3$	25. $^-10$	35. $^-1000$	45. $^-81$
16. 5	26. $^-30$	36. $^-873$	46. $^-240$
17. 1	27. 45	37. 342	47. $^-342$
18. 7	28. 72	38. 16	48. 61
19. 0	29. $^-17$	39. $^-72$	49. $^-100$
20. $^-6$	30. 100	40. 249	50. 91
21. 8	31. $^-200$	41. 21	51. 82

Subtracting integers – to subtract an integer, add its opposite. Solve the following problems.

1. 5 – 9

2. ⁻3 – 8

3. 0 – 4

4. ⁻2 – 0

5. 14 – ⁻5

6. ⁻9 – 12

7. 12 – 37

8. 3 – ⁻7

9. ⁻5 – ⁻7

10. 0 – ⁻7

11. ⁻5 – ⁻5

12. ⁻17 – 9

13. ⁻13 – ⁻4

14. 42 – ⁻15

15. ⁻6 – 2

16. ⁻4 – ⁻10

Multiplying integers – the product of two positive or two negative integers is positive. The product of a positive integer and a negative integer is negative. The product of any integer and zero is zero. Solve the following problems.

17. 2 x ⁻1

18. ⁻9 x 0

19. ⁻8 x ⁻9

20. ⁻1 x 4

21. 10 x ⁻2

22. 20 x 4

23. ⁻15 x 3

24. ⁻3 x ⁻17

25. ⁻6 x 6

26. ⁻3 x 8

27. 5 x ⁻9

28. 4 x 0

29. ⁻7 x ⁻11

30. 2 x ⁻30

31. ⁻6 x ⁻13

32. 12 x ⁻6

33. ⁻4 x ⁻3

34. 5 x 7

35. ⁻8 x ⁻5

36. 6 x ⁻2

37. ⁻13 x 2

38. ⁻10 x ⁻6

39. 5 x ⁻12

40. ⁻19 x 0

41. 4 x 10

42. ⁻1 x ⁻1

43. 5 x 5

44. ⁻8 x ⁻6

45. 9 x 7

46. ⁻12 x ⁻5

47. 3 x ⁻7

48. 2 x 9

Dividing Integers – the quotient of two positive or two negative integers is positive. The quotient of a positive integer and a negative integer is negative. The quotient of zero divided by any other integer is zero. An integer can not be divided by zero.

49. ⁻18 ÷ 9

50. ⁻24 ÷ ⁻4

51. 81 ÷ ⁻9

52. ⁻26 ÷ 2

53. 16 ÷ ⁻2

54. ⁻64 ÷ 8

55. ⁻7 ÷ 1

56. 84 ÷ ⁻4

57. ⁻30 ÷ ⁻5

58. 42 ÷ 6

59. 0 ÷ ⁻9

60. ⁻46 ÷ ⁻2

61. 56 ÷ ⁻7

62. 6 ÷ ⁻3

63. ⁻28 ÷ 7

64. ⁻48 ÷ 3

65. 24 ÷ 3

66. 72 ÷ ⁻8

67. 9 ÷ 3

68. ⁻8 ÷ 4

69. 18 ÷ 9

70. 36 ÷ 6

71. ⁻36 ÷ 6

72. ⁻15 ÷ ⁻5

Rational Numbers – When two integers are added, subtracted or multiplied the answer is an integer; however, the quotient of two integers is not always an integer. A <u>rational number</u> is any number that can be written as the quotient of two integers. NB: 0 can never be used as the denominator of a quotient. Any repeating decimal as a quotient of two integers can be shown as the fact $0.\bar{1} = \frac{1}{9}$ and $0.\overline{01} = \frac{1}{99}$. Numbers such as $\sqrt{2}, \sqrt{3}$ and π cannot be written as the quotient of two integers. These are called irrational numbers. It is possible to add, subtract, multiply or divide with rational numbers. The answer is stated as positive or negative using the same rules that apply when performing operations with integers (the answer is usually written in lowest terms.)

To evaluate mathematical expressions, remember the mnemonic device, <u>Please Excuse My Dear Aunt Sally</u>. First, working from left to right, do all work with parenthesis, then exponents. Continue working left to right, then do all the multiplication and division; next addition and subtractions, still working from left to right.

Example: $^-3 \bullet 5 + 2 = {}^-15 + 2 = {}^-13$

$2\frac{1}{2} \div (5 + 5) = \frac{5}{2} \div 10 = \frac{5}{2} \bullet \frac{1}{10} = \frac{1}{4}$

1. $0 - 6\frac{1}{2} + {}^-3$

2. $9 - 10.2 + {}^-8.6$

3. $^-4.1 \bullet {}^-5.2 \div 4$

4. $6.2 \bullet 3 \bullet \frac{-1}{2}$

5. $16\frac{1}{8} \div 14\frac{1}{3}$

6. $^-37.6 \bullet .03$

7. $\frac{-3}{8} \div {}^-3 \bullet \frac{4}{5}$

8. $2 + [48 \div (12 + 4)] - 16$

9. $\dfrac{5 + [4 \bullet 3 (2 + 1)] + 4}{19 + {}^-10}$

10. $^-28 \div 7 + 2\frac{1}{3}$

11. $35 + \dfrac{50 + 25}{5 \bullet 5} - (8 + 11)$

12. $7\frac{1}{10} + {}^-7.25 - 11.39$

13. $11 - 18.6 + {}^-3\frac{3}{10}$

14. $^-1.75 \bullet {}^-3.4$

15. $5\frac{2}{3} \bullet 9.81 \bullet 0$

16. $4\frac{2}{3} \div \dfrac{{}^-6}{7} \bullet \frac{9}{10}$

17. $^-5\frac{5}{6} \div 2\frac{1}{3}$

Solving Equations. Equations with integers are solved in the same way equations with whole numbers are solved. The same integer may be added or subtracted from both sides of an equation. Both sides of an equation may be multiplied or divided by the same integer.

Example:

$$a + 5 = {}^-3$$
$$a + 5 - 5 = {}^-3 \ {}^-5$$
$$a = {}^-8$$

Check:
$$a + 5 = {}^-3$$
$${}^-8 + 5 = {}^-3 \text{ True}$$

> Subtract 5 From both Sides.

Solve the equation.

1. $n + 7 = 3$

2. $x + 9 = {}^-6$

3. $b + 20 = 5$

4. $p - 5 = {}^-4$

5. $z - 7 = {}^-9$

6. $t - 12 = {}^-10$

7. $b + 38 = {}^-5$

8. ${}^-9t = 9$

9. ${}^-1y = 45$

10. $n - 36 = {}^-17$

11. $6d = {}^-54$

12. ${}^-4k = 28$

Equations are open mathematical sentences. It is customary to represent unstated values (missing numbers) with letters. These letters are referred to as variables. When simplifying expressions combine like terms.

Examples:

1) If $a = \frac{1}{2}$, $x = 4$ and $y = 2$ Solve $5x(2a - 5y)$

$$5x(2a - 5y) = 5 \bullet 4 (2 \bullet \tfrac{1}{2} - 5 \bullet 2) = 20(1 + 10) = 20(11) = 220$$

2) Distributive Property $3(x + 2y) = 3x + 3 \bullet 2y = 3x + 6y$

3) Combine like terms $6m - 4m + 3p = (6 - 4)m + 3p = 2m + 3p$

Write the mathematical equation or solve the equation.

1. Fifty-seven minus nine

2. Eight more than a number q

3. $s + 14 = 57$

4. $w - 23 = 75$

5. The product of a number x and 7

6. $b + 36 = 91$

7. A number a divided by 15

8. $r - 38 = 23$

9. $y + 18 = 77$

10. $93 - c = 53$

11. $3t = 78$

12. $\frac{m}{4} = 84$

relationship among the sides of right triangles. In a right triangle, the longest side is called the **hypotenuse**. The other sides are called **legs**. Count the squares drawn on each side of the triangle. The sum of the squares of the legs is equal to the square of the hypotenuse.

Pythagorean Theorem: $a^2 + b^2 = c^2$
$3^2 + 4^2 = 5^2$
$9 + 16 = 25$

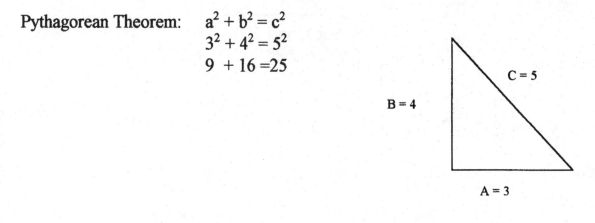

Write an equation to find the missing number, then solve the equation.

1.

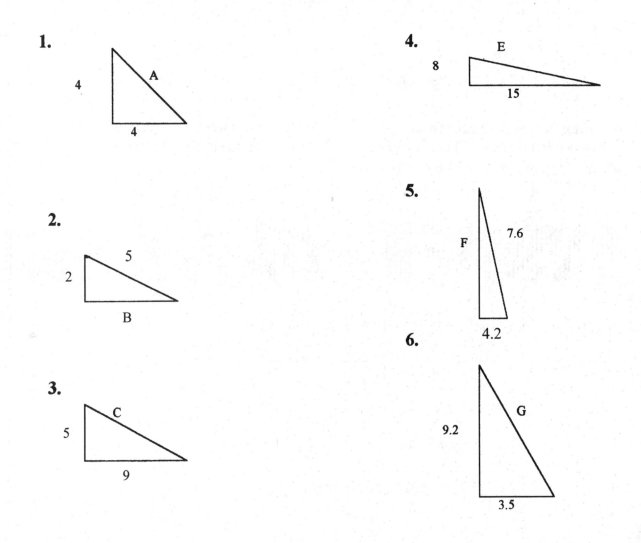

2.

3.

4.

5.

6.

Social Studies

6th Grade in Review

- Geography • History • Economics
- Government • Charts • Graphs • Maps • Tables

Creating a Compass Rose

A Compass Rose is used to measure directions. It is a circle on which points are marked to indicate direction and/or degrees. Each degree mark represents a direction; due north is at 0°, south at 180°, east at 90°, and west at 270°.

Materials List
Heavy paper
Pencil and eraser
Ruler
String
Tape
Paper Plate
Glue
Scissors
Markers
Compass

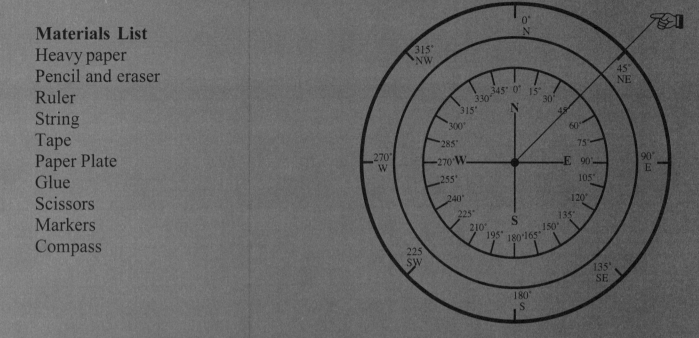

Procedure:

1. Use a compass to draw a circle 3" in diameter.

2. Draw two perpendicular diameters and label **N**, **S**, **E**, and **W**.

3. Fill in and mark every 15°'s. See example above.

4. Cut out the compass rose.

5. Make a small hole in the center of the compass rose with the point of the compass.

6. Thread an 8" piece of string through the hole and tape to the back of the compass rose.

7. Lay the compass rose in the center of the plate and glue in place.

8. With the ruler and pen, mark **0°, 45°, 90°, 135°, 180°, 225°, 270°,** and **315°**on the edge of the plate.

9. Label these marks **N, NE, E, SE, S, SW, W,** and **NW**.

Plotting My Own Course

Directions: Here's a chance to make your own game!

Take a piece of poster board or large sheet of paper. On the paper draw a bird's eye view of your town, a park, a zoo, or an amusement park. With an arrow indicate magnetic north on the map. Be sure to create a legend for the map. Place your compass rose so that 0° N and magnetic north are aligned. Hold the compass rose in place while you pull the string taut. Next locate at least five places on your map. Then record the degree mark that the string passes over on the compass rose. Place a large dot at this point on the map to mark the spot. On a separate sheet of paper, record the degree mark and the direction. After you have marked and recorded all five locations, check your plot course.

When everything is accurate, give your map, plot course and compass rose to someone else. Ask this person to follow your plot course to see if he/she can recreate your path. Tell the person to be sure that 0° N and magnetic north on the map are aligned. Pulling the string taut, move it over the first plot point in your plot course. Name the point that the string passes over (i.e., the lion's cage or whatever is on your map). Continue through all the points that have been plotted.

Now that you have been successful, trade places and have the other person plot a course. Then, you try to follow the plot course that has been created.

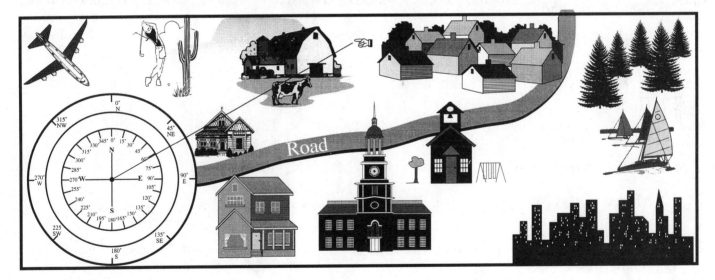

Hints:
- Make sure that the string is tight.
- Double check that the string is directly over the spot to be marked.
- Always center the compass rose over the last spot that you have plotted before continuing to next plot.
- If the string crosses more than one dot, retry each spot until you can align the next plot point.

North America (global grid page 89). First, use your color pencils to shade in each country of North America. Next, label the countries and major bodies of water.

Latitude and Longitude. Remember lines extending east and west are called lines of *latitude.* Lines extending north and south are called lines of *longitude.* All of North America is located in the Northern Hemisphere, north of the equator which is located at 0° latitude. North America is also located in the Western Hemisphere, west of the Prime Meridian which is 0° longitude. Together, lines of latitude and longitude comprise the *global grid.* The global grid helps to locate any place on earth. Should you know the approximate latitude and longitude of a location, it can be found by first placing your finger on the point where the equator and prime meridian cross. Next, move your finger east or west along this parallel to the point where it crosses the correct meridian. To find the latitude and longitude of a specific place, find the location on a map and reverse the process.

Use the steps above to match the following locations:

_____ 1. Hispaniola

_____ 2. Victoria Island

_____ 3. Baffin Island

_____ 4. Newfoundland

_____ 5. Cuba

_____ 6. Panama Canal

_____ 7. Hudson Bay

_____ 8. Gulf of Alaska

_____ 9. Gulf of Mexico

_____ 10. Mexico City, Mexico

_____ 11. Washington, D.C.

_____ 12. Vancouver, B.C.

_____ 13. New Orleans, LA

_____ 14. San José, Costa Rica

_____ 15. Nassau, Bahamas

A. 20°N, 100°W

B. 09°N, 80°W

C. 49°N, 56°W

D. 18°N, 73°W

E. 10°N, 84°W

F. 38°N, 77°W

G. 70°N, 100°W

H. 23°N, 90°W

I. 30°N, 90°W

J. 60°N, 90°W

K. 70°N, 72°W

L. 48°N, 123°W

M. 22°N, 80°W

N. 58°N, 145°W

O. 25°N, 78°W

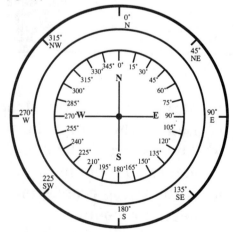

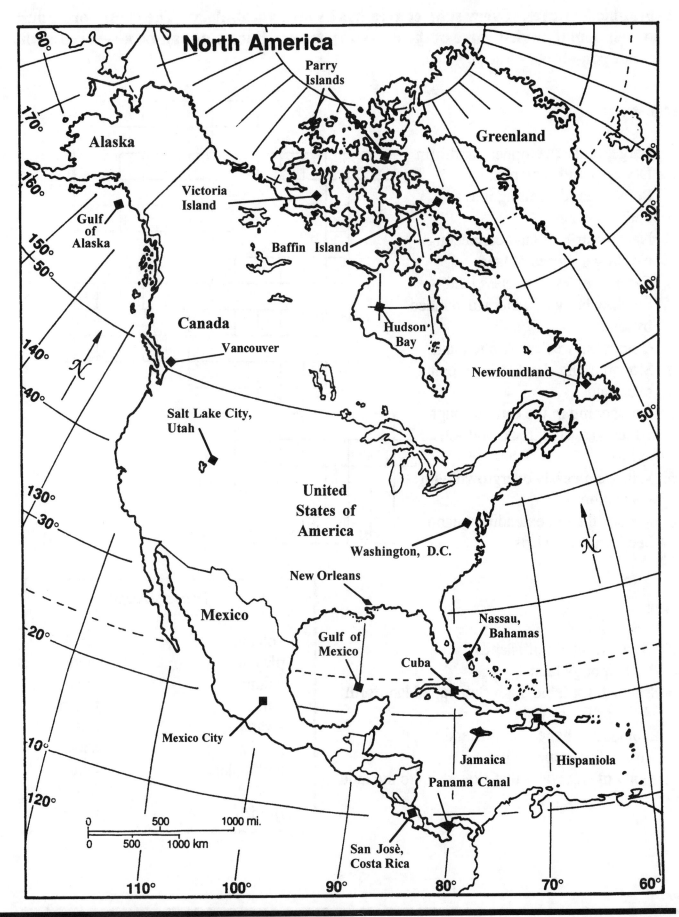

North America

Parry Islands

Alaska

Greenland

Gulf of Alaska

Victoria Island

Baffin Island

Canada

Vancouver

Hudson Bay

Newfoundland

Salt Lake City, Utah

N

United States of America

Washington, D.C.

N

New Orleans

Mexico

Gulf of Mexico

Nassau, Bahamas

Cuba

Mexico City

Jamaica

Hispaniola

Panama Canal

San Josè, Costa Rica

0   500   1000 mi.

0   500   1000 km

60°
170°
160°
150°
140°
130°
120°
110°
100°
90°
80°
70°
60°
50°
40°
30°
20°
20°
30°
40°
50°
10°

Geographic Features. Every subject area has its own vocabulary. The crossword puzzle below will help to review some of the necessary terms. Each clue can be answered with a term that you already know.

Across

1. Large, high, flat topped landform
3. Dry area with few plants
5. Point of land pointing into a body of water
7. Narrow strip of land connecting two larger pieces of land
8. Extensive, level, treeless land
9. Shallow body of water surrounded by land
10. Cold, vast, treeless Arctic plain
11. Slow moving sheet of ice moving over land
12. An opening in the earth through which gas, lava, rock, and ash escape
16. Wild land nearly overgrown with vegetation
18. Arm of the sea extending inland between steep cliffs

Down

2. Group or chain of islands
4. Wet, spongy land
6. Spanish for table, high flat topped landform
13. Body of fresh water
14. Doughnut shaped coral island
15. Small, flat topped hill
17. Body of salt water that extends in to the land

Word Bank

volcano	jungle
plateau	lagoon
isthmus	mesa
gulf	tundra
swamp	butte
glacier	cape
archipelago	lake
atoll	desert
fjord	prairie

Provinces, Territories, and Capitals. On a separate sheet of paper, identify the numbered physical and political geographic features on the Canadian map below. Your list will include provinces, territories, capitals, major bodies of water, islands and mountains. Use a world atlas for assistance.

Canada

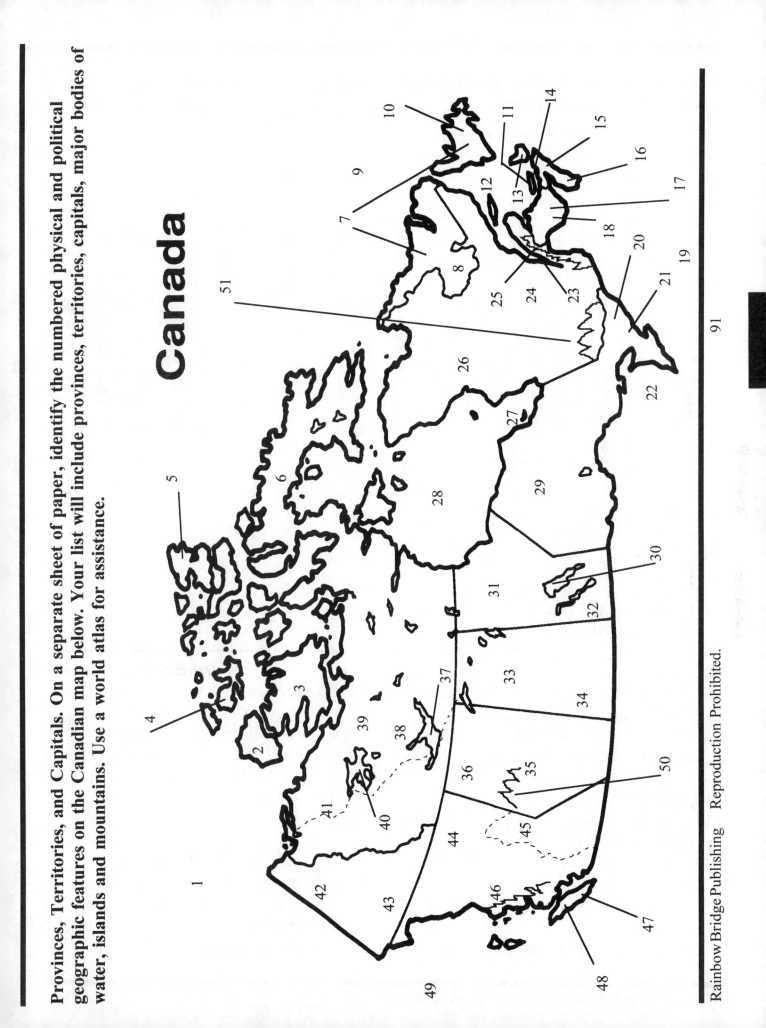

Solve this crossword puzzle to refresh your knowledge about Canada. Use the clues below to complete the puzzle.

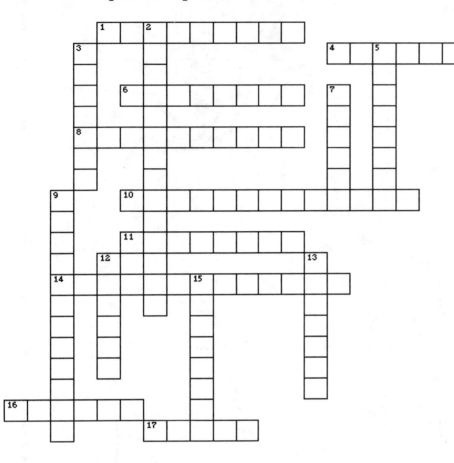

Across

1. Canada has the longest _____ of any country in the world.
4. The word _____ means "eaters of raw meat."
6. Canada Day, July 1, marks the day in 1867 when Canada was given _____.
8. Only _____ (continent) is more sparsely populated than Canada.
10. _____ _____ is Canada's political leader.
11. In Nova Scotia, _____ (music) are often played during festivals.
14. Canada has a central _____ government.
16. Canada is the _____ largest country in the world.
17. In N.S., men occasionally dress in _____.

Down

2. Another name for the Northern Lights.
3. _____ is the national anthem.
5. Gold was discovered on the _____ River in 1896.
7. _____, or "real people," live in the Arctic north.
9. In 1982, Canada was given complete _____.
12. Most people in Quebec speak _____.
13. After the French and Indian War, _____ gained control of Canada.
15. Next to Paris, _____ is the largest French speaking city in the world.

Fast Facts about Canada. Use the clues in the word search to find the famous people, places, and things in Canadian History. The names may be written up, down, or diagonally. They may read from left to right, right to left, top to bottom, or bottom to top. Circle the names in the scramble of letters below.

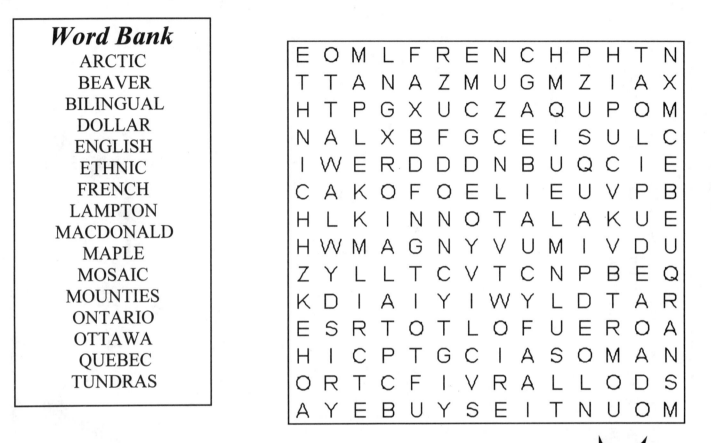

Word Bank

ARCTIC
BEAVER
BILINGUAL
DOLLAR
ENGLISH
ETHNIC
FRENCH
LAMPTON
MACDONALD
MAPLE
MOSAIC
MOUNTIES
ONTARIO
OTTAWA
QUEBEC
TUNDRAS

E	O	M	L	F	R	E	N	C	H	P	H	T	N
T	T	A	N	A	Z	M	U	G	M	Z	I	A	X
H	T	P	G	X	U	C	Z	A	Q	U	P	O	M
N	A	L	X	B	F	G	C	E	I	S	U	L	C
I	W	E	R	D	D	D	N	B	U	Q	C	I	E
C	A	K	O	F	O	E	L	I	E	U	V	P	B
H	L	K	I	N	N	O	T	A	L	A	K	U	E
H	W	M	A	G	N	Y	V	U	M	I	V	D	U
Z	Y	L	L	T	C	V	T	C	N	P	B	E	Q
K	D	I	A	I	Y	I	W	Y	L	D	T	A	R
E	S	R	T	O	T	L	O	F	U	E	R	O	A
H	I	C	P	T	G	C	I	A	S	O	M	A	N
O	R	T	C	F	I	V	R	A	L	L	O	D	S
A	Y	E	B	U	Y	S	E	I	T	N	U	O	M

Clues

1. Sir John A. _____ was elected the first Prime Minister of Canada in 1867.
2. John George _____ was the first governor-general of all British North America.
3. Canada has two official languages _____ and _____.
4. The basic monetary unit is the Canadian _____.
5. A red _____ leaf is the central symbol on the Canadian flag.
6. The capital of Canada is _____ located in _____ province.
7. _____ is Canada's oldest city.
8. The _____ Islands are _____, places too cold and dry for trees to grow.
9. Canada's 1981 Constitution declared it a " _____ land."
10. Canadians describe their country as a _____ of various _____ groups.
11. Three important symbols of Canada are the _____ (Royal Canadian Mounted Police), the maple leaf, and the _____.

States, Capitals and Locations. Take a blank sheet of paper and fold it in half. Label one half "States," and the other "Capitals." Number from 1 (*one*) to 50 (*fifty*). Set a timer for five minutes. Matching the number on the map to the number on the paper, see how many states and capitals you can identify.

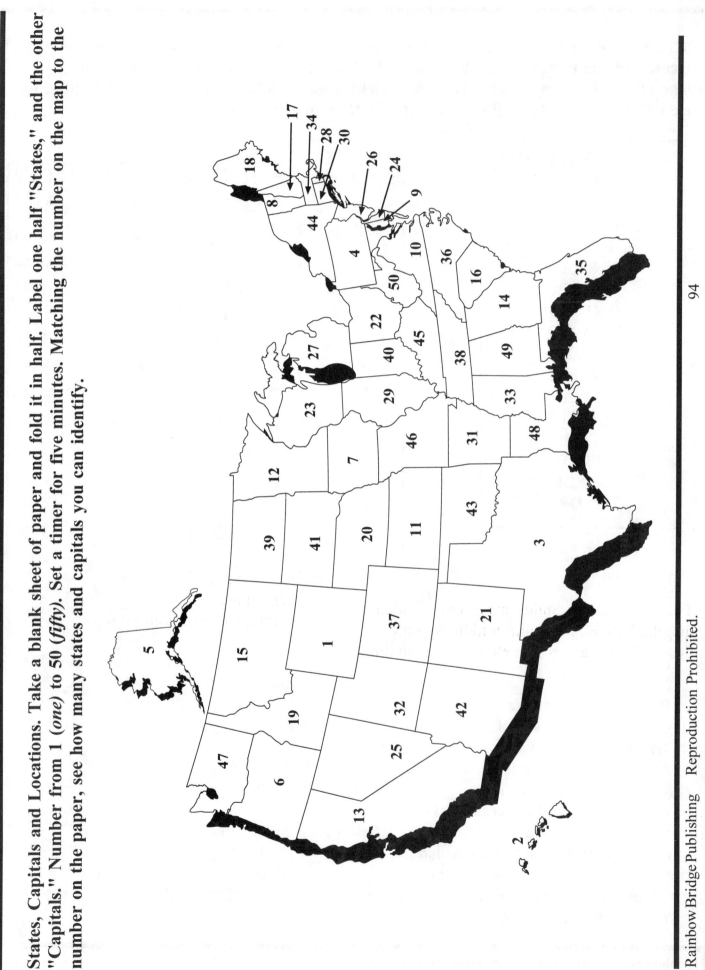

U.S. Regions. The fifty United States are often divided into a series of regions. This activity explores the region known as the Northeast. Each of these eleven states will be found in the Northeast Word Search. The eleven questions and each state has a place in one of the sub-regions.

Northeast Region Word Search

```
K Q E X H E R A W A L E D T S
S R M A R Y L A N D G F N S S
N T O Q W H B F G L F O N J U
E C T Y J D H F W M M E J D T
W G U E W V U S Q R W I F N U
J U R S S E A U E H D T E A C
E A I L I U N V A R Y U A L I
R S D U Y J H M Z G C H I S T
S R Q L L Q P C M Y D N L I C
E N H I Z S M E A A V S E E E
Y I M A H W J K H S I R N D N
L F V I L B E T T U S N J O N
S W R X P J S I Q H P A E H O
C E L Z K K P Y L B K I M R C
I O M A I N A V L Y S N N E P
```

1. The northern most eastern state is
   _____.
2. State divided by the Chesapeake Bay is
   _____.
3. Smallest state in the Union is _____
   _____.
4. _____ is known as the "Empire State."
5. State that is home of the Liberty Bell is
   _____.
6. Famous for granite quarries is _____.
7. The first state is _____.
8. John Adams was born in the state of
   _____.
9. Mystic Seaport is located in the state of
   _____.
10. Mount Washington, Manchester and Nashua are in _____.
11. Atlantic City is a popular resort city in
    _____.

The Northeastern States are further divided into the New England and Middle Atlantic States. Place each of the eleven states in the proper sub-group.

New England   **Mid-Atlantic**

_____   _____
_____   _____
_____   _____
_____   _____
_____

Northeastern States

Pennsylvania	New York
Connecticut	Massachusetts
Vermont	Maine
Delaware	New Jersey
Maryland	New Hampshire
Rhode Island	

Regions. Using a blank sheet of paper, identify the numbered state and its capital from the Southern Region. Use an atlas for assistance.

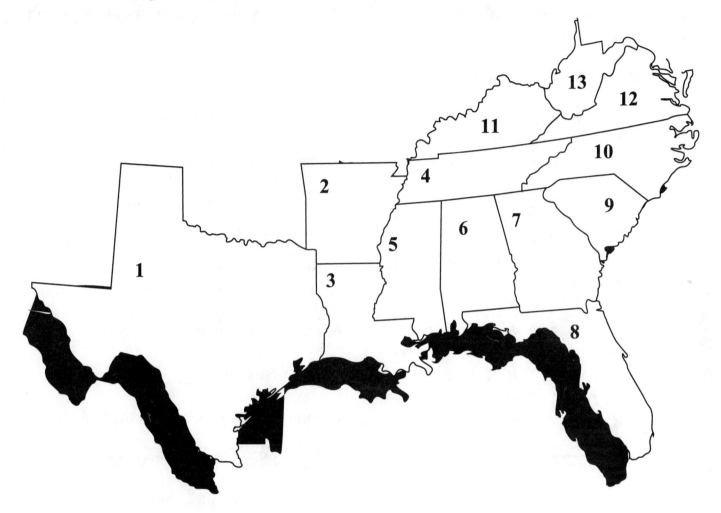

What state is located between each of the two states named?

Louisiana	_____	Alabama
Kentucky	_____	Virginia
Alabama	_____	South Carolina
Florida	_____	Mississippi
West Virginia	_____	North Carolina
Mississippi	_____	Kentucky
Georgia	_____	North Carolina
Tennessee	_____	South Carolina
Texas	_____	Mississippi
Arkansas	_____	North Carolina

Region. The clues below will help to identify each of the states located in the Midwest. Write the two-letter abbreviation (postal code) for each state.

1. This state has the panhandle, the Will Rogers Memorial, and the Chisholm Trail. _ _
2. The Big Sioux, Missouri, Mississippi, and Des Moines Rivers flow through this state. _ _
3. This state has two distinct sections divided by one of the Great Lakes. _ _
4. Fort Leavenworth, Fort Riley, and the Eisenhower Library and are located here. _ _
5. Oshkosh is the name of one of this state's cities. _ _
6. Where would you find Mount Rushmore and the Badlands? _ _
7. The source of the Mississippi River is in which state? _ _
8. The Great Serpent Mound is located in the same state as the city of Cincinnati. _ _
9. This border state has several Indian reservations and the city of Fargo. _ _
10. Anyone wanting to visit the Gateway Arch, the Pony Express Stables, and the city of Hannibal would travel to this state. _ _
11. The Lewis and Clark Expedition, the Pony Express, the Mormon Trail and the Oregon Trail all cross in this state. _ _

On a separate sheet of paper, identify each Midwestern state and its capital. Use an atlas or map for assistance.

Regions. The Western States cover the greatest area. Two of these states, Alaska and Hawaii, are not contiguous (connected). Place the number of each state in Column One next to its capital in Column Two and an important city in Column Three.

State	Capital	City
1. Alaska	___Salt Lake City	___Laramie
2. Arizona	___Helena	___Eugene
3. California	___Honolulu	___Barrow
4. Colorado	___Cheyenne	___Hilo
5. Hawaii	___Olympia	___Yuma
6. Idaho	___Sacramento	___Fresno
7. Montana	___Carson City	___Ketchum
8. Nevada	___Phoenix	___Great Falls
9. New Mexico	___Denver	___Reno
10. Oregon	___Juneau	___Wenatchee
11. Utah	___Santa Fe	___Boulder
12. Washington	___Boise	___Gallup
13. Wyoming	___Salem	___Provo

United States Government. The U.S. Constitution guarantees a balance of power between the three branches of government at all levels of government. On the tree below, fill in a branch of the government on each of the tree branches.

Fill in the U.S. Constitution chart below.

BRANCH _____ _____ _____

WHO _____ _____ _____

WHAT _____ _____ _____
_____ _____ _____
_____ _____ _____

HOW _____ _____ _____
_____ _____ _____
_____ _____ _____

The Flag of Mexico

Research the story of the Mexican flag. Color the flag using color pencils. Then, write a short paragraph below explaining its meaning.

_____

_____

_____

_____

_____

_____

_____

_____

Central America, the isthmus stretching from Mexico to Columbia, contains seven independent nations. Use color pencils to shade in each country in a different color. Then, label it and use a ✪ to indicate each capital. Finally, label the capitals.

Central America

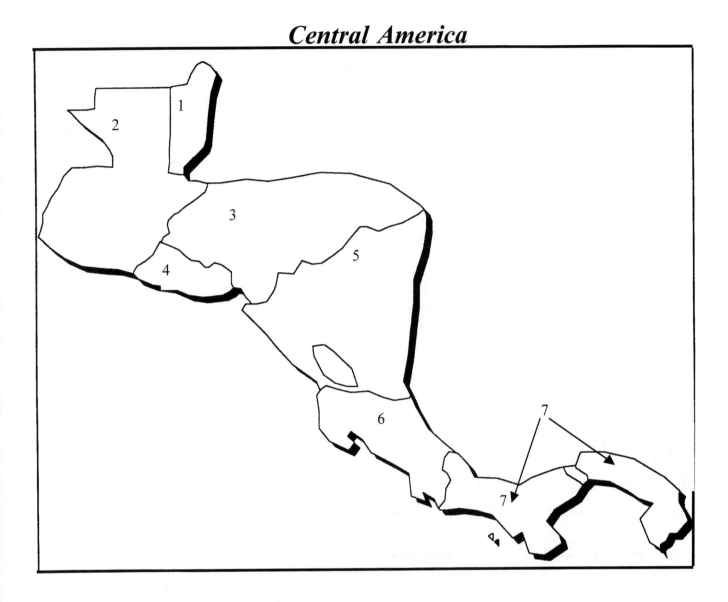

Create a Travel Brochure

Each of the Central American countries has an interesting history and culture as well as unique physical geography. Choose one of the seven countries you would like to learn more about. On a separate sheet of plain paper, create a travel brochure for the country. Areas to be included are the following: capital city and its interesting attractions, the country's scenery, plants, animals, cultural, historical facts and sites. When this information is collected, arrange it in a brochure and decorate it with the country's flag, and other appropriate symbols and decorations. The internet home page for each country is an excellent source of information.

Caribbean Islands and Nations. Using your encyclopedia, atlas, or any other reference materials fill in the blanks, using the word bank below.

The many islands of the Caribbean are really partially submerged peaks of a mountain range. These "chains" are called Archipelagoes, the major islands groups in this area are the (1)_____, the Greater and Lesser Antilles, the Leeward and (2)_____ Islands. The significant bodies of water in the Caribbean are the Atlantic Ocean, the (3)_____, Gulf of Mexico, and the Straits of Florida. The tropic of Cancer is north of Cuba and through the (4)_____ and the Bahamas Islands. The second largest island in the area is (5)_____; French speaking Haiti and the Spanish speaking Dominican Republic are independent nations located on it. Colonialism has left its mark throughout the (6)_____. Many of the smaller islands are still territories of the U.S. or (7)_____ powers. (8)_____, French, Spanish and English languages and place names continue to show the impact of those who followed Columbus to the "New World". A limited number of safe passages for ships through the islands make shipping lanes very predictable. (9)_____ is the name given to the shores of lands bordering the Caribbean. Caribbean nations are tiny by world standards but have high population densities especially in larger cities along the vast coastlines. (10)_____ continues to be a problem as high birth rates and the disappearance of plantation agriculture prevent the development of a middle class.

Word Bank

Caribbean	Poverty
Bahamas Islands	Hispanolia
Caribbean Sea	Dutch
European	Rimland
Windward	Straits of Florida

Islands in the Caribbean Sea

South America - On the map below, label each country in South America and its corresponding capital.

Morse Code

Alfred Vail was a friend of Samuel F. B. Morse who provided him with money for his experiments with the telegraph. On January 6, 1838 Morse and Vail demonstrated the telegraph at the Speedwell Ironworks in Morristown, NJ. The Morse code, a system of dots and dashes to represent each letter of the alphabet and numerals zero through nine, is used to send messages over long distances. Even today people use this system to signal emergencies when other systems are unavailable.

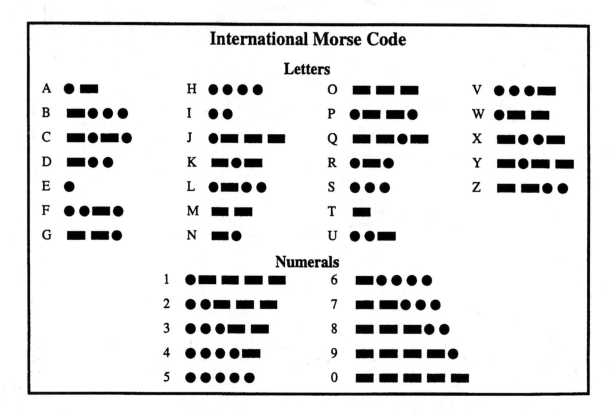

Use the above chart to translate the first message sent by Morse on May 24, 1844.

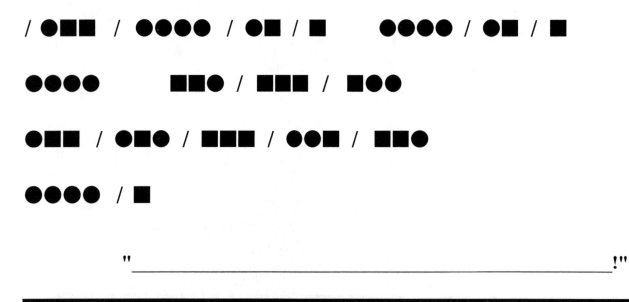

"_____!"

Africa from A to Z: For each letter of the alphabet identify at least one physical or political feature on the continent of Africa.

Materials – maps of Africa – atlas or the internet

A is for _____

B is for _____

C is for _____

D is for _____

E is for _____

F is for _____

G is for _____

H is for _____

I is for _____

J is for _____

K is for _____

L is for _____

M is for _____

N is for _____

O is for _____

P is for _____

Q is for _____

R is for _____

S is for _____

T is for _____

U is for _____

V is for _____

W is for _____

X is for _____

Y is for _____

Z is for _____

A
F
R
I
C
A

Western and Eastern Europe. The European continent is divided both physically and culturally into Western and Eastern Europe. Since the breakup of the USSR, the countries of Eastern Europe have now been expanded to include several countries in northern Asia. At the time of this printing, the former Yugoslavia is still somewhat in a state of transition so your list may not agree with the one printed in your book.

Using a world atlas, label the countries and capitals on the map below. On a separate sheet of paper, create two columns. Label one **Western Europe** and the second, **Eastern Europe**. Place each country in the correct column.

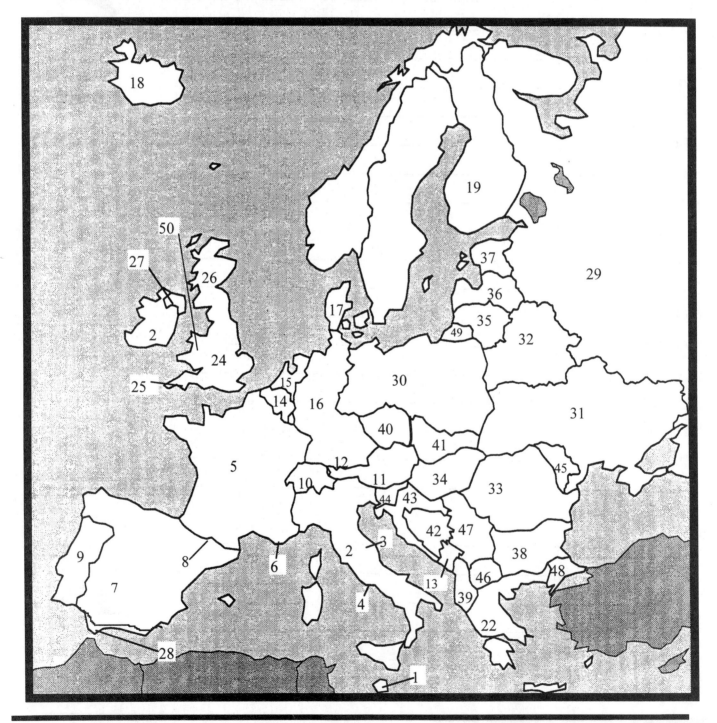

Think like an Egyptian. The kings of Egypt, who from the time of the New Kingdom until the fall of Egypt in 525 BC, were known as pharaohs. The pharaohs were worshipped as gods. These mighty rulers had as their principal duty the establishment of *Ma'at* (truth, order, and justice throughout the land).

Choose a specific pharaoh to research. Use the information to complete the mind map below. Redraw on a blank sheet of paper.

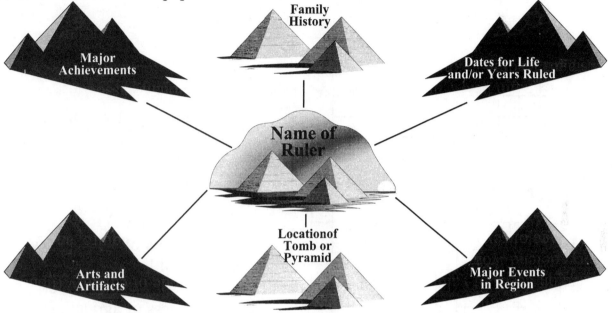

Family History

Major Achievements

Dates for Life and/or Years Ruled

Name of Ruler

Arts and Artifacts

Location of Tomb or Pyramid

Major Events in Region

Egyptians believed that every person had a physical body and a *Ka* (soul or spiritual personality). They also believed that both aspects of the person remained in the tomb. Included in the tomb at the time of burial was everything the person needed or valued in life to provide comfort in his/her eternal home. Since life after death was thought to mirror this life, only better, so the *Ka* was provided a body (the mummy) and the finest of food, drink, furniture, clothing . . .

Spend a few minutes considering what things you would choose to have entombed with your mummy and *ka*. Everything need not be tangible. On a separate sheet of paper, create your list. List all of the items you want and why each would be included. On a second piece of paper, recreate the list but limit your list to the top fifteen items that you would need to be satisfied with for all eternity.

Ancient Greece. The people of ancient Greece had many gods and goddesses, which included gods of music, war, and wisdom. The Greeks also created many myths about their gods which gave explanations for things that happened in their real world. Therefore, these myths became the basis for Greek religion, poetry, music, art, and theater. Use the resource list of gods and goddesses below to complete the Ancient Greek crossword puzzle.

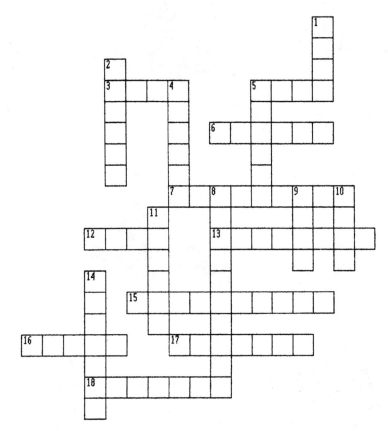

Clues

Down

1. Supreme ruler of the gods
2. Mother of Achilles
4. Goddess of wisdom
5. God of poetry, music, & prophecy.
8. God of fire
9. Goddess of the rainbow
10. God of love
11. Messenger of the gods
14. Goddess of agriculture

Resource Guide

Hermes
Zeus
Poseidon
Iris
Apollo
Demeter
Aphrodite
Eros
Thetis
Hades
Cronus
Hera
Athena
Ares
Artemis
Hephaestus
Persephone
Erinyes
Hebe

Across

3. Goddess of motherhood
5. God of war
6. Father of Zeus
7. Goddess of beauty and love
12. Goddess of youth
13. God of the sea
15. Queen of the underworld
16. God of the dead
17. Goddess of hunting
18. Avengers of evil doing

The Roman Timeline: Latium, on the west coast of Italy, was the site of a group of villages near an island in the Tiber River. This location was chosen because it was a convenient place to cross the Tiber River. Here, according to legend, in 753 BC, Rome was founded by Romulus after he killed his twin brother Remus. Romulus became Rome's first king. Kings ruled Rome until 510BC. Rome then became a republic, governed by a group of citizens, the Senate. The city was defended by a wall as well as a strong army.

The Roman soldier (pictured below) is a true symbol of the Roman Empire. The soldier forms a timeline of part of Roman history. Match the events below with the correct dates by writing the corresponding letter in the blank beside the date given. Use any of your reference books to help you with this timeline.

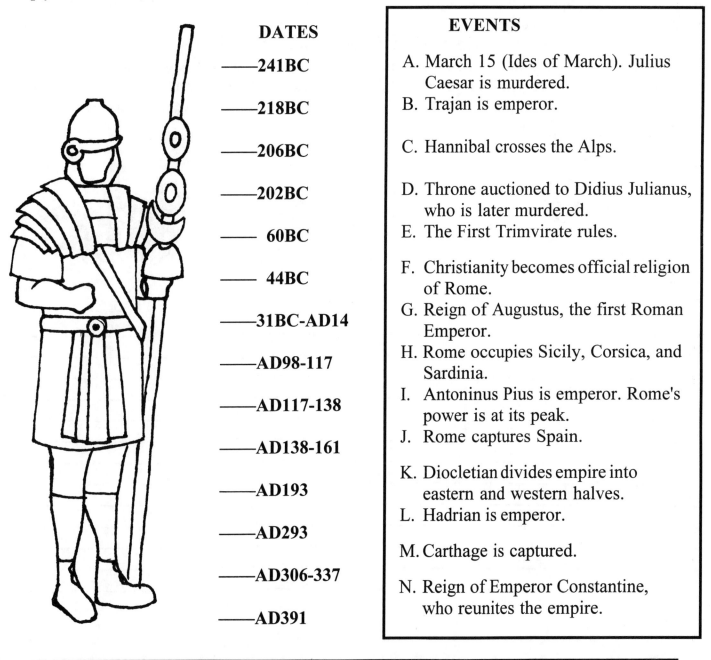

DATES

——241BC

——218BC

——206BC

——202BC

—— 60BC

—— 44BC

——31BC-AD14

——AD98-117

——AD117-138

——AD138-161

——AD193

——AD293

——AD306-337

——AD391

EVENTS

A. March 15 (Ides of March). Julius Caesar is murdered.
B. Trajan is emperor.

C. Hannibal crosses the Alps.

D. Throne auctioned to Didius Julianus, who is later murdered.
E. The First Trimvirate rules.

F. Christianity becomes official religion of Rome.
G. Reign of Augustus, the first Roman Emperor.
H. Rome occupies Sicily, Corsica, and Sardinia.
I. Antoninus Pius is emperor. Rome's power is at its peak.
J. Rome captures Spain.

K. Diocletian divides empire into eastern and western halves.
L. Hadrian is emperor.

M. Carthage is captured.

N. Reign of Emperor Constantine, who reunites the empire.

Knights and Weapons

In 1066, the Norman French, who came on horseback, were called knights by the English whom they conquered. The English began to refer to any man who could fight on horseback as a knight. Every knight had a master whom he served either in war related or routine service. Soon the knights began to outfit themselves in expensive armor and weapons whose value limited knighthood to the wealthy. However, a man could achieve the rank of knight based on deeds of valor. All knights swore to uphold the code of chivalry (uphold Christianity, defend women and protect the poor and weak).

At the age of seven, a boy became a page, at twelve or thirteen, a squire, and finally in a ceremony called an accolade, he became a knight. Any knight who was dishonorable or broke his vows was stripped of his knighthood in a mock burial ceremony for in that time "a knight without honor is no longer alive."

In modern times knighthood is either inherited or an honor bestowed by a monarch in recognition for services to one's country and the crown. Today a male knight is called Sir. His wife is referred to as Lady and a female who is knighted is called a Dame.

In each column below list skills, duties and weapons traditionally associated with each of the three stages leading to knighthood.

Page

Squire

Knight

Kingdoms of Ancient Africa. Ancient Africa because of its great geographical diversity was the site for many kingdoms. These kingdoms flourished in sub-Saharan Africa between 751BC when Piankhi, King of Kush, conquered Egypt until about AD1600.

For each kingdom below fill in the details to support each main idea.

Kush

Where _____

When _____

History _____

_____

Resources _____

Accomplishments _____

_____

Ethiopia

Where _____

When _____

History _____

_____

Resources _____

Accomplishments _____

_____

Great Kingdoms in Ancient Sub-Saharan Africa

Mali

Where _____

When _____

History _____

_____

Resources _____

Accomplishments _____

_____

Songhai

Where _____

When _____

History _____

_____

Resources _____

Accomplishments _____

_____

Modern Africa is generally considered to have begun with the arrival of the Portuguese and the beginning of the slave trade out of Africa in the late 1400's.

Choose one of the topics below to research and write a **first person** account about it. You may want to write this account in the style of a diary entry.

1. Being captured by slaves and transported to the sea coast.
2. The voyage known as the "Middle Passage," either as a slave or as a crew member.
3. Fighting in the resistance against European conquest.
4. Life under apartheid either as a black or white South African.
5. If you were an African leader today, what would you try to accomplish for your country and its citizens?

Middle East Match-Up. Each of the statements in Column A describes or defines a word in Column B. Place the letter from Column B in the space before its definition in Column A.

Column A

_____ 1. Wedge-shaped, Sumerian writing

_____ 2. An upright carved stone slab

_____ 3. A local leader who often launched raids

_____ 4. Words of God written soon after Muhammad's death

_____ 5. Well-watered area within desert region

_____ 6. Religion in Middle East; means "surrender to God"

_____ 7. Muslim place of worship

_____ 8. Place where Muhammad rose to heaven

_____ 9. Belief in one god

_____ 10. Islamic holy war

_____ 11. Israeli legislator

_____ 12. Exile of the Jews from Palestine

_____ 13. Christians believe that Jesus is the _____

_____ 14. Pious Jews, called Essenes, wrote and hid the _____

_____ 15. Nomadic desert dwellers

_____ 16. Holy city for Christians, Jews and Muslims

_____ 17. European Christians' wars against Moslems

_____ 18. The Byzantine Empire was ended by the _____

_____ 19. Jewish state whose birthday is May 14, 1948

_____ 20. Organization of Petroleum Exporting Countries

Column B

A. Dead Sea Scrolls
B. Koran
C. Jihad
D. Mosque
E. Ottoman Empire
F. Stele
G. Diaspora
H. OPEC
I. Bedouin
J. Islam
K. State of Israel
L. Cuneiform
M. Knesset
N. Sheik
O. Crusades
P. Monothesism
Q. Messiah
R. Oasis
S. Dome of the Rock
T. Jerusalem

TIME OUT: Name five of the Middle Eastern countries and their capitals.

_____

_____

_____

The Renaissance. The term *Renaissance* refers to a "rebirth" or a rediscovery. It is the continuation of learning and creativity of the classical ages that had slowed during the Middle Ages. Hallmarks of the Renaissance were as follows: 1) celebration of the individual, rather than the group, 2) interest in the ideas of ancient Greece and Rome, 3) enjoyment of worldly pleasure, and 4) the rejection of the simple life of feudal times.

For each group of people below, decide what is the common tie between them (i.e., poets).

1. Michelangelo, Buonarroti, Leonardo da Vinci, Sandro Botticelli, Raffaello Santi (Raphael), Rembrandt van Rijn.

1. _____

2. Nicolaus Copernicus, Galileo Galilei, René Descartes, William Harvey, Isaac Newton.

2. _____

3. Dante Alighieri, Geoffrey Chaucer, Niccolò Machiavelli, Miguel de Cervantes, William Shakespeare.

3. _____

4. Martin Luther, John Calvin, Pope Leo X, King Henry VIII, Pope Paul III, Ignatius of Loyola.

4. _____

5. Elizabeth I, Catherine the Great, Maria Theresa, Isabella, Catherine de Medici.

5. _____

6. Venetian Republic, Kingdom of Naples, Papal States, Siena, Firenze.

6. _____

7. Blaise Pascal, Peter Heinlein, Otto von Guericke, Evangelista Totticelli, Johannes Gutenberg.

7. _____

8. Henry VII, Louis XIII, Philip II, Peter the Great, Frederick the Great, Joseph II.

8. _____

9. John Donne, Edmund Spencer, Ludovico Ariosto, Joachim du Bellay, Pierre de Ronsard.

9. _____

10. Guillaune Dufay, Gilles Binchois, Clement Janequin, Heinrich Isaac, Giovanni Gabrieli.

10. _____

11. Luca Marenzio, Thomas Morley, Claudio Monteverdi, Jean d'Ockeghem, Josquin des Prez.

11. _____

Age of Exploration. A Portuguese prince, Henry the Navigator, worked to spark the Age of Exploration. European countries sent out explorers to find new trade routes, look for gold, establish new colonies, and/or spread Christianity. Fill in the surname of each of the explorers to complete the crossword puzzle.

Across

3. Made voyages to the West Indies and South America for Spain and Portugal (1497-1503). Amerigo _____.
5. Explored a river and bay in North America (1609-1611) later named for him. Henry _____.
9. Sailed around Africa to India; Brazil. Pedro _____.
10. Explored the eastern coast of North America (1524). Giovanni _____.
11. Made contact with Inca Empire (1531) Francisco _____.
12. First Englishman to sail around the world (1577-1588) Sir Frances _____.

Down

1. Led expedition across Panama; sighted the Pacific Ocean (1513) Vasco _____
2. Landed in Newfoundland (1497-1498) John and Sebastian _____.
4. Explored Florida (1513). Juan _____.
6. Explored eastern coast of North America the Great Lakes (1603-1616). Samuel ?
7. Conquered the Aztec Kingdom of Mexico (1519-1521). Hernando _____
8. First to circumnavigate the world; sailed for Spain (1509-1522). Ferdinand _____
9. Made four voyages to West Indies (1492-1504). Christopher _____.
10. First European to reach India by sea (1498). Vasco _____.
12. First European to sail around Africa. (1487-1488). Bartolomeu _____.

Europe and North Asia in Modern Times. Each item in the chart below can be classified as either the cause or the effect of another item that should be in the chart. Use the items filled in to help you decide what is missing.

CAUSE	EFFECT
1. Industrial Revolution	
2. Absolute monarch Social class structure Formation of National Assembly	
3.	Peter the Great "opened a window to the West" by building port city of St. Petersburg.
4. Most Russians were serfs (later peasants) and as such were landless and often hungry.	
5.	Under Stalin's rule, Russia became a totalitarian country.
6. Europe divided into two major alliances (Central Powers & Allied Forces) Archduke Franz Ferdinand assassinated	
7.	Rise of Adolf Hitler and the Nazi Party.
8. Hitler broke friendship treaty with Stalin and attacked Soviet Union. USA entered war on the side of the Allies.	
9.	Formation of the United Nations.

Creating a historic timeline. A timeline can be compared to a number line with the Birth of Christ at the zero position. On a sheet of blank paper, use a straight edge and a pencil to create a number line. Arrange each of the events listed according to chronological order.

1. 1500 BC   The Sahara becomes a desert as a result of climatic change.
2. AD 750   Teotihuacan is destroyed.
3. AD 1761   British gained control of India from the French.
4. AD 1917   Russian Revolution.
5. 202 BC   China is united by the Han Dynasty.
6. 776 BC   First recorded Olympic Games held in Greece.
7. AD 1614   First Europeans begin to explore the coast of Australia.
8. AD 1175   First Muslim Empire is founded in India.
9. 1200 BC   Jews are sent out of Egypt and settle in Palestine.
10. AD 641   Arabs conquer Egypt.
11. 753 BC   Legendary founding of Rome.
12. c AD 1200 The Mali Empire flourishes in West Africa
13. AD 1789   The French Revolution begins
14. AD 1776   U.S. Declaration of Independence signed
15. AD 1989   Communist governments fall in Eastern Europe.
16. AD 1863   Gold rush in New Zealand.
17. c 2590 BC Cheops builds the Great Pyramid at Giza in Egypt.
18. 0   Birth of Jesus Christ.
19. c AD 790   Vikings make the first raids on Britain.
20. AD 1760   Britain wins territory in Canada from the French.

Choose one event from the list above to find out more information. In the space below write a short description detailing the event. Possible resources could include encyclopedia, topical books at the library, the Internet, parents or other adults.

Title _____

_____

_____

_____

_____

_____

Doodling:

TO DRAW OR SCRIBBLE AIMLESSLY

Social Studies

7th Grade Preview

- Geography · Charts · Graphs
- Maps · Tables

Test Your Summer Que

Answer the following questions in order to spell out a message.

_____ 1. If blackberries are still green when they are red, write **H** in the left hand margin. If not, write **Z**.

_____ 2. If brown cows give white milk which makes yellow butter, write **A** in the left hand margin. If not, write **W**.

_____ 3. If paper can be made out of wood, write **V** in the left hand margin. If not, write **P**.

_____ 4. If Leap Year has 366 days, write **E** at the left. If not, write **A**.

_____ 5. If a ground hog is a pig that lives in the earth, put an **H** at the left. If not, write **A** there.

_____ 6. If the letter **M** comes before the letter **K** in the alphabet, write **R** in the left margin. If not, write **G**.

_____ 7. If the Atlantic Ocean is the largest ocean in the world, write **P** at the left. If not, write **O**.

_____ 8. If Beethoven was deaf the last years of his life, write **O** at the left. If not, write **T**.

_____ 9. If basketball is a major sport, write **D** at the left. If not, write **S**.

_____ 10. If the first day of summer is called the Spring Equinox, write **K** at the left. If it is called Summer Solstice, write **S**.

_____ 11. If seventy is larger than seventeen, write **U** in the left margin. If not, write **T**.

_____ 12. If Edison invented electricity, write **P** in the left margin. If not, write **M**.

_____ 13. If Francis Scott Key wrote our national anthem, put an **M** in the left margin. If he didn't, put an **X**.

_____ 14. If Mr. Gettysburg wrote the Gettysburg Address, put **B** in the left margin. If not, put **E**.

_____ 15. If the Pilgrims had never seen corn until they came to America, put **R** at the left. If they had, put **Z**.

_____ 16. If this is the final question in this quiz, put **!** at the left. If not, put a **?**.

The message is "_____ ___ _____ _____!"

GETTING A HEAD START IN THE 7TH GRADE: Most schools concentrate on the study of geography. A common choice of regions to study in the seventh grade are Latin America, the Caribbean, Asia, and Oceania (also called Pacifica). Since students are expected to identify each of the countries and its capital with the location, this preview of the book includes maps of all the areas commonly studied. You will need a current atlas to complete the map activities.

North American Map. Label all of the countries and capitals of North America and the major bodies of water in and around the continent. Draw in and label the major rivers, mountains and any other significant geographic features of the continent.

North America

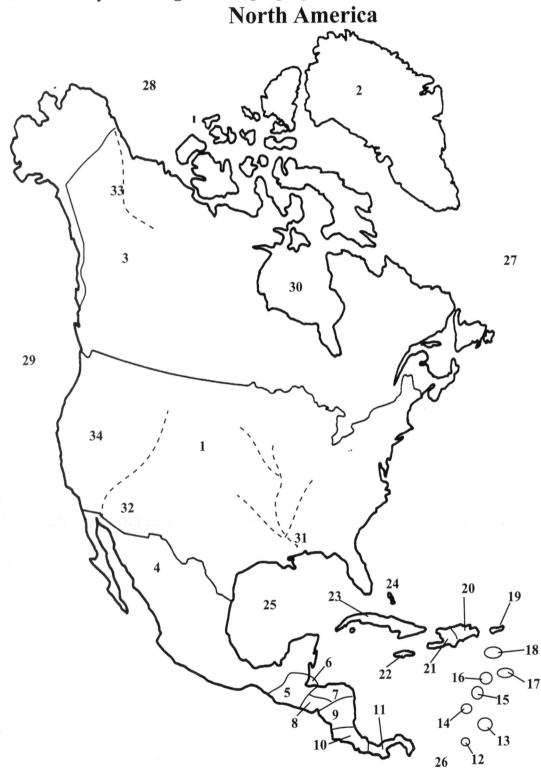

Caribbean Map. Label the major bodies of water, Tropic of Cancer, major countries their capitals, and major islands. Use color pencils to label: *blue* for water, *green* for countries, *red* for capitals, and *orange* to draw the Tropic of Cancer. Consult a world atlas for assistance.

Caribbean Map

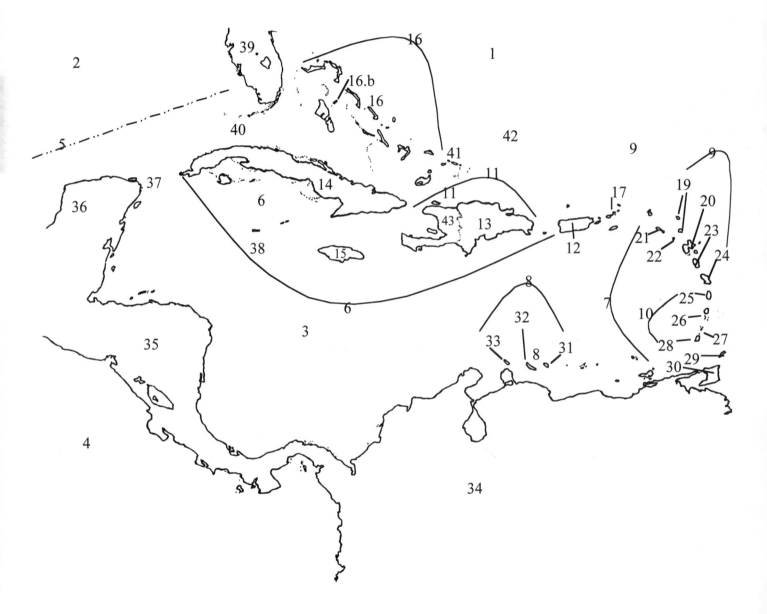

South American Map. Draw in and label the major rivers, mountains, lakes and forests of South America. Label each country and its capital or capitals. Draw in the Equator. Label the major bodies of water surrounding South America. Use an atlas for help.

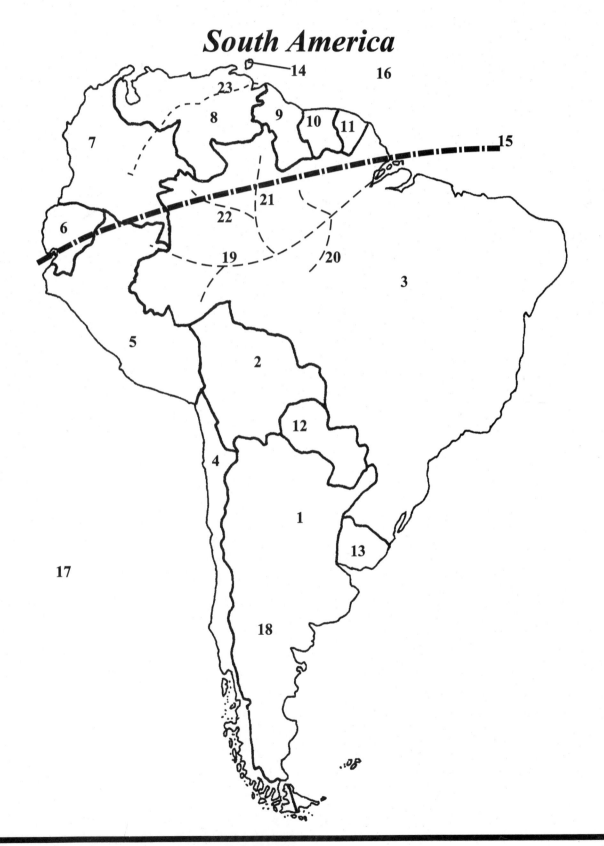

South America

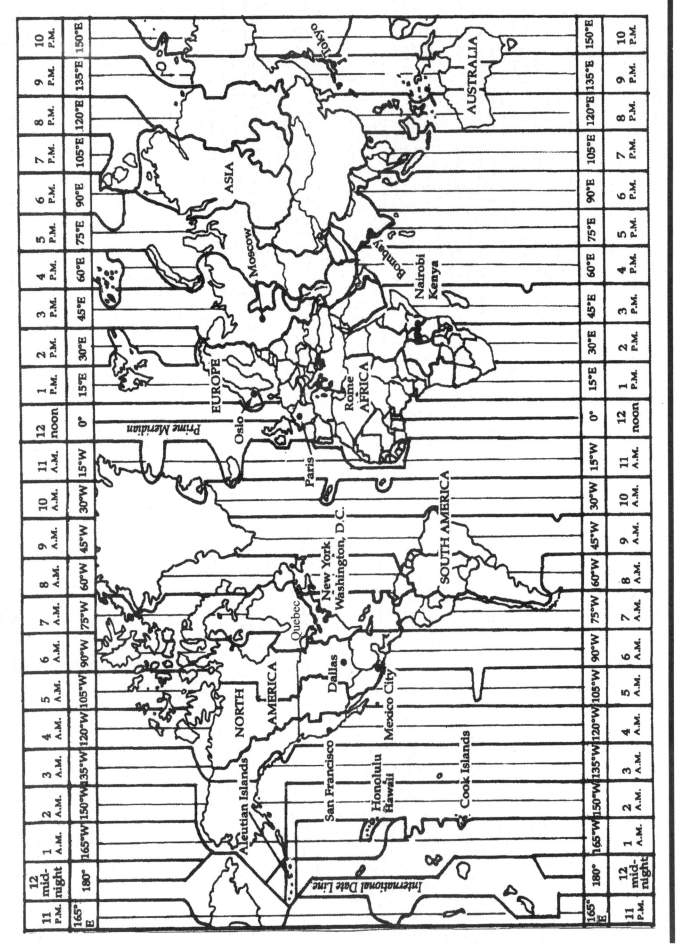

International Time Zones. Use the time zone map on the previous page to help answer the following questions. **Answer all questions as if time were stopped exactly as recorded on the map.**

1. How many times zones are there? _____ Why do you think this number was chosen? _____

2. Time zones are calculated based on lines of _____ with _____ ° in each zone.

3. If time is calculated as hours plus or minus from 12 noon at the Prime Meridian, what line of longitude would be at the center of this time zone? _____

4. On this map, it is 12 noon in Greenwich, England (Greenwich Mean Time is also called Zula Time and is the reference point for all zones). What time is it in:
   A. San Francisco, California, USA _____
   B. Moscow, Russia _____
   C. The Cook Islands _____
   D. Mexico City, Mexico _____
   E. Hobart, Tasmania, Australia _____
   F. Quebec, Canada _____

5. Since the earth rotates from east to west, subtract 1 hour for each 15° moving _____ and add 1 hour for each 15° moving _____.

6. 180° west or east is the International Date Line; the east is 12 hours behind, so by crossing the line there is a difference of _____ hours or _____. If you cross the line from west to east, you gain a day but crossing from east to west you _____ a day.

7. The continental US or lower 48 has _____ time zones. Canada has _____ time zones.

8. What time zone do you live in? _____ Which time zone is *east* of you? _____ Which time zone is *west* of you? _____

9. How many degrees of longitude are included in the complete time zone map of the earth? _____ °

African Map. On a separate sheet of paper, use the numbers to label each country, its capital or capitals and major bodies of water in and around Africa. Use a world atlas for assistance.

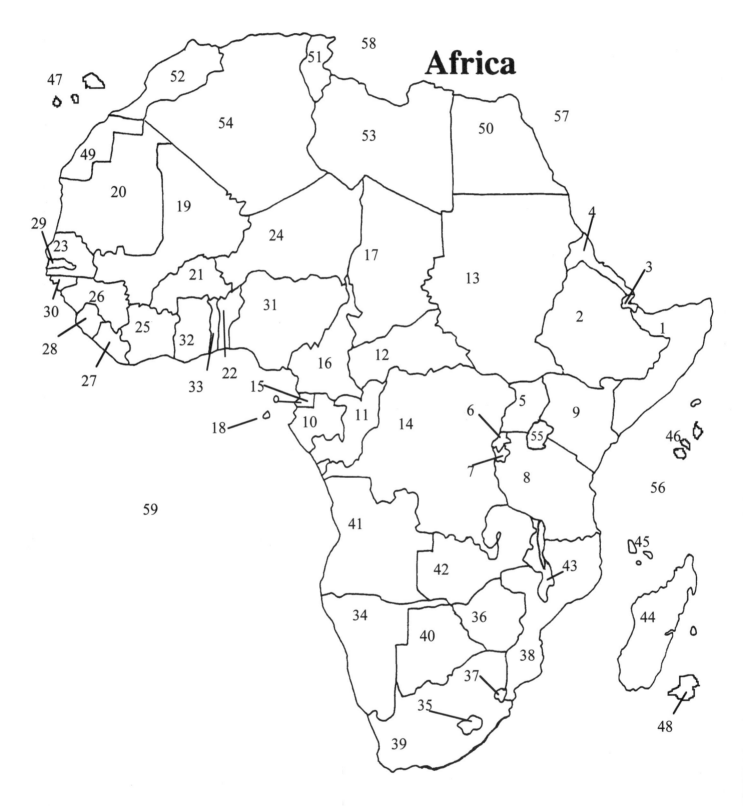

Africa

Asian Map. On a separate sheet of paper, label the countries, capitals, major bodies of water, mountains and any other significant geographic features of Asia. Finally, do not overlook the island nations that surround the mainland. Consult a world atlas for assistance.

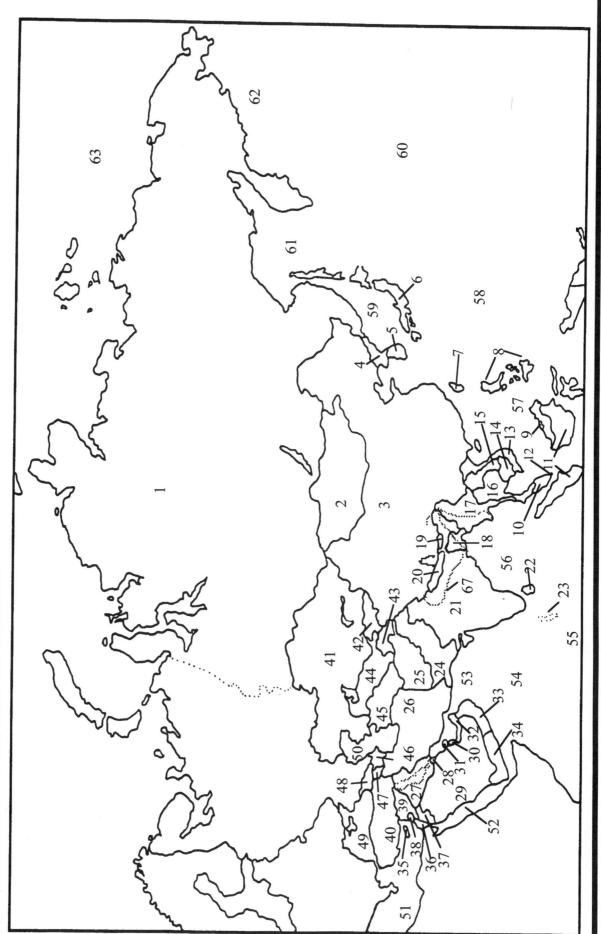

Oceania Map. Label the countries, capitals, major islands and island groups. Label the territories of Australia and their capitals. Label the two main islands of New Zealand. Consult a world atlas for assistance.

Oceania

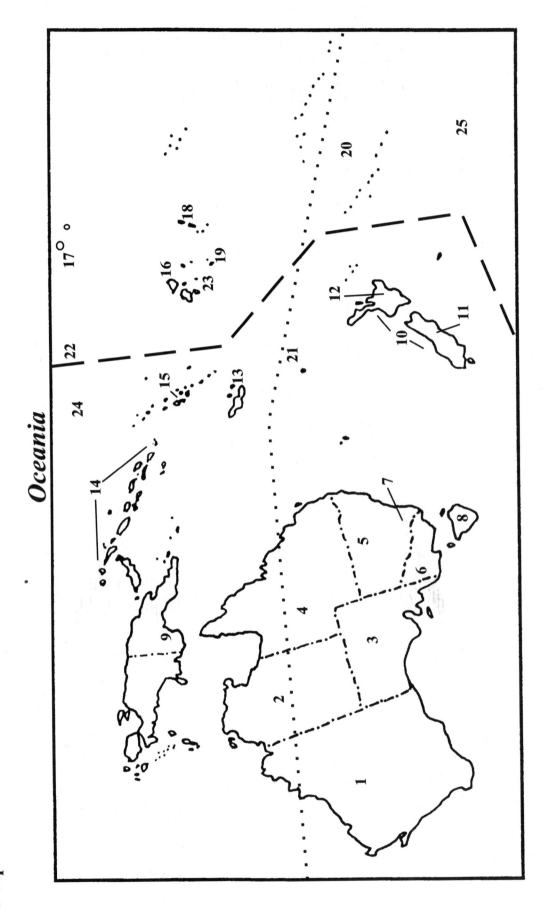

Science
6th Grade in Review
- Life Science • Earth Science
- Biological Science • Physical Science

Warning: Rainbow Bridge Publishing recommends that the experiments in this section be performed under adult supervision.

And the answer is...

You think some of your answers are silly. Check out some of the answers actually given by sixth graders on their science tests.

"Water is composed of two gins: Oxygin and Hydrogin. Oxygin is pure gin. Hydrogin is gin and water."

"When you breathe, you inspire. When you do not breathe, you expire."

"H2O is hot water, and CO2 is cold water."

"When you smell an odorless gas, it is probably carbon monoxide."

"Three kinds of blood vessels are arteries, vanes, and caterpillars."

"Blood flows down one leg and up the other."

"The moon is a planet just like the earth, only it is even deader."

"Mushrooms always grow in damp places and so they look like umbrellas."

"The pistol of a flower is its only protection against insects."

"The alimentary canal is located in the northern part of Indiana."

"The skeleton is what is left after the insides have been taken out and the outsides have been taken off. The purpose of the skeleton is something to hitch meat to."

"A fossil is an extinct animal. The older it is, the more extinct it is."

"Equator: A managerie lion running around the Earth through Africa.

"Planet: A body of Earth surrounded by sky."

"Vacuum: A large, empty space where the Pope lives."

"Before giving a blood transfusion, find out if the blood is affirmative or negative."

"To remove dust from the eye, pull the eye down over the nose."

"For dog bite: put the dog away for several days. If he has not recovered, then kill it."

"For asphyxiation: apply artificial respiration until the patient is dead."

"For head cold: use an agonizer to spray the nose until it drops in your throat."

"To keep milk from turning sour: keep it in the cow."

Science as Art

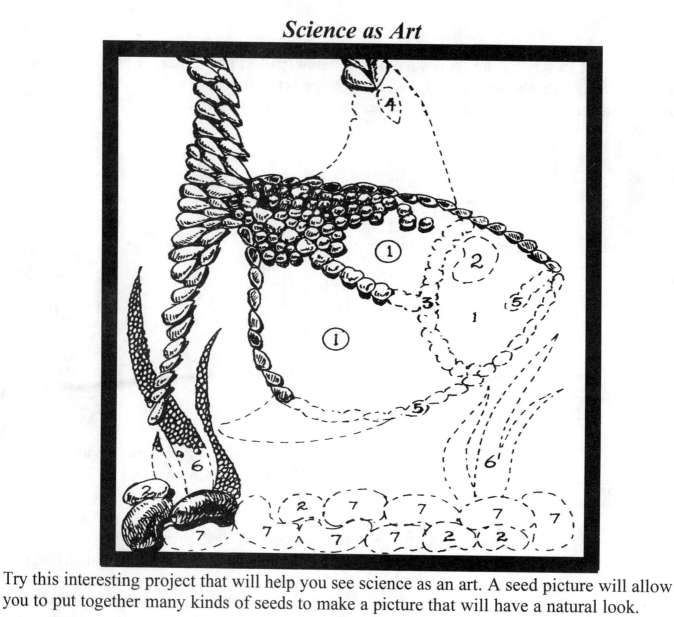

Try this interesting project that will help you see science as an art. A seed picture will allow you to put together many kinds of seeds to make a picture that will have a natural look.

Materials

1. *Seeds, dry beans, and peas*
2. *Heavy construction paper or oaktag paper*

3. *Rubber cement or paper glue*
4. *Pencil and an eraser*

Directions:

1. With a pencil, draw a picture on the heavy sheet of paper. Try not to make your picture too complicated. Why not draw an animal, a plant, or a fish?
2. Put some glue or rubber cement along the most important lines in your picture. Place your largest seeds on these lines.
3. Choose areas of your picture where each type of seed would look best. Next, spread the glue over each section, and then put the other seeds in place.
4. When you have finished, put your "seed picture" away for the glue to dry. After the glue has dried, shake the picture so that the seeds that weren't glued properly fall off. Reglue any seeds that have fallen off. Finally, you may spray a fixative to make your picture permanent.

Living Things. In solving the crossword puzzle below, you will have review terms necessary for successfully completing some of the Life Science activities. Use the clues below to complete the crossword puzzle with information about living things.

Down

1. A member of a kingdom of living things that have one cell with a very simple structure.
2. Ranging or grouping things together based on similarities.
5. A theory that explains why living things change: _____ selection.
6. The largest category in the classification of living things.
7. A member of a kingdom of living things that do not move about but do make their own food.
10. A member of a kingdom of living things that resemble plants but do not have leaves or flowers.
12. A member of a kingdom of living things that resemble both plants and animals in some ways.
13. A member of a kingdom of living things that have many cells, are able to move and sense their environments, but do not make their own food.

Across

3. The process of change in living things that occurs over a long period of time.
4. A scientist that studies plants.
8. No longer living or existing.
9. A guide for identifying living things.
11. A change in structure or behavior that helps a living thing survive in its environment.
14. A group of living things that have certain like characteristics.

General Science. Let's have some fun! You have heard of the game Trivial Pursuit. Now, let's play Science Pursuit. You will have various questions, and each will have a value point assigned. Test your general science knowledge of the following questions.

1. What planet, discovered in 1930, is named after the god of the lower world?

   (10 Points)

2. What does "equinox" mean? (20 Points)

3. How does a deciduous tree differ from a non-deciduous tree? (25 Points)

4. Explain why the whale is a mammal and **not** a fish. (40 Points for all 4 reasons)

5. What do sugar, sand, salt and snowflakes all have in common? (10 Points)

6. How many legs does a spider have? (5 Points)

7. Who invented the telescope? (15 Points)

8. Who was the first European in North America to sight the Pacific

   Ocean? (35 Points)

9. Do snakes close their eyes when they sleep? (20 Points)

10. Who invented the phonograph? (10 Points)

11. Name the first man to walk on the moon. (10 Points)

12. When Wilson Bentley photographed 1000 snowflakes, what two discoveries did he

    make? (15 Points)

13. Name a marsupial found in the USA. (20 Points)

14. Explain why it rains. (35 Points)

15. How long is a year on the planet Mercury? (25 Points)

16. Why don't snakes close their eyes? (10 Points)

17. What planet, discovered in 1846, is named after the Greek god of the sea? (10 Points)

HOW DID YOU DO?   **POSSIBLE SCORE: 315**   **MY SCORE** _____

Genius	280 to 315
Expert	200 to 279
Student	151 to 200
Curious	101 to 150
Novice	0 to 100

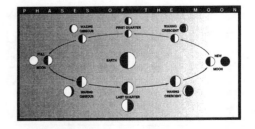

The Water Cycle. Water travels in an endless cycle. Energy from the sun causes water in earth's oceans to evaporate. Hot air rises and carries water vapor up into the cooler atmosphere. Here water vapor forms clouds. Water falls from the clouds as rain or snow. Animals drink water or obtain it by eating plants. Both plants and animals use or store some water and return the rest to the environment. Plants release water through their leaves. Animals release water with waste products. Water evaporates, and the cycle continues.

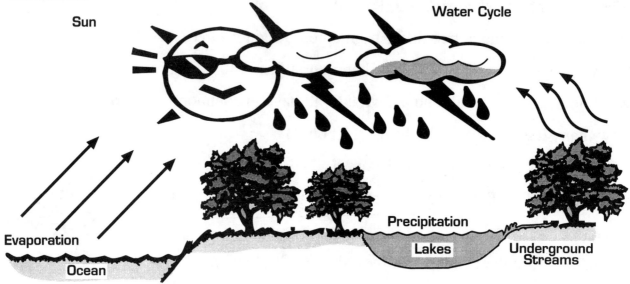

The answer to each of the questions below is included in the word search. Fill in the blank and then circle the words in the puzzle.

```
C A B S O R B S A H W F P
U L Q D T O U G V H R R D
L N O J N V I B J O E N A
U Y D U L R A K Z C V E Y
U Y X E D B B E I W S Z L
E V V E R S N P L U W W I
A B Y F B N I Y H D R F G
N T U Z Z T E K P Y E D H
A Z O F A T Z A E X H N T
E L Z T I K Q M T L R U X
C M I N C S J H I H C S T
O O T Q C V R E T A W Y Q
N N E C E S S A R Y H V C
```

WATER CYLCE CLUES

1. Rivers empty into the _____.
2. The earth has more _____ than land.
3. Water cycles are _____ for all life.
4. Snow is a _____ state of water.
5. Water travels in a _____.
6. The _____ are really water vapors.
7. Springs come from _____ the ground.
8. The ground _____ water.
9. The _____ evaporates water.
10. Evaporation occurs during _____ hours.
11. Water falls to the earth in the form of _____.

Water Pollution - Water pollution is caused by solids, bacteria and chemicals found in water supplies. In this experiment comparisons will be made of solids found in various water sources.

> You will need the following materials:
> Coffee filters (cone shape work best)
> Small jars (at least 3)
> Magic marker
> Large jar (1)
> Funnel
> Pencil & eraser
> Labels (sticky labels or plain paper & tape)

Procedure:
1. Use small jars to collect samples from various local water sources (streams, ponds, puddles...)

2. Place filter in funnel and place the funnel in the mouth of the large jar.
   Pour one of the jars of water through the filter in the funnel.

3. Remove the filter and label the sight of collection on the filter with a marker.

4. Repeat steps 2 & 3 with each sample. Note: Mark each filter with collection data.

5. Create a chart to compare the amount and colors of the filtered material and the kinds of particles caught by the filters.

A. Which sample had the most solids in it?

B. Which had the least?

C. What might account for the differences?

D. What other observations can be made?

WARNING !!
Water that has been filtered will look cleaner than before it was filtered. Filtering is one of the first steps in the water purification process, but filtering does not make water safe to drink. Harmful bacteria and chemicals may still be in the water. Don't drink the water!

Time Travel. Albert Einstein theorized that if the rate is accelerated a point will be reached where time would slow down. Some scientists think that it is possible to accelerate to a point that would make time go in reverse. Science fiction writers use this theory when they suggest time travel either backward or forward. This theory of time travel requires traveling faster than the speed of light. Light travels at about 186,000 miles per second. Is it possible to travel this fast? What would a time machine look like? Where in time would it travel? What adventure would await the time travelers?

In the space below, write a story of time travel. On a separate sheet of paper, draw and label a time machine.

_____
_____
_____
_____
_____
_____
_____
_____
_____
_____
_____
_____
_____
_____
_____
_____
_____
_____
_____
_____
_____
_____
_____

Growing Crystals. Crystals are regularly shaped, repeating units of chemicals. Some crystals are unique in shape and formation. This experiment in crystal growing must be carried out in the <u>open air</u> or a <u>well-ventilated room.</u>

Materials needed:

12-18 charcoal briquettes (plain, no lighter fluid)
Thick paper bag
Hammer
Measuring cup
1 cup laundry bluing (either liquid or mix in order to make 1 cup)
Water

4 disposable plastic containers (2 cups or greater)
Measuring spoon
1/3 cup of each: salt, borax, Epsom salts
3 tablespoons unscented household ammonia
Food coloring

Procedure:

1. Place the charcoal in the bag. Use the hammer to break into small pieces. (Be sure to get your parent's permission as to where to do this project.)
2. If bluing is dry, mix powder with equal amount of water. If liquid, add about 6 tablespoons of water to it.
3. For each of the mixtures, in a separate container, mix 1/3 cup of bluing, plus 1/3 cup of water and 1 tablespoon ammonia with the 1/3 cup of salt, borax or Epsom salts. Do one mixture at a time and rinse the container before reusing.
4. Place 1/3 of the charcoal in a container and pour one of the solutions over it. Add a drop of food coloring on top of the coals. Put the container somewhere that is safe and where it can sit undisturbed for a day.
5. Repeat with each of the solutions for a total of three. Label each as to salt, borax or Epsom salts.
6. **Do not move the containers! The crystals will break easily.**

The crystals will form on the surface of the charcoal, which has absorbed some of the water, allowing the crystals to form. The other ingredients mixed together to form the crystals. As the water was absorbed by the charcoal, small particles of the salts evaporated out of the water and bonded in a repeating pattern. Millions of these small particles join together to form the crystal shapes. Notice that each type of chemical forms a crystal with a different and characteristic shape.

Draw and label each of the crystal structures. What observations can you make for each of them?

Investigating Our Earth. Use the words in bold print in the box below to complete the crossword puzzle. If necessary, use your dictionary to look up the definitions.

continental drift	fault	Richter scale	tension
Pangea	synclines	lava	compression
seismograph	fracture	magnitude	mantle
plate tectonics	anticlines	waves	core

CLUES

ACROSS

5. Molten rock that flows across the surface of the earth
10. Theory stating that present-day continents drifted to their present locations
12. The innermost layer of the earth
13. Giant continent that included all of earth's present-day land masses
14. The force that pulls rocks apart at plate boundaries and normal faults
15. The middle layer of the earth's interior
16. The form in which energy travels in an earthquake

DOWN

1. A break in the crust along which rock moves
2. The force that pushes rocks together at plate boundaries and reverse faults
3. Areas where the crust bends down
4. Relative strength of an earthquake.
6. Theory that earth's surface is divided into plates that move
7. A scale that rates the strength, or magnitude, of an earthquake
8. Instrument that records vibrations caused by movements within the crust
9. A break in the crust
11. Areas where the crust bends upward

Chemical Reactions. A *mixture* is made when two or more materials are combined with no reaction. An example: mixing salt, sand and sugar. A *solution* is created when one material dissolves in another with no reaction. An example: salt or sugar in warm water. A *reaction* occurs when two materials combine to form a new substance.

Materials:

    Clear plastic cups
    Water
    White vinegar
    Baking soda
    Plastic spoons
    Paper towels

Procedure:
1. Place a cup on the paper towel and fill half-way with water.
2. Stir in several spoonfuls of baking soda. Stir continuously until the solution is clear.
3. Predict what will happen when vinegar is added.
4. Pour 1/4 cup of vinegar into the solution.
5. Draw what happened when the vinegar was added.

What's the Matter—creating a polymer?

Materials:

    Borax
    Water
    White glue
    Food coloring
    Plastic spoons
    Plastic, self-sealing bag
    Paper towel

Procedure:

1. Dissolve 1/2 cup of borax in 1 quart of very hot water. Set aside to cool.
2. Place 2 spoonfuls of water in a plastic bag.
3. Add 3 spoonfuls of white glue.
4. Seal the glue; then, squish and squeeze to mix.
5. Open the bag and add 2 spoonfuls of borax solution. (Be sure to use a clean spoon.)
6. Seal the bag, making sure to push out all excess air.
7. Observe the changes that occur as you squish and squeeze the bag.
8. When totally thickened, remove the "gloop," roll and stretch.

Layers of the Earth. Label and color each layer of the earth model below.

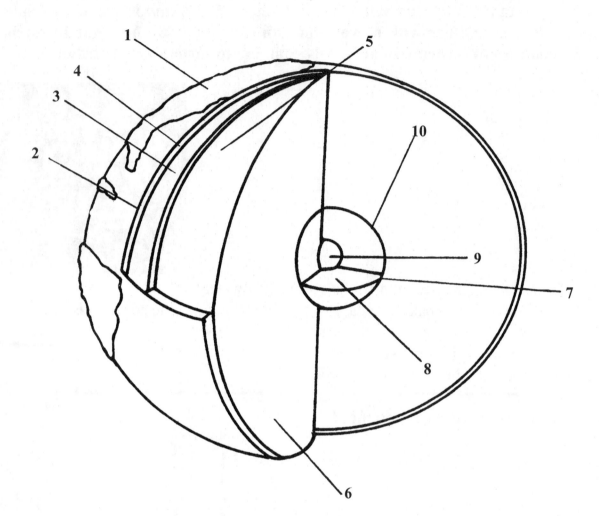

The outside of the earth is called the (1) _____. The crust is part of the earth that we see, live on, and explore. The (2) _____ _____ separates the crust from the top part of the mantle. The (3) _____ is the upper layer of the earth including the crust and the cooler part of the upper mantle. The (4) _____ is about 1,802 miles thick and is composed of silica, iron, magnesium, and other minerals. The (5)_____ is hot and plastic or semi-solid and approximately 186 miles thick. It is the layer between the brittle crust and upper mantle and the more solid (6) _____. The (7) _____ of the earth consists of the (8) _____ _____ which is about 1,400 miles thick and appears to be liquid. The (9) _____ _____ is approximately 800 miles thick and appears to be solid. It is very hot, with temperatures between 7,200 and 9,000 degrees Fahrenheit. The (10) _____separates the earth's mantle from the outer core.

asthenosphere	Mohorovicic discontinuity	outer core
lithosphere	mesosphere	Gutenberg discontinuity
crust	core	mantle
inner core		

Static Electricity. The English word *electricity* comes from the Greek word for amber, *elecktron*. Ancient Greeks discovered that when a piece of fur was rubbed over a chunk of amber, the amber would pick up straw, hair and various other fine, lightweight items. Rubbing stocking feet across a carpet and then touching someone or something like a door knob will release a static charge. Things with the same charge push away from each other while things with opposite charges will attract each other.

Materials:

    Tissue paper torn in tiny pieces
    Several pieces of cloth (i.e., wool, felt, nylon, or silk)
    A collection of small "stuff" (i.e., nail, comb, paper clip, glass chip, etc.)

Procedure:

    Note: This experiment will work best in a cool, dry environment.

1. Choose one object and one cloth scrap. Rub the object vigorously with the cloth.
2. Hold the object close to the tissue paper. If the object attracts the tissue paper, it has been charged with static electricity. Record your results on a blank sheet of paper.
3. Repeat with the same object and each piece of cloth. Record each result. Be sure to wipe the object with your hand after each trial. Test to make sure this has removed the static charge before beginning the new trial.
4. Repeat for each object with each fabric scrap. Hint: Some items may need to be warmed in your hands before it will accept the charge.
5. After all trials have been completed, decide which types of substances are easiest to charge with static electricity.

Magic Rabbits. Did you know that you can use rabbits to show the magic of static electricity? No, you won't pull them out of a hat, but make them jump at your command!

Now, try this:
Lay 2 thick books several inches apart on a table. Rest a sheet of glass from a picture frame on the books. Cut out some tiny paper rabbits and put them on the table under the glass. Now, really concentrate on the rabbits. Then mumble a few magic words to build up your spectators. Rub the glass with some silk or flannel. Bingo! **The rabbits do come alive!**

Well, here's how it is done:
When you rub the glass, you give it a static charge. The glass attracts the rabbits. They pick up the same charge while they stick to the glass. Now they are pushed away by the glass; therefore, they jump back down. Want to try it again?

Heat Flow. Look at the pavement on a hot summer day. Shimmering just above the ground the hot air can be seen rising from the hot ground. A desert mirage is actually an example of this heat flow.

Materials:
> Large jar
> Small bottle
> String
> Food coloring
> Cold water
> Hot water

Procedure:
1. Tie a string around the neck of the bottle.
2. Fill a large jar with cold water.
3. Fill a small bottle with hot water and a strong dash of food coloring.
4. Slowly and carefully lower the bottle into the jar holding onto the string. Lower the bottle to sit on the bottom of the jar. DO NOT ALLOW THE BOTTLE TO TIP OVER. Record the results on a separate sheet of paper.
5. Empty the bottle and the jar. Reverse steps 2 and 3. Repeat step #4 and record the results.
6. Try repeating the above steps but color the water in the jar. Now record your results.

As water is heated, it expands and rises. Cooler water is heavier and sinks to the bottom.

Did you know? A glass of hot water looks fairly innocent; however, there is a lot going on inside it. Add just a pinch of sawdust and watch the way it moves around.

Next, put the sawdust into a glass container that can be heated on the stove. *Ask your Mother or Dad to help you.* Watch the sawdust as the water heats up and record results.. As water at the bottom heats up, it rises, taking the sawdust with it. Cooler water moves down to take its place and be heated. What would happen if a microwave oven were used? Try it and record the results. Compare the two.

A wood, rubber or metal spoon? Why do you stir soup on the stove with a rubber or wooden spoon? If you leave a metal spoon in the pot for a few minutes and then touch it, you will know why! So we can easily say that some things pick up heat much faster than others.

Mass and Weight. All *matter* shares several general properties: *mass, weight, volume* and *density*. Matter has three common phases: solid, liquid and gas.

    Mass—the amount of matter contained in an object.

    Weight—the measurement of the force of gravity exerted on an object.

Mass does *not* change when an object is moved from place to place. Weight *will* change because the force of gravity changes. Use the chart below to determine your weight on each of the planets. Remember: Although an object's weight changes from planet to planet, the mass remains constant. For example, the surface gravity of the moon is 1/6 that of the Earth. What would be your weight on the moon? _____

Planet	Weight Calculation	Results
Mercury	weight x .38	
Venus	weight x .89	
Earth	weight x 1.0	
Mars	weight x .38	
Jupiter	weight x 2.7	
Saturn	weight x 1.1	
Uranus	weight x .8	
Neptune	weight x 1.2	
Pluto	weight x .01	

Inertia—Newton's first law of motion. A body at rest will remain at rest until some outside force moves it. The force applied to overcome inertia must be greater than the forces acting to keep the body at rest. Inertia is the property of mass to resist change in motion. No two pieces of matter can occupy the same space at the same time.

All matter has mass. Matter can achieve a weightless state.
This can be proven by swinging a bucket of water in a vertical circle. The water does not come out at the top of the arch because it does not have weight at the top of the arch. It does, however, still have mass. Perform this gravity defying experiment outside.

Volume is the amount of space something occupies. The mathematical formula for expressing volume is length times width times height. (V = L x W x H). Some objects allow for increase and decrease of volume, for example, a balloon that expands and deflates air. Water displacement is a method for measuring the volume of a solid.

Materials:

>Measuring cup or beaker
>Water
>Small, heavy object

Procedure:

1. Fill the beaker about half full of water; record volume (amount) of water (value a).
2. Predict the volume of the object (a small rock works well).
3. Sink the object in the cup until it is totally submerged. Measure the volume of water plus the object together (value b).
4. Subtract original volume from the new volume (b - a). The difference is the volume of the solid object.

Space exists between all particles. This is easy to visualize in the case of solids. A full cup of rice will still allow for the addition of water. The difference between the cup of water before and after adding to the cup of rice is the volume of space between the grains of rice. It is more difficult to visualize the space between particles of liquids. Slowly pour 1/2 cup of water into 1/2 cup of rubbing alcohol. The new volume is slightly less than one cup.

Density or specific gravity is the amount of matter packed into a given volume of space. Density is calculated as the mass of an object divided by the volume of water it displaces. Formula: Density equals mass divided by volume (D = M ÷ V).

A good demonstration for density requires a large container filled with water and a can of soda plus a can of diet soda, both 12 oz. Place both cans in the water. The regular soda is denser because of the sugar and will sink while the diet soda will float. Wave bottles demonstrate that liquids have different densities.

Materials:

>Clear bottle or jar with tight fitting lid
>>(plastic jar is fine)
>Mineral or vegetable oil

>Water
>Food coloring
>Light weight add ins (toothpick boat, paper clip, small plastic charm)

1. Clean the bottle or jar; be sure to remove all labels.
2. Fill the bottle about 1/2 full of oil.
3. Fill with water and add a few drops of food coloring.
4. Add charms, tighten cap, and invert bottle or jar.
5. Slowly move the bottle or jar back and forth on its side; observe the wave action.

Facts about plants. **Tropism is the bending movement of a plant as a reaction to its environment. Plants experience tropism as a reaction to gravity, light or water.**

Geotropism—the way a plant responds to gravity.
Phototropism—the way a plant responds to light.
Hydrotropism—the way a plant responds to water.

Plants grow from different beginnings—seeds, cutting, tubers, or bulbs, but all follow a definite pattern of growth. Baby plants will grow to be like adult plants. Plants have different needs for temperature, sunshine, water and soil. Try a recycle garden.

Materials:

Collection of seeds and cuttings from kitchen and around your house	Tiny pieces of charcoal (no lighter fluid)
	Vermiculite
Various containers for planting (egg cartons, old flower pots)	Sand
	Water spritzer
Potting soil	Humus

Procedures:

1. Citrus seeds—soak the seeds overnight; mix sand and potting soil. You may use a fruit shell for initial sprouting or use other small "pots." Place layer of potting mixture in pot, add seeds, and cover with 1/2 inch of potting mixture. Spray each day with water; water well twice a week. Transfer young plant to a sturdier container.

2. Root vegetable tops—carrot, beet, turnip; cut, retaining 1 inch of foliage and 1 inch of the root. Plant in sandy soil and keep moist, not wet. Alternative: A. set in a shallow pan of water (about 1/2"); add tiny pieces of charcoal to keep water sweet. B. Trim the foliage; cut the root 2 inches from the top and hollow out the center; hang upside down like a basket. Keep the center filled with water.

3. Irish potato, sweet potato or yam—make sure the potato is fresh, not heat dried. Look for sweet potatoes with a few whiskers. Cut the potato in half. Insert toothpicks around the circumference of potato just above the cut (may be left whole with toothpicks inserted around the center). Place tapered end down in a jar suspended by means of toothpicks. Fill the jar with water. Place in a dark area until the roots sprout. Then, move into the light. Keep the water level constant. The plant may be left in water or transplanted into soil allowing green sprouts to remain above the soil. Alternatives: Add food color to the water; choose a yam with purple eyes. Cut the white potato in sections, each with an "eye" or two; plant in rich earth and keep moist (needs lots of light). Potato Porcupine: slice off the top of an Irish potato and carve out a hole leaving plenty of meat for side walls. Insert 4 toothpicks to serve as legs. Attach eyes (either wiggly eyes or small white paper circles each held in place with a map tack). Fill cavity with soil and sprinkle with chives, grass or other spiky seeds. Water often; it will sprout in about 10 days.

Facts about Plants continued.

4. Seeds—bird seed, pepper, pumpkin, squash, melon. Punch small holes in the bottom of a container for drainage. Fill the container with soil and then sprinkle the seeds on the soil. Cover with 1/4 inch of soil. Keep soil moist.

5. Beans, peas, lentils—*Method 1*: Spread in a single layer on a saucer; moisten but do not float seeds. Keep moist and in the sun. The seeds will sprout in about 10 days. *Method 2*: Soak 2-3 hours until the beans swell. Roll drawing paper or other heavy weight paper and line a 1 pound clear glass jar. Trim the paper at the mouth of the jar. Place the soaked beans 1/2 inch down between the jar and the paper. Pour 1" of water into the jar. Keep the paper wet. Place in a dark place to germinate. Then, bring into the light. Lay sprouted beans on the soil. Keep moist.

6. Pineapple tops, avocado and other pits, apple and other fruit seeds. Experiment to see what you can grow.

Capillary Action—the process by which water travels up the stems to the leaves and flows through the veins (vascular bundles) in the stem of the plant.

Materials:

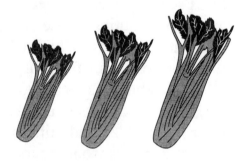

    Celery stalks with leaves and/or white flowers
       (daisy, carnation or chrysanthemum)
    Food coloring (red or blue)
    2 clear glass containers (drinking glasses or jars)
    Water
    Knife

Procedure:

1. Fill each glass with water. Then add 8-10 drops of food coloring to one glass.

2. Slice about 1/2 inch from the bottom of each stalk or stem. Carefully slit the bottom of each stalk or stem.

3. Place the bottom of one celery stalk and/or flower stem in the glass of clear water and another in the colored water. Record your observations about the stalk or stem, leaves, and flowers.

4. Set the experiment aside overnight.

5. Record your observations about the stalk and/or stem, leaves, and flowers.

6. Cut a one inch piece from the bottom of the stalk or stem. Draw what you observe. The colored dots are the vascular bundles that go up the stem.

7. Repeat the experiment using different flowers. Are the patterns of the vascular bundles in the stems the same or different?

Note: The stems of monocots and dicots are different. Vascular bundles of dicots are arranged in a circle. The vascular bundles of monocots are arranged in a more complex pattern.

Classifying Living Things (taxonomy or systematics). Aristotle classified all living things into two groups—Plants and Animals. There are, however, many organisms that do not fit easily into either of these categories. A Swedish scientist, Carolus Linnaeus, developed a five kingdom system of classification:

1. Monera: Bacteria (single celled, microscopic creatures with no nucleus) and blue-green algae.
2. Protista: Single celled organisms.
3. Fungi: Organisms usually formed from spores.
4. Plants: Contain chlorophyll, use process of photosynthesis to manufacture their own food (starch) and have cell walls primarily of cellulose.
5. Animals: Can move; all parts not just tips of bodies grow. Do not make their own food and have different chemical composition.

Some scientists argue for a six-kingdom system, since no one is sure how to classify viruses. Currently there is a debate as to whether or not viruses are even alive.

TIME OUT: Web Pictures. Walking into a spider web is not a pleasant experience. Collecting webs is interesting and informative. Use the same procedure for each web you collect.

Materials:
> Unoccupied spider web
> Scrap or newspaper
> Spray paint (white works well)
> Contrasting construction paper

Procedure:
1. Check web for signs of life and the wind for its direction.
2. Tear a piece of scrap/newspaper so that it can be slipped behind the web without touching the web. Use care so the web is not torn.
3. Spray the web toward the paper and away from the wind. Carefully, gently slip paper from behind the web.
4. Press the construction paper to the web and pull toward you. A web of a contrasting color should appear on the paper. Allow to dry completely.
5. Collect as many different webs as you can. Compare the webs. Can spiders be identified by their webs?
6. Use web pages to create a scrapbook or use the pictures to decorate a wall.

Kingdom I Monera—Humans tend to associate bacteria with disease. This a false belief. Most bacteria are benign or even essential for maintaining life. Some of the harmful bacteria are usually present in the human body and are harmless unless the normal body defenses are weakened and the bacteria multiply extensively.

Bacteria come in a variety of sizes, shapes and colors. Cyanobacteria are the most colorful; while phototrophic green and purple sulphur bacteria are interesting both for their color and the fact that they grow only under anaerobic conditions. Pseudomonads are classified as "microbial weeds" because of their ability to feed on organic nutrients that are useless as a food source by any other organisms; this class includes the bacteria used to clean up oil spills and to decompose pesticides.

A world without bacteria would be a world without decay and decomposition. Bodies would wear out and die but would not decay. Interesting areas for research include the following: How do bacteria "work"? How do they "infect" a host? How do antibiotics "work?" Methanogens are poisoned by oxygen. How are they useful? Nearly all bacteria have cell walls. How does this influence their life cycle?

What does a bacteria look like?

Below are three descriptions for the basic bacteria shapes. Draw each in the box provided.

1. Bacilli are rod-shaped and usually are solitary. Some also form long chains. They look like cooked rice grains.

2. The cocci are spherical bacteria. They are shaped like balls and can be found singly or in pairs or in long chains or clusters like grapes.

3. Spirilla, spirochetes, and vibrios are curved bacteria. The spirilla are shaped like corkscrews, the spirochetes are shaped like spirals, and the vibrios are shaped like commas.

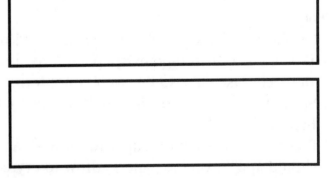

| *Salmonella typhi* | *Shigella bacillus* | *Escherichia coli* | **Streptomyces** | **Methanogens** |

Kingdom II Protista—also called protozoa . These single celled microscopic organisms have a nucleus and characteristics of the plants and/or animals. Most live in water but they also live inside animals. Protista come in many forms and have very different abilities.

Match the descriptions below with the correct drawing.

1. The amoeba looks like a blob. It moves by stretching its pseudopod (false foot) out of its body. Amoebas live in fresh or salt water, soil and other organisms.

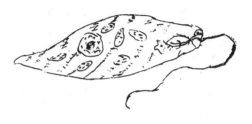

2. The euglena contains chlorophyll so it is a green flagellate. It lives in stagnant pond water and moves by means of long, whip-like flagella. In the light it produces its own food; in the dark it feeds by means of phagocytosis, a process of surrounding the food with its body.

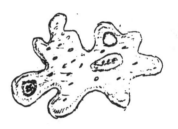

3. The paramecium is slipper-shaped and flaps its cilia (small, hair-like projections around the outside of its body) to move back and forth through the water. Paramecium are found in fresh water.

4. The stentor is a ciliate like the paramecium. Locomotion is achieved with membranelles (rows of tightly packed cilia which function as a single unit).

5. The trypanosoma is a zoomastigote. The organism looks like a tiny, short, fat snake. Locomotion is by means of a whip-like flagella.

Kingdom III Fungi—Yeast, mushrooms, toadstools, penicillium and truffles are all members of this kingdom. Fungi come in a multitude of sizes, shapes, and colors. They can be one-celled and microscopic or many celled and quite large, poisonous, harmful, edible or useful. Some fungi are parasites which absorb nutrients. Some fungi are saprophytes (absorb their nutrients from dead plant or animal matter, thus aiding in the decay process). Among the most positive functions of fungi are the ability to make bread rise, cause the blue or green streaks in cheese, or make medicine. Some are highly prized as food.

Note: Lichens are a combination of an alga and a fungus. They are hardy, with the ability to grow under very adverse conditions (cold, bare rocks, etc.), but they cannot survive air pollution.

Growing Fungi I

Materials:

Slice of bread	Spoon
Small piece of fruit	2 saucers
Water	Paper towel

Procedure:
1. Dampen the paper towel and fold to cover 1 saucer. Place the bread on a saucer and place it in a warm dark place.
2. Place a piece of fruit (a slice works best) on a saucer and place it in a warm, dark place.
3. Observe daily and record your observations. Compare and contrast the two experiments; use illustrations.

Experiment II

Materials:

Package of dry yeast	2 Quart bowls
Warm water (110°F)	Magnifying glass
1 Tablespoon of sugar	

Procedure:
1. Pour yeast into the bowl. Observe through the magnifying glass. Record your observations with illustrations.
2. Pour 1 cup of warm water and 1 tablespoon of sugar on the yeast. Stir well until the yeast and sugar are dissolved. Place mixture in a warm spot and allow to rest for 15 minutes. Observe with a magnifying glass and record your observations with illustrations.
3. Place 1/2 the mixture in a second bowl. Return original bowl to the same warm spot. Place the second bowl in the refrigerator. After 15 minutes rest, compare the two bowls. Observe and record your findings with illustrations.

Kingdom IV Plants—Plant types vary widely, but most to them share three common characteristics:
   1. Usually green.
   2. Have roots or rootlike structures that hold them stationary.
   3. Produce their own food.

Roots may take one of several forms depending upon the growing situations: compact root systems close to the surface absorb water quickly; tap roots are thickened roots which store food for the plant; fibrous roots are branched and spreading and go very deep into the ground.

In addition to roots, plants have stems which support the plant, store food, and allow for movement of materials through vessels called xylem. Xylem is dead (wood) and contains tubelike vessels for transporting water and minerals from the roots through the stem to the plant's leaves. Another type of plant vessel is the phloem. It is alive and also made of tubelike vessels which move food from the leaves to other parts of the plant. The third major plant part is the leaf. Leaves come in all sizes, shapes, thicknesses and textures, but all serve as the plant's organ for trapping sunlight and making food.

Additionally, plants may be classified as vascular or non vascular. Reproduction may be through spores or more commonly seeds either in cones (gymnosperms) or fruit (angiosperms). Plant reproduction is also in two classes: asexual (vegetative from roots, stems or leaves) or sexual (spores or seeds).

Classification of Plants

Materials:

Absorbent paper
Collection of leaves
Construction or plain white paper
Glue

Markers
Leaf Chart (on next page)
Hole Punch
Brads

Procedure:
1. Place each leaf between two sheets of absorbent paper and press under a heavy weight (books work well) on a flat surface.
2. When the leaves are flat and dry, mount each on a separate sheet of paper. Place the leaf tip near the top, leaving room to write at the bottom.
3. Write each category name on each sheet.
4. Compare the leaf to the samples in each of the four categories, and label it accordingly.
5. Create a cover for the leaf book.
6. Carefully line up all pages and punch holes; insert brads or alternately tie with ribbon, yarn or string.

Leaf Classification Chart

Use this chart to complete the activity on the previous page.

SHAPES. Leaf shapes are either:

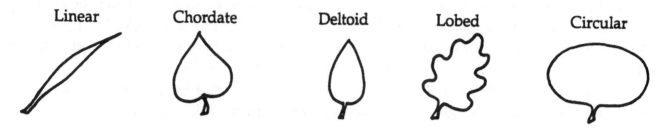

Linear   Chordate   Deltoid   Lobed   Circular

MARGINS. The edges of the leaves are called margins. Margins are either:

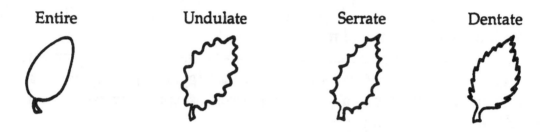

Entire   Undulate   Serrate   Dentate

MOSAIC. The way the leaves are arranged on the stem is called the leaf mosaic. The mosaic is either:

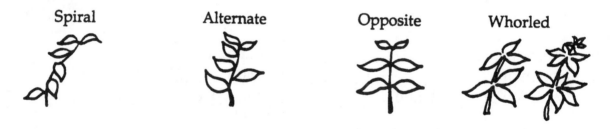

Spiral   Alternate   Opposite   Whorled

VENATION. The leaf venation, or the way the veins of the leaf are arranged, is either:

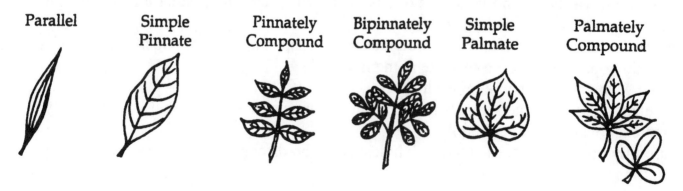

Parallel   Simple Pinnate   Pinnately Compound   Bipinnately Compound   Simple Palmate   Palmately Compound

Kingdom V—Animals show symmetry (matching sides). This symmetry may be radial (matching parts top to bottom radiating from the center but not left to right); or bilateral (matches side to side). Two groups of animals with radial symmetry are classified as radiata: Cnidaria which have stinging cells on their tentacles called cnidocytes. After stinging their prey, the tentacles are used to push it into their mouth. Ctenophora are the largest animals that use cilia for locomotion and catching their food. All animals are multicellular. They ingest their food; most store their carbohydrates as glycogen (sugar). Some animals can regenerate new parts. Vertebrates are animals with backbones. Some animals bear live young while others lay eggs. Forms of locomotion include walking, swimming and flying.

Answer the animal facts below to complete the crossword puzzle.

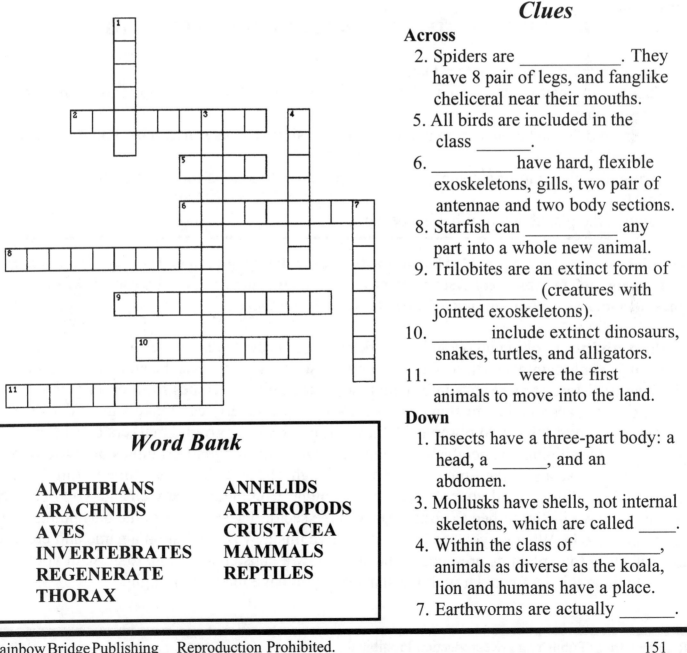

Clues

Across

2. Spiders are _____. They have 8 pair of legs, and fanglike cheliceral near their mouths.
5. All birds are included in the class _____.
6. _____ have hard, flexible exoskeletons, gills, two pair of antennae and two body sections.
8. Starfish can _____ any part into a whole new animal.
9. Trilobites are an extinct form of _____ (creatures with jointed exoskeletons).
10. _____ include extinct dinosaurs, snakes, turtles, and alligators.
11. _____ were the first animals to move into the land.

Down

1. Insects have a three-part body: a head, a _____, and an abdomen.
3. Mollusks have shells, not internal skeletons, which are called ____.
4. Within the class of _____, animals as diverse as the koala, lion and humans have a place.
7. Earthworms are actually _____.

Word Bank

AMPHIBIANS   ANNELIDS
ARACHNIDS   ARTHROPODS
AVES   CRUSTACEA
INVERTEBRATES   MAMMALS
REGENERATE   REPTILES
THORAX

Day and Night. Day and night are the result of the earth's rotation on its axis. The sun's light comes to Earth in waves of different lengths, some visible and some short UV (ultra violet) waves that are invisible. The UV rays are one cause of skin cancers in humans; sunscreens offer protection from these rays. The amount of protection offered is indicated by the SPF number (sun protection factor). The higher the SPF number the greater the protection.

Materials:
>   Scissors
>   Tape
>   Photosensitive paper
>   Sunscreens with different SPF ratings

Procedure:

WARNING: DO STEPS 1, 2, AND 3 OUT OF DIRECT LIGHT.

1. Cut plastic wrap slightly larger than photosensitive paper.
2. Place photosensitive paper on a flat surface and cover with plastic wrap. Tape to hold the wrap in place.
3. Design and "paint" a picture on the plastic wrap using various sunscreens. Label the SPF number of each.
4. Expose the above to bright sunlight (follow package directions for recommended exposure time).
5. Remove the plastic wrap. What happened?

The night sky has always provided humans with an ever changing show and is a source of mystery and imagination for observers. Astronomers and astronauts spend their lives trying to answer questions such as "What's in space?" and "Is anybody out there?"

Night Activity: Looking up on a clear, dark night can provide the viewer with an evening of inexpensive entertainment. Binoculars and/or a telescope will increase the amount of visible information. Most of mankind's information about the universe comes from observation. Anyone who takes the time to study and record the sky regularly can make a great discovery. Choose a piece of the sky to observe. Delineate it by choosing ground markers to set the parameters (a tall pine, the neighbor's chimney, a light pole are good examples of **stationary** markers). Choose a specific time to observe each night (be sure that it is a time in full dark). Study and carefully record your sky sector each night. Comment on any change you observe. When you have distinguished the bright stars in the sector, try to visualize them as points in a dot to dot puzzle. What do you see in the sky? Give this new constellation a name and create a fanciful story to explain its presence in the sky. Draw a constellation map to go with your story. Include this in a booklet with the star maps you have made each night.

Fish. Fish is the name commonly given to 3 classes of Vertebrates: Agnatha (includes lampreys and hagfish); Chrondrichtyes (includes sharks, skates, and rays) and Osteichthyes (true fish including tuna, gar and trout). Should you or someone you know catch a fish or if you purchase a whole fish, you can actually dissect it and do your own illustrations. When the real thing is not available, use the word bank and illustrations provided to label the exterior and interior parts of this generic fish.

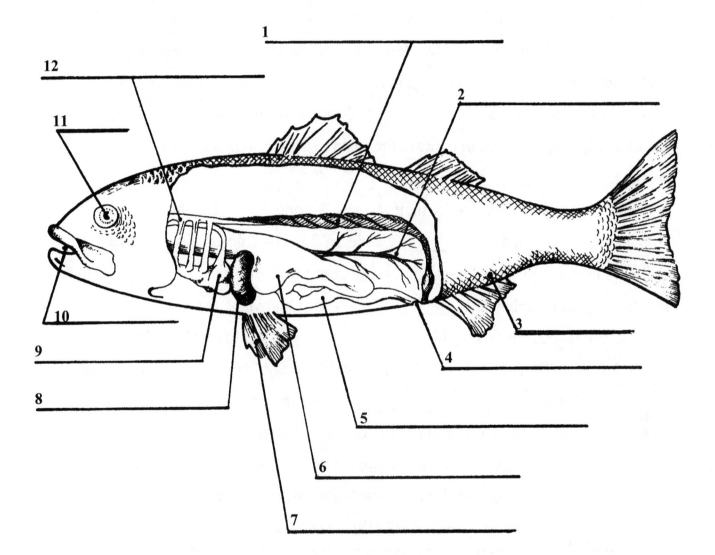

Word Bank

anus	heart	mouth
dorsal aorta	intestine	ovary
eye	kidney	scale
fins	liver	stomach

Volcanoes

As you read the following excerpt on volcanoes, use the word bank below to fill in the blanks.

_____ believe that the earth's crust is broken into about twenty pieces called _____. The continents have been moving or drifting for millions of years. The edges of some plates are moving toward each other. As one edge bends and dives beneath another, a _____ is formed. As the diving edge descends into the earth's extremely hot _____, it begins to melt forming _____. Magma is the substance that by rising and breaking through the earth's crust forms _____. Volcanoes are mountains that are formed by the piling up of molten materials from beneath the earth's surface. The upper or above-riding plate crumples to form a _____ range.

Volcanic cones are classified by their shapes. Among the most common are the _____, _____ and _____ cones. While all volcanoes contain the same basic parts, the parts may be given different names, for example: a magma _____ may also be called the magma chamber; the _____ is also known as the pipe; _____ are central vents. Volcanoes may have side vents and _____ as well as the central vent.

There are over 500 active volcanoes in the world today; more than half are located in "The Ring of Fire" which encircles the _____ Ocean. The western coast of North and South America and the Eastern coast of Asia and Oceania make up "The Ring of Fire."

_____ rock, one of the three major types of rock, is formed by the hardening of _____ magma. Magma that does not reach the earth's surface as _____ erupting from a volcano can form other igneous rock structures underground.

Word Bank			
cinder	Geologists	molton	shield
composite	Igneous	mountain	trench
conduit	lava	Pacific	volcanoes
craters	magma	plates	
fissures	mantle	reservoir	

Watch for the Weather Words. Can you find the 20 weather words in this word search? The names may be written up, down, or diagonally. They may be read from left to right, right to left, top to bottom, or bottom to top.

```
H S O C L O U D S A B V F W V D R D
T U S D O W K S Y D V L H K R J D P
Z N M A A A G L B I K O J A J E K Y
C S E I M N Q L J H G M Z D D W H Z
H N T C D R R D J Y C Z M U Y I K A
G O Y R U I I O P K I E L H Y N X M
W W A N Q L T A T L T C M G Z D E E
Q G I F H V I Y B E C K O Q V H G R
N N W F X L K T O O Y Q U L T X C U
O P M E G Y S R C H D V Q C S N S T
O T R H M T O E Q O U R A R V J U A
H S G S R L S C M V N R I Y L G R R
P D M A I U K I T K D Q R Z H D R E
Y V T G L G R W G F E X O I Z Y I P
T U I U F N P Z K F S Q B W C L C M
S S M Y S F D H A F X N I A R A E E
T U S T A T I O N A R Y O K P F N T
C H V A O K N C I R T E M O R A B E
```

Word Bank

Stratus
Cumulus
Cirrus
Noctilucent
Humidity

Typhoon
Barometric
Wind
Temperature
Airmass

Occluded
Stationary
Clouds
Rain
Snow

Drizzle
Blizzard
Tornado
Hurricane
Meteorologist

Earthquakes. Earthquakes occur every 30 seconds somewhere in the world. If you do the multiplication, you will discover that means over one million quakes a year. Seismographs all over the world record this activity. Recordings are made based on the primary and secondary waves produced by the quake. The relative strength or magnitude of the quake is measured by the Richter Scale, the higher the magnitude, the stronger the quake. In fact, each number represents a quake 32 times stronger than the next lower one.

Fill in the blank in each statement below. Then find the term in the Word Bank.

1. The instrument used to measure the strength of an earthquake is a _____.

2. Shaking of the ground is called an _____.

3. Seismic waves originate _____.

4. A _____ is a crack in the earth's crust where movement has occurred.

5. _____ is the name given a seismic sea wave.

6. Directly above the focus of a quake is the _____.

7. The downhill movement of rocks or mud is a _____.

8. The secondary quakes following a main shock are the _____.

Word Bank

fault
after shocks
seismograph
Tsunami
earthquake
focus
epicenter
landslide

F	E	A	R	T	H	Q	U	A	K	E	F
S	O	A	I	M	A	N	U	S	T	A	A
W	E	C	B	Z	Z	U	J	S	U	F	P
R	U	I	U	X	I	C	Q	L	T	E	E
E	C	X	S	S	C	Z	T	E	D	U	D
T	S	D	H	M	A	Z	R	U	L	C	I
N	I	H	D	K	O	S	E	M	M	B	L
E	F	C	M	T	H	G	T	J	G	V	S
C	T	P	B	O	Y	G	R	L	Y	E	D
I	V	D	C	L	J	T	Z	A	K	U	N
P	I	K	M	M	G	I	U	Z	P	E	A
E	S	F	Z	E	X	I	R	H	D	H	L

WHO LIVES IN A TREE? You might like to make predictions before you complete this activity. Have you ever considered the fact that a tree is like an apartment building with a variety of organisms living in each tree? You do not need to travel to a rain forest to explore this idea, only as far as your yard or a neighborhood park!

Materials:

A tree   Hand lens
Ruler   Color pencils
Recording sheet

Procedure:
1. Once you have chosen a tree, use it to study each day for 3 or 4 days.
2. Study the bark, leaves, branches, and roots of the tree very carefully.
3. Record each organism that you find. The hand lens will help you see more clearly. Draw what you see. Include insects, birds, fungi, and small plants.
4. Measure and record the size of each organism you find. You need only draw one but count and measure all that you see.
5. Write a short report about your observations. You may choose to repeat steps 1 through 4 with another tree. Then write a report comparing and contrasting your findings from each tree that you studied.

Marvelous Mixtures

Modeling Materials

Dough—Combine 4 cups of unsifted all purpose flour, 1 cup salt, $1\frac{1}{2}$ cups water in a bowl. Mix thoroughly with hands. If too stiff, add water. Knead the dough for at least 7 minutes. Form into the desired shapes and bake in a preheated 350° oven until golden brown (about 15-45 minutes depending on thickness). Remove from the pan and cool. You may paint with acrylics, poster paints or water colors. Spray with clear varnish or other shine producing fixative. Colored dough is obtained by kneading food coloring into unbaked dough.

Jewelry Clay—Mix 3/4 cup of flour, 1/2 cup of salt, 1/2 cup of cornstarch. Mix the ingredients together. Now gradually add warm water until the mixture can be kneaded into shapes. Make beads by rolling the dough into little balls, piercing the balls with toothpicks, and allowing the balls to dry. Paint and string the beads.

Cooked Salt—Mix 2 parts salt to 1 part corn starch and 1 part water. Cook over a low heat, stirring vigorously until the material is stiff. Allow it to cool before molding. Small pieces will air dry in about 36 hours.

Play Dough—Mix 8 cups of flour, 2 cups of salt, and 3 tablespoons of vegetable oil with enough water to make a soft dough. Add food coloring. Store in covered plastic container.

Glue

Pour 1 pint of skim milk into a glass or enamel sauce pan and add 1 cup of white vinegar. Heat and stir until the lumps are formed. Pour coagulated milk into a bowl and allow it to cool. Discard the excess water that forms. Now add 1/4 cup of cool, clean water and 1 teaspoon of baking soda. Pour into a small squeeze type bottle or small cover glass jars.

Finger Paint

In an old pot, mix 2 cups of flour and 2 teaspoons of salt. Slowly mix in 3 cups of cold water and stir until the mixture is smooth. Pour in hot water and then place over a low heat. Then bring the mixture to a boil. Stir as needed. Boil until the mixture is clear. Divide the mixture into separate covered containers. Add food coloring to each and beat until smooth.

MILLENNIUM

One Thousand Years

Where were you on New Year's Eve? Were you one of the 2 million people who went to Times Square in New York City to watch "the New York apple" drop? Did you travel down under to Australia to ride in a boat around the harbor? Or did you go to China, the country that invented fireworks, to watch one of the world's greatest fireworks displays? No matter where you were — New York, Australia, China, or even in your home town — you were a part of one of the world's greatest celebrations. You were part of welcoming in the New Millennium!

What exactly is a millennium? A millennium is one thousand years. Can you imagine what the world was like one thousand years ago? I assure you, it was a lot different than today! One thousand years ago there were no cars, electricity, computers, telephones, flashlights, airplanes, fax machines, not even plastic water bottles! There was no NBA nor NFL, and the thought of roller-blading would have been as outrageous as thinking that eating carrots will make you grow to be seven feet tall! Over the last thousand years our world has changed in many, many ways. And because it has changed, you and I are able to use things in our life today that help us and make us happy.

In this section, we will explore different events, inventions and people that occurred and lived during the last one thousand years. As you can imagine, many, many things have happened to help shape the world we live in, so, keep in mind that the following pages list only a few. As we explore, imagine yourself discovering a new way to tell time, or inventing a new instrument or a faster computer. It's kind of fun imagining this, but it's even more fun imagining yourself in the New Millennium. Project yourself into the future. What do you see yourself doing? What do you think our world will look like in another one thousand years?

TIME

What is time? Why do we track it? How is it used in our lives?

There are sixty seconds in every minute. No matter who you are or what you are doing, time is the same for everybody. The difference in time is how people use it. In the same minute that Michael Jordan may have shot 30 free throws (2 seconds per free throw), your neighbor may have walked down his or her driveway to pick up the mail. In this same minute, a Mayan girl in Guatemala may have made a doll to sell to tourists and you may have been studying for your math test. What is time, and how is it used in your life?

Everybody has had special things happen to them during their lives. A timeline is a list of these important events in our lives or in the lives of others. These events can be the same as your friends', but they can also be very different. Events that are important to you may not be as important to someone else, but it is this personal experience that makes the events so special!

Activity: Choose from the suggestions listed below and use some of your ideas to create your own timeline on the following page. Use the boxes on the timeline for writing or illustrating the important events in your life. Be sure to include the dates. When you are finished, cut out the timeline and connect the events of your life.

My birth date.

My first day of school.

My first pair of e-mail.

My first words.

My first slumber party.

My first social experience.

My first broken bone.

My first set of stitches.

My first sport.

My first pet.

My first musical instrument.

My first friend.

My first vacation.

My first steps

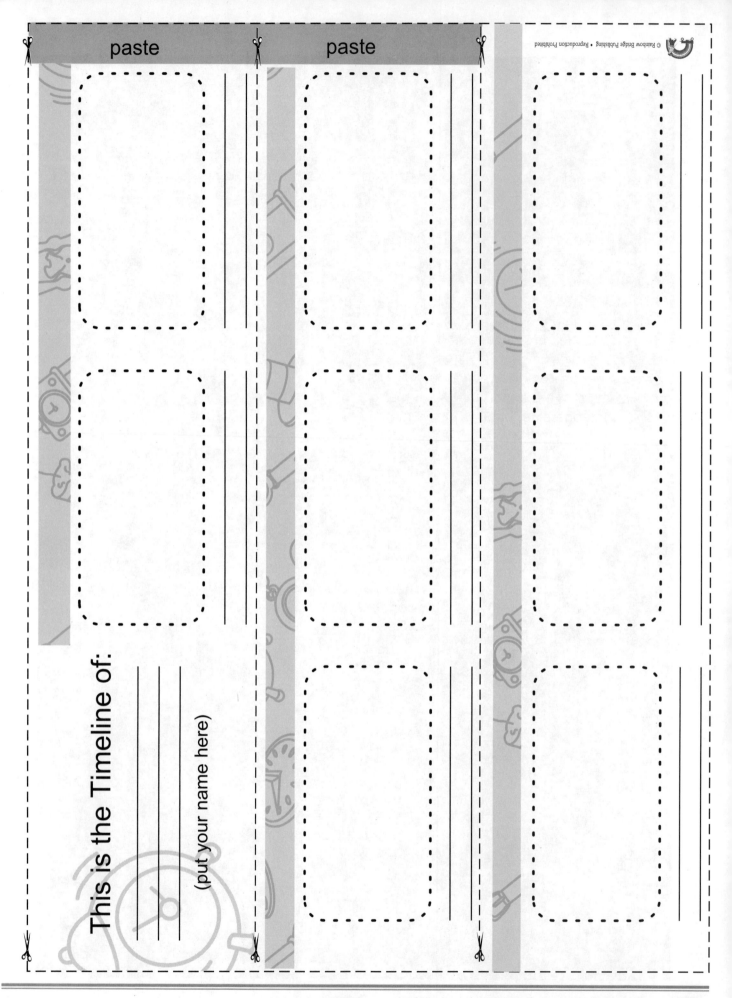

paste

paste

This is the Timeline of:

(put your name here)

Summer Bridge Activities • TIME & TECHNOLOGY SECTION

1000's-1300's

A Time of Discovery and Conquest

1026

Do Re Mi Fa So La Ti

Guido D'Arezzo, an Italian monk and music teacher, developed DO, RE, MI, FA, SO, LA, TI.

DO=10 RE=17 MI=28
FA=93 SO=16 LA=37
TI=2

Use the seven notes of the musical scale to figure out the math solutions. Sing your results to the musical scale.

DO+MI=
MI+FA=
SO+FA=
DO-TI=

Mechanical Water Clock

Design a clock that would show the difference between a.m. and p.m. What do you call it?

_____

_____

_____

1090

Mechanical clock driven by water invented by Su Sung in China.

1114

First Trade Fair

International Trade Fairs were first held in France.

On a separate sheet of paper, write a first-hand descriptive paragraph on a fictional experience at the first International Trade Fair. Use all five senses to describe the excitement of the vendors as they showed potential buyers their inventions and ideas for the very first time.

1202

The use of zero is introduced to Europe from India by Italian mathematician Leonardo Fibonacci.

How many zero's are there in one million?

zero

1337

The beginning of the Hundred Years' War, which was a series of battles between the French and the English. The war actually lasted 116 years.

Hundred Years' War

On a separate sheet of paper, write a treaty to end a war. Make sure it represents both sides and clearly states what each side must do in order to insure that fighting does not begin again. Your treaty should explain why you think war started and it should address the damage the war caused to the nations and people involved. You may use a real war or make one up on your own. Your essay should be no longer than 250 words.

1400's - 1500's

A Time of Exploration

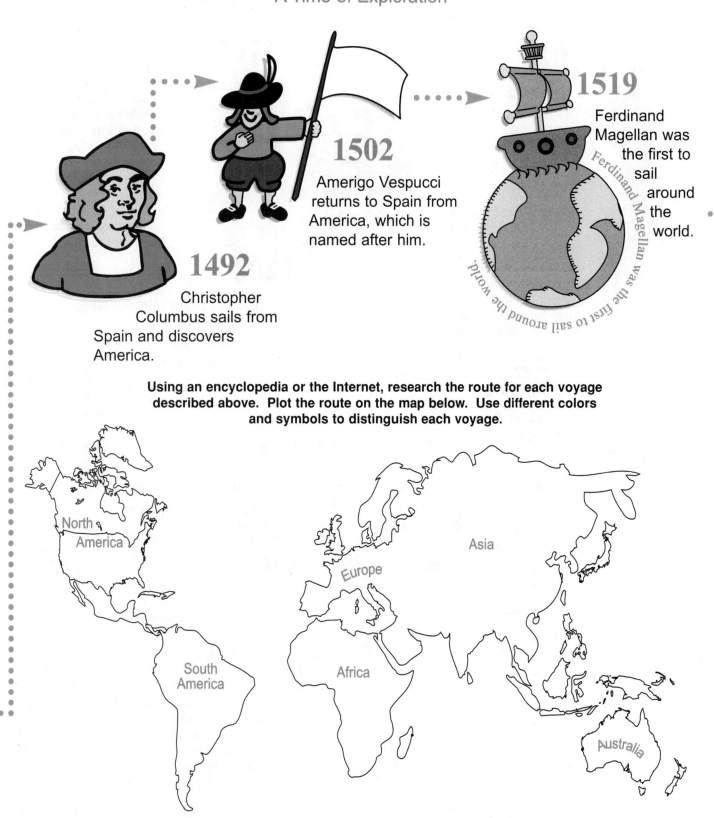

1502

Amerigo Vespucci returns to Spain from America, which is named after him.

1519

Ferdinand Magellan was the first to sail around the world.

1492

Christopher Columbus sails from Spain and discovers America.

Using an encyclopedia or the Internet, research the route for each voyage described above. Plot the route on the map below. Use different colors and symbols to distinguish each voyage.

North America

South America

Europe

Asia

Africa

Australia

1600's

A Time of Discovery

1607

John Smith founded Jamestown, the British colony of Virginia in America. Captured by a Native American tribe and condemned to death, Smith is saved by Pocahontas, the chief's daughter.

What would Pocahontas had to have said to her father and tribe to save the life of John Smith? Can you think of any other modern day couples or groups of people, real or fictional, that have had to overcome differences in order to be together? List three.

_____

_____

_____

1620

The first submarine was invented by Dutch physicist Cornelis J. Drebbel. It was made of wood!

1620

The Mayflower ship arrives in New England.

Use an encyclopedia or the Internet to help you draw a sketch of the New England shoreline.

Summer Bridge Activities • TIME & TECHNOLOGY SECTION
© Rainbow Bridge Publishing • Reproduction Prohibited

1700's

A Time of Liberty and Independence

1776

The Declaration of Independence was signed.

We the People

Ask a parent or guardian to explain what the Declaration of Independence means. Write down what your rights and responsibilities are in your family.

1790

Benjamin Franklin died at the age of 84. He was the 15th child and had 16 brothers and sisters. He was an inventor, statesman, and he signed the Declaration of Independence. He is credited for discovering that lightning is electricity as well as inventing bi-focal glasses and the lightning rod. Ben was the owner of one of the first public libraries, took one of the first successful hot air balloon rides in Paris and wrote many books, including *Poor Richard's Almanac*.

1760

The first roller skates were worn by Joseph Merlin in London, England.

1709

Bortolomeo Cristiforio, an Italian keyboard maker, invents the piano.

The first piano.

My bright idea and how it works.

Use an encyclopedia or the Internet to find out how many strings a Baby Grand piano has?

WEB SEARCH

Draw a picture of your own invention and tell how it works.

1800's

A Time of Excitement

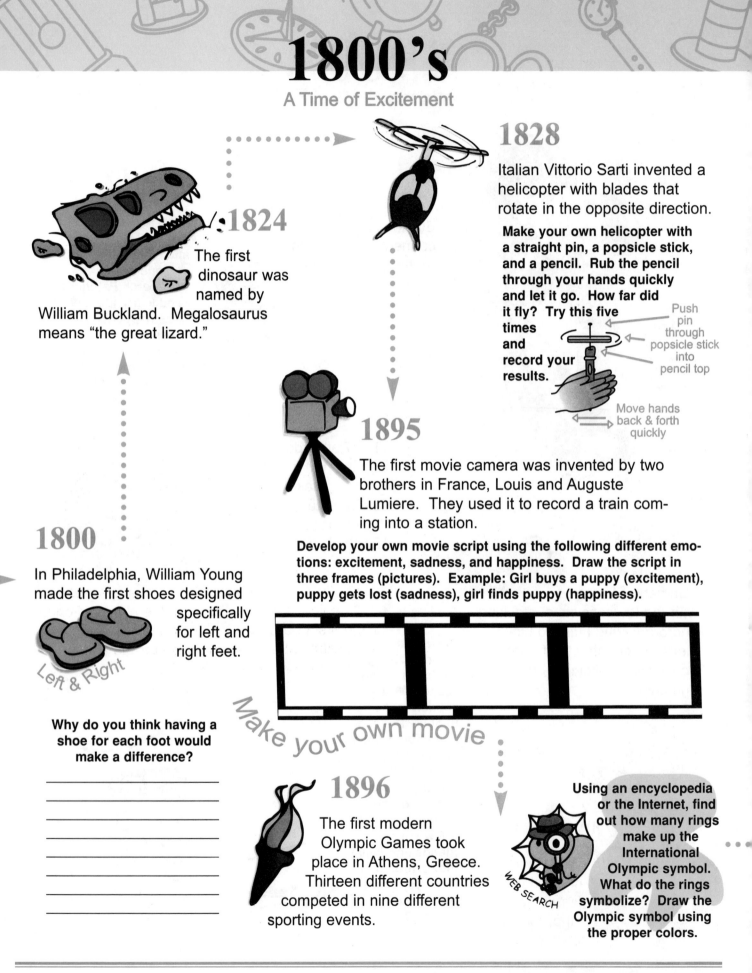

1828

Italian Vittorio Sarti invented a helicopter with blades that rotate in the opposite direction.

Make your own helicopter with a straight pin, a popsicle stick, and a pencil. Rub the pencil through your hands quickly and let it go. How far did it fly? Try this five times and record your results.

Push pin through popsicle stick into pencil top

Move hands back & forth quickly

1824

The first dinosaur was named by William Buckland. Megalosaurus means "the great lizard."

1895

The first movie camera was invented by two brothers in France, Louis and Auguste Lumiere. They used it to record a train coming into a station.

Develop your own movie script using the following different emotions: excitement, sadness, and happiness. Draw the script in three frames (pictures). Example: Girl buys a puppy (excitement), puppy gets lost (sadness), girl finds puppy (happiness).

Make your own movie

1800

In Philadelphia, William Young made the first shoes designed specifically for left and right feet.

Left & Right

Why do you think having a shoe for each foot would make a difference?

_____
_____
_____
_____
_____
_____
_____

1896

The first modern Olympic Games took place in Athens, Greece. Thirteen different countries competed in nine different sporting events.

WEB SEARCH

Using an encyclopedia or the Internet, find out how many rings make up the International Olympic symbol. What do the rings symbolize? Draw the Olympic symbol using the proper colors.

1900's

A Time of Action

1959

Skateboards were invented by Bill and Mark Richards by connecting wheels to the bottom of long wooden boards.

Log onto the NASA website at www.NASA.com, and explore the NASA online facility. Research Pathfinder and learn about what has happened to the mission since it was originally launched. **Has NASA found any signs of life on Mars? Where else does NASA plan to explore?**

WEB SEARCH

1997

The Pathfinder probe successfully lands on Mars. The first photographs taken from Mars by the remote-controlled Sojourner are sent back to Earth via satellite.

The Sojourner

1955

The popular toy LEGO was invented in Denmark. Playing with the toy consists of stacking and organizing building block pieces to construct different objects like buildings, bridges and ships.

Draw your favorite Disney character in this scene. Write a caption in the bubble. Pretend that your cartoon is going to be placed in the Sunday comic section of the newspaper. Show your friends and family the cartoon to get their responses. Do they understand it?

TRASH

1924

Walt Disney created the first cartoon strip, *Alice in Cartoonland*.

Doodling:

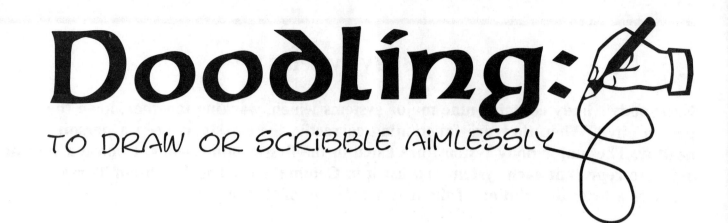

TO DRAW OR SCRIBBLE AIMLESSLY

Science

7th Grade Preview

- Life Science
- Earth Science
- Biological Science
- Physical Science

Body Systems

Everybody's body contains nine major systems which, working together, keep the person alive. When they are functioning correctly, these systems keep a person healthy. The major body systems are listed in the first column below. Choose a specific organ to represent each system and list it in Column Two. Then, Column Three requires a brief description of the major function of that organ.

SYSTEM	MAJOR ORGAN	FUNCTION
Circulatory		
Digestive		
Endocrine		
Excretory		
Muscular		
Nervous		
Reproduction		
Respiratory		
Skeletal		

Light and Sound. If we are fortunate, we can see and hear, two very important senses. But how are sound and light produced? What do the terms light and sound mean? You may recall that sound is a form of energy produced by vibrating matter, and light is a form of energy that radiates from atoms when they are violently disturbed by heat or electricity. Light and sound are forms of energy that produce waves that can be visible as well as invisible.

Study the following Word Bank on the ear and eye. Then, place each word found in the Word Bank under the picture of the ear or eye.

Word Bank

thunder	Hz	convex	iris
music	anvil	photoelectric	violet rays
ultraviolet	lens	auditory nerve	decibel
intensity	optic	tone	luminous
ultrasonic	fluorescent	mirror	infrared rays
candle flame	pupil	spectrum	cone
illumination	cochlea	percussion	photon
listen	retina	incandescent	prism
harp	vibration	farsightedness	hologram
sonar	timbre	concave	laser
	pitch	X-rays	stirrup

Contracting a Disease. It is *easy* to contract a disease. The crossword puzzle below can be solved by correctly matching each disease with the organ it affects.

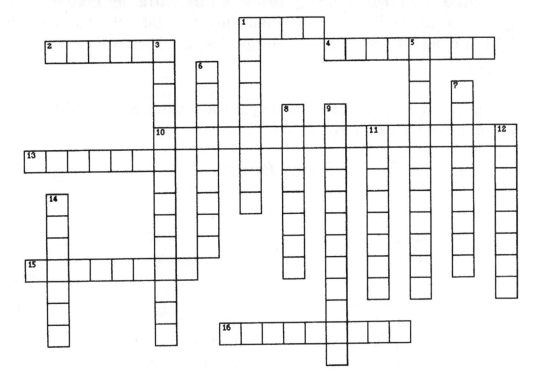

Clues

Diseases of the central nervous system:
    10A   12D

Respiratory System
    5D   6D

Immune System
    1A

Digestive System
    13A   15A   16A   9D   14D

Skin
    4A

Skeletal System
    1D   9D

White Blood Cells
    11D

Eyes
    8D

Heart
    3D

Thyroid Gland
    2A

Disease Bank

Digestive System
    cholera, colitis, hepatitis, diabetes, dysentery

Diseases of the central nervous system
    multiple sclerosis, shingles

Eyes
    glaucoma

Heart
    rheumatic fever

Immune system
    AIDS

Respiratory system
    tuberculosis, influenza

Skeletal system
    arthritis, osteoporosis

Skin
    impetigo

Thyroid gland
    goiter

White blood cells
    leukemia

Animal and Plant Cells. All plants and animals are constructed of many cells functioning together. All cells have commonalties but there are also specific differences which allow identification and classification of a cell either plant or animal. Two have been drawn below. Label all of the parts by using the word bank for clues. Some words may be used twice.

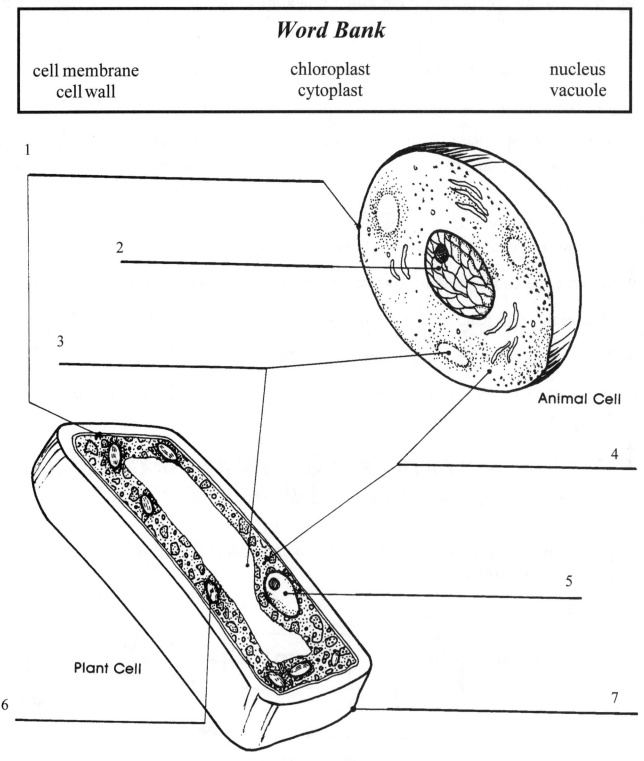

Word Bank

cell membrane	chloroplast	nucleus
cell wall	cytoplast	vacuole

1

2

3

Animal Cell

4

5

Plant Cell

6

7

Feeding Your Robot. A computer program lists instructions, telling the computer what to do. It is very important that each instruction be exact, concise, sequential and precise. Any errors in the writing will prevent the program from running smoothly and/or completing the task assigned. Robots are able to function because of this programming. To learn more about programming and the importance of precise language try to write a program for making a peanut butter sandwich.

First: Break down all steps and supplies needed to accomplish the goal.

Second: List them in the order to be prepared.

Third: Enlist a friend to be the "robot." Your friend must execute each command precisely as you give it (remember your friend is a robot and not capable of independent reasoning).

Fourth: Your program will have "bugs." Note each of these basic flaws (problems that prevent the robot from completing the sandwich).

Fifth: Rewrite the entire program correcting the errors you encountered.

Sixth: Repeat the command trial, again noting the command flaws.

Seventh: Rewrite the entire program eliminating the "bugs."

Eighth: Continue steps six and seven until the program can be successfully executed (the robot make a peanut butter sandwich).

NOW YOU UNDERSTAND WHY PROGRAMMERS ARE HIGHLY SKILLED AND WELL PAID!

Creating a flow chart may help. It is most helpful to draw the chart before each rewrite. Flow charts help to prevent errors.

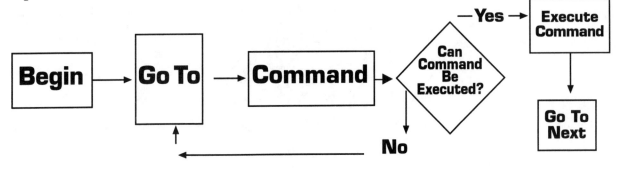

Constructing a Pinhole Viewer. Light travels in straight lines enabling scientists to predict its behavior during reflection and refraction. Many instruments and devices make use of this property. In this experiment, you will construct a pinhole viewer.

Materials:

Small coffee can (with a plastic top)
 with a small clean, round hole
 punched into the center
 of the closed end
Rubber band

Piece of waxed paper or
 tracing paper slightly larger
 than the open end of the can
Candle and matches
Piece of cardboard (6 cm x 6 cm)

Procedure:

1. Holding the can up to your eye, look through it. Make sure the hole is small (about 1 mm), clean and centered.
2. Now place the piece of waxed or tracing paper over the open end of the coffee can. Use the rubber band to hold it in place.
3. With the lit candle, place a few drops of wax on the small piece of cardboard. So that the candle will remain upright, place it onto the cardboard.
4. Place the candle and cardboard on the top of a table or cabinet.
5. Hold the pinhole viewer so that the pinhole points toward the burning candle. Place the viewer so that a reflection of the candle is seen on the paper screen. (You may want to turn off the lights and close the shades or blinds for this part of the experiment.) Draw the image that you see on the paper screen (in the drawing below).

Drawing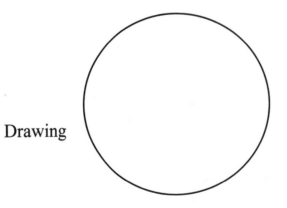

Conclusions:

1. If the lighted candle is larger than the pinhole, can you explain why the image is formed on the screen? _____

2. In the drawing is the image right side up or upside down? _____

3. Could this pinhole viewer be changed into a pinhole camera? Explain. _____

_____

Doing the Impossible. Each of these tricks is actually an experiment about finding a center of gravity.

1. Kneel on the floor and place your elbow in front of your knee. Make sure your elbow touches your knee. Stretch your arm and hand out flat. Have someone place a deck of cards (in its box) a match box or similar item, on end and touching your finger tips. Now, kneel up straight and fold your arms behind your back, grasping your elbows. Bend forward and push over the box with your nose, retaining your balance. Slowly straighten back up.

2. Use a broomstick for this activity. Bend down and place the broomstick under your bent knees. Crook your elbows around it. Have someone place an apple or pear, stem end up, on the floor in front of you at a distance of approximately 18". Lean forward, using your hands for balance. Pick up the apple or pear with your teeth. Slowly return to your original position.

3. Try this gravity activity. Stand with your left side facing the wall. Put your left foot and cheek against the wall. Lift your right foot.

4. Place a quarter between the crossed tines of two forks. Balance the quarter's edge on the sharpened point of a pencil.

5. Place two people of different weights on a teeter-totter. Make sure your subjects are old enough to participate and understand the principles involved. Have both people raise their legs. What do you observe? How can you make the teeter-totter balance? Think of as many solutions as possible, including the use of a third person.

Which of these activities were you able to do? Explain what happened that allowed or prevented you from accomplishing each activity. Challenge a friend or neighbor to try the "tricks."

_____
_____
_____
_____
_____
_____
_____
_____

Creating a Science Fiction Tale. Science fiction has long been a favorite topic of both authors and readers. Choose *one* of the prompts to create an illustrated science fiction tale. Note: this would be an ideal activity to do on your computer. Use the word processing feature and make use of spelling and grammar check options.

1. Tell the story of the invention of some modern-day device and its uses.

2. You have won a ticket for a free trip to another planet (known or unknown). Write about where, why, what, who, and how. Perhaps you might choose to do this as a series of journal entries.

3. Invent a land. Name it for someone special. Describe life in this new land (weather, plants, animals, "people," and their lifestyle). Create an adventure set in this environment.

4. You have an "alien" friend who is visible only to you or who appears as an "earthling" to everyone else. Write a story about your adventures. Tell how and why the friendship ends.

5. Discoveries of the next millennium: How are they discovered? What are they? In what way are they important?

6. A large meteor strikes the earth. What happens?

7. Doctors discover the secret of immortality. How does this affect life on earth?

8. Robots now do all the required manual and repetitive work for humans. What would various members of your family do to fill their days?

9. Scientists learn to control "mother nature." What would this do to life on earth? You may see this as a positive, negative or mixed blessing.

10. Create your own science fiction adventure.

ANSWERS

Page 2 They slept at night.

Page 3 1. S, 2. F, 3. S, 4. S, 5. F, 6. F, 7. S, 8. F,
9. S, 10. S, 11. advertisement, 12. busiest, 13. leisure,
14. appreciate, 15. changeable, 16. athletic, 17. protein,
18. occasion, 19. statement, 20. Druggist, 21. classical,
22. occupation

Page 4 1. C, 2. B, 3. A, 4. B, 5. D, 6. A, 7. C, 8. B,
9. D, 10. . . . meeting. declarative, 11. . . . 3:00?
interrogative, 12. . . . meeting. imperative,
13. . . . podium? interrogative, 14. . . . members.
declarative, 15. . . . hour. declarative, 16. . . . lot!
exclamatory, 17. . . . expenses. imperative, 18. . . .
school. declarative

Page 5 Character Sketch: Answers will vary. 1. P boys run,
2. C team plays, 3. P Toni and sister ride, 4. C band
practices, 5. S You were, 6. P They have decided jog, 7.
P girls are going, 8. S judging was held, 9. P pennies are,
10. C crowd stands

Page 6 1. quan/ti/ty, 2. ham/burg/er, 3. par/a/troop/er, 4.
laugh/ter, 5. dis/ap/point, 6. im/me/di/ate, 7. yearn, 8.
sus/pi/cion, 9. re/cess, 10. neg/a/tive, 11. ir/reg/u/lar, 12.
es/tab/lish, 13. branch, 14. fre/quen/cy, 15. o/rig/i/nal
Paragraphs: (Answers may vary.) In the past, people in
Europe and America danced their traditional folk dances at
fairs, festivals, weddings, and celebrations. Folk dances are
very old, and the steps have been passed down from parents to
children for hundreds of years. Today they are mostly
performed by dance groups in national costumes.

In other parts of the world, people have traditional
dances which they perform at festivals or use to tell stories of
their gods and heroes.

Page 7 1. C, 2. N, 3. H, 4. E, 5. A, 6. G, 7. M, 8. P,
9. B, 10. I, 11. F, 12. K, 13. Q, 14. O, 15. J, 16. D,
17. L. Word Search below.

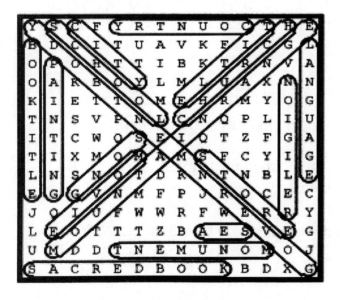

Page 8 1. bored, 2. herd, 3. They're, 4. allowed, 5. passed,
6. suite, sweet, 7. whether, weather, 8. principal, principle,
9. Write, 10. capital, 11. from her new boyfriend, 12. about
the Oregon Trail, 13. on vacation to the Grand Canyon, 14.
for the problems on this test, 15. behind us, 16. underneath
your coat, 17. in the morning with breakfast with lunch
18. around the corner across the street from the dry cleaners

Page 9 1. c, 2. b, 3. d, 4. a, 5. b, 6. c, 7. c, 8. d, 9. a, 10. d,
11. b, 12. a, 13. c, 14. d, 15. a

Page 10 1. C, 2. S, 3. C, 4. S, 5. C, 6. S, 7. S, 8. C, 9. C,
10. S, 11. whom, 12. who, 13. Whom, 14. who, 15. who,
16. whom, 17. whom, 18. who, 19. whom, 20. who

Page 11 1. love bicycles transitive, 2. took tour transitive,
3. rode intransitive, 4. climbed hills transitive, 5.
explained rules transitive, 6. misunderstood intransitive,
7. ignored customers transitive, 8. is suspect transitive,
9. assigned projects transitive, 10. followed trail transitive
Paragraph: Answers will vary.

Page 12 1. really likes, 2. always goes, 3. never gives, 4.
quickly burned, 5. very tired, 6. hard studied, 7. quickly
work, 8. too tired, 9. Suddenly heard, 10. easily worked
11. France, Italy, Switzerland, Austria, 12. piano, organ,
violin, 13. hamburgers, french fries, salad, ice cream, 14.
door, block, gate, 15. clear, exact, 16. Mrs. Walker, Ms.
Grant, 17. Nevada, Utah, Colorado, 18. dishes, stories,
19. chicken, ribs, 20. swimming, tennis, hiking, bicycling,

Page 13 1. Carla, 2. report, 3. libraries, 4. Sweden,
5. students, 6. coats, 7. students, 8. heartbeat, 9. George,
10. Sara and Juanita. **The following activities are circled:**
11. several, 12. Red, yellow, blue, 13. those, priceless,
14. historical, 15. contest, green, 16. bright, unusual,
17. These, science, best 18. quiet, studious, 19. beautiful,
clever, Spanish, 20. five, hard, steady

Page 14 The following conjunctions are circled: 1. but,
2. Because, 3. or, 4. Either, or, 5. When, 6. Neither, nor, 7.
and, 8. Although, 9. but, 10. since, 11. receives, 12. makes,
13. do, 14. is, 15. were, 16. has, 17. look, 18. are, 19.
practice, 20. share

Page 15 1. Whew, 2. Goodness, 3. Wow, 4. Hurrah, 5. Oh,
6. Gosh, 7. Alas, 8. Ugh, 9. Well 10. My, 11. Ouch, 12.
Gracious 13. Your, 14. hers, 15. mine, 16. my, 17. its, 18.
ours, 19. Their, 20. your.

See the next page for the Interjection Word Search.

Page 15 Interjection Word Search

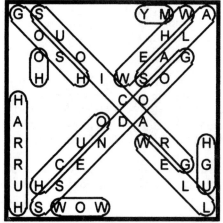

Page 16 1. Chuck answered, "I really like studying about Russia." 2. "My parents were very impressed with my report on Russia," Tyler remarked. 3. "Can you think of any Russian foods that you would like?" asked Mrs. Slaton. 4. "Oh, no," groaned Isaac, " I don't want to eat Russian food for lunch." 5. "I know the Russians make great chocolates," said Margaret. 6. "Could you take care of my two cats," asked Mrs. Thomas, "while I'm on vacation." 7."I will be on vacation for two weeks," said Mrs. Thomas. 8. Mrs. Thomas asked, "Will you also water my plants about every three days?" 9. "Is there anything you would like me to bring you while I am in Mexico?" said Mrs. Thomas. 10. John said jokingly, "Could you bring me a real taco?" 11. , the principal, Dr. Marshall 12. Jessica friend 13. , Mrs. Kelly, English teacher 14. , Marshall and Tony, sixth graders 15. , a team sport, Basketball 16. , Leon and Jose, basketball players 17., the largest in the mall, department store 18. , a new model, home computer 19. , the guest speaker, Robert Carrell 20. , my father's brother, Ward

Page 17 1. good, 2. polite, 3. easily, 4. interesting, 5. Surely, 6. hard, 7. slowly, 8. beautiful, 9. thoroughly, 10. Badly. **Possible Answers:** 11. in - not costing a lot of money, 12. co - to work together, 13. dis - to think wrong, 14. im - living or lasting forever, 15. dis - to take no notice of someone or something, 16. im - that cannot be, exist or happen, 17. in - not genuine or honest, 18. dis - to make ill-satisfied; 19. in - cannot be seen; 20. un - not stressed; 21. im - not courteous; rude; 22. un - does not have a job or work; 23. re - to make up for; 24. ir - not standard in shape; timing; 25. un - vacant; 26. im - to put into or confine in a prison; 27. re - to stimulate (the memory); 28. dis - to go against the rules or someone's wishes; 29. dis - to injure the credit or reputation of; 30. trans - to remove (a plant) from one place and plant it in another.

Page 18 1. youngest, 2. clearest, 3. latest, 4. fastest, 5. greatest, 6. more frequently, 7. darker, 8. hardest, 9. silliest, 10. tallest, 11. prettiest, 12. most wisely, 13. highest, 14. closer, 15. happier, 16. lay, 17. sat, 18. lain, 19. rises, 20. risen, 21. sit, 22. laid, 23. set, 24. laid, 25. raised.

Page 19 1. ate, direct object, 2. offered, indirect object, 3. wrote, direct object, 4. bought, indirect object, 5. fed, indirect object, 6. gave, indirect object, 7. told, direct object, 8. gave, direct object, 9. feeds, indirect object, 10. sold, direct object 11. 2, 12. 8, 13. 3, 14. 5, 15. 1, 16. 7, 17. 4, 18. 6, 19. 1, 20. 6, 21. 3, 22. 2, 23. 7, 24. 4

Page 20 Possible Answers: 1. Angela did not tell anyone about her failing grade on the math test. 2. Walter had gone hardly ten steps when his name was called. 3. Nobody ever had a more interesting job of interviewing television guests. 4. Cynthia said that she hadn't read anything about Ms. Jane Pittman. 5. My grandfather doesn't do anything all day long. **Paragraph:** Answers will vary.

Page 21 1. backward, 2. ignorance, 3. scarce, 4. careful, 5. nonfiction, 6. illogical, 7. extravagant, 8. pardon, 9. discourage, 10. temporary, 11. succeed, 12. waste.

August 10, 2000

Dear Aunt Emily and Uncle Bob,

Thank you so much for my twelfth birthday party. All of my friends really enjoyed the pizza and skating party at Sal's Skating Palace.

Mom and Dad must have told you that I wanted a pizza and skating party. I have heard from almost everyone who attended. What a great time!

As soon as the pictures are developed, Mom and I will send you some of the prints. I can't wait to see them!

Thanks again for such a wonderful birthday party.

Love,
Marsha

Page 22

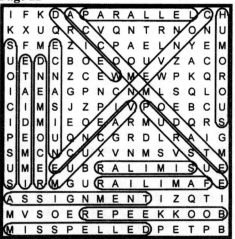

Page 23 1. Haley, school? 2. Well, Tuesday, June 6. 3. book, words, 4. report; (or report.) 5. Roberts, teacher, 6. Diana, Wales, Paris, France, 31, 1997. 7. today: Cook, Holbrook, 8. paint! 9. Starks: 10. Sincerely, 11. grades; (or grades.) 12. me, 13. following: contents, body, illustrations, sources? 14. C 15. G 16. F 17. D 18. B 19. A 20. E

Page 24 Answers will vary.

Page 25

1. My mother is a teacher.

2. The custodian swept, washed, and waxed the floors.

3. Dad prepared them some spaghetti.

4. Our new school has a large, bright gym.

5. The new girl with blonde hair plays in our school band.

6. Finally, the small blue plane radioed the tower.

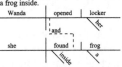

7. Wanda opened her locker, and she found a frog inside.

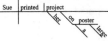

8. Sue printed her project on a large poster.

9. Dr. Jones, the principal, announced the winners.

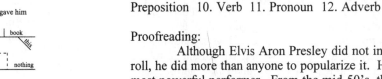

10. He gave me this book, but I gave him nothing.

Page 26 1. happier, happiest 2. more beautiful, most beautiful 3. weaker, weakest 4. more talented, most talented 5. louder, loudest 6. more slowly, most slowly 7. farther, farthest 8. more quietly, most quietly 9. more politely, most politely 10. higher, highest 11. funniest 12. extremely 13. more carefully 14. sure 15. good 16. better 17. more attentively 18. warmer 19. more expensive 20. taller 21. greatest 22. bigger 23. fastest 24. oldest 25. least 26. best 27. harder

Page 27 1. Those 2. that 3. Those 4. those 5. this 6. those 7. them 8. those 9. these 10. this 11. they're - they are 12. can't - can not 13. you're - you are, aren't - are not 14. haven't - have not, we'll - we will 15. we're - we are 16. won't - will not 17. couldn't - could not 18. I'm I am

Page 28 & 29 1. C 2. A 3. B 4. D 5. C 6. A 7. B 8. D 9. D

Page 30 I.A. Conquering the wilderness I.B. Establishing the frontier II. Moving Westward II.B. How the pioneers traveled III.A pioneer settlement III.A. A pioneer home III.B. Education and religion III.C. Law and order III.D. Social Activities IV.A. The wagon trail IV.B Life on the trail

Page 31 1. D 2. A 3. C 4. B 5. A 6. C 7. B 8. D 9. A 10. B 11. D 12. B 13. D 14. A 15. C 16. B 17. A 18. D

Page 32 20. A 21. C 22. D 23. B 24. A 25. C 26. A 27. C 28. D 29. B 30. A 31. B 32. A 33. C 34. D 35. B 36. B 37. C 38. B 39. A 40. D 41. A

Page 34 Answers will vary.

Page 35 1. West Palm Street, Houston Mill Road 2. Salt Lake City, Utah 3. Rome, Venice, Italy 4. Nile River, Mediterranean Sea 5. Washington D.C., Lincoln Memorial 6. Mount Logan, Canada 7. Asia 8. C 9. A 10. D 11. A 12. B 13. C 14. D 15. A 16. B

Page 36 1. F 2. S 3. S 4. F 5. S 6. S 7. F 8. F 9. F 10. S 11. Dickens' 12. guardsmen's 13. newspapers' 14. year's 15. Margaret's 16. Harrison's 17. sister's 18. characters' 19. teachers' 20. nations' 21. Harris' or Harris's 22. Vincent's 23. children's 24. referee's 25. governor's

Page 37 1. appeal 2. doesn't 3. fascinates 4. was 5. is 6. walk 7. are 8. likes 9. was 10. wishes Personal Narrative: Answers will vary.

Page 38 1. Pronoun 2. Interjection 3. Adverb 4. Noun 5. Adjective 6. Conjunction 7. Verb 8. Adjective 9. Preposition 10. Verb 11. Pronoun 12. Adverb

Proofreading:

Although Elvis Aron Presley did not invent rock 'n roll, he did more than anyone to popularize it. He was rock's most powerful performer. From the mid-50's, the "King's" vocal mannerism, sideburns, and attitude made him an international hero of the young.

During his lifetime, Elvis sold more than four hundred million records. He had forty-five golden hit records. Elvis also appeared in thirty-two movies.

When Presley died on August 16, 1977, at the age of forty-two, many mourners journeyed to Memphis, Tennessee, Presley's home, to pay their last respects. Elvis left behind an almost immeasurable influence on popular music.

Page 39 1. your 2. His 3. our 4. Her 5. theirs 6. its 7. mine 8. my 9. their 10. hers 11. studies, believe, 12. me, Ralph, 13. lunch, 14. said, record, 15. Harrison, 16. story, 17. test, 18. This, suppose, 19. Blake, 20. Plains, Time Out: Answers will vary.

Page 40 1. Its 2. There 3. you're 4. Whose 5. to 6. won 7. your 8. They're 9. one 10. two
Descriptive Paragraph: Answers will vary.

Page 41 Answers will vary.

Page 42 1. ADJ that his grandmother knitted 2. ADV If you listen carefully to the directions 3. ADV until I could play the selection perfectly 4. N what the problem is 5. ADJ that my mother lost 6. ADV when he attends a basketball game 7. N whoever would listen 8. ADV as he read the winners 9. threw 10. begin 11. drunk 12. shown 13. known 14. lent

Page 44

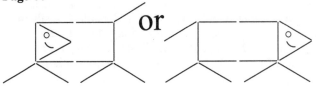

Page 45 1. 30,000+7,000+50+7 2. 10,000,000+2,000,000+ 300,000+40,000+5,000+600+80+9 3. 100,000+80,000+ 7,000+40+2 4. 6,000,000+800+60+2 5. 50,000+1,000+8 6. 9,000,000+900,000+90,000+9,000+900+90+6 7. 5,000+400+10+2 8. 60,000,000+8,000,000+800,000+ 80,000+8,000+200+20+2 9. 800,000+5,000+600+3 10. 7,000+7
Party Time: 1. $20 2. Graduation: 5+30=$35 for spring, 15+25=$40 for graduation 3. Spring: more money on cups 4. Spring: about $70, Graduation: about $69 5. About $1

Page 46 1. 200 2. 700 3. 2000 4. 6800 5. 200 6. 9100 7. 1000 8. 9000 9. 15,000 10. 58,000 11. 131,000 12. 772,000 13. 9,000,000 14. 10,000,000 15. 6,000,000 16. 1000 17. 300 18. 130 19. 1100 20. 2700 21. 150 22. 21 23. 15 24. 2 25. 5 26. 8 27. 3 28. 16 29. 647 30. 1 31. B

Page 47 1. One hundred eighty seven thousand six hundred fifty three 2. Eighty seven million four hundred sixty thousand thirty 3. Two hundred twenty two million three hundred thirty three thousand one hundred eighty nine 4. One billion two hundred thirty four million five hundred sixty seven thousand eight hundred ninety 5. Five hundred forty three billion two hundred one million sixty five thousand four hundred eighty three 6. 397,433 7. 509,877 8. 549,911 9. 98,937 10. 8,650 11. 302,296 12. 833,952 13. 108,270 14. 249,425 15. 330.96 16. 5391.41 17. 66.89

Page 48 1. 12 2. 4, 6, 8, 10, 12 3. 22, 33, 44, 55, 66, 4. 50, 75, 100, 125, 150 5. 14, 21, 28, 35, 42 6. 32, 48, 64, 80, 96 7. 400, 600, 800, 1000, 1200 8. 20, 30, 40, 50, 60 9. 80, 120, 160, 200, 240 10. 300, 450, 600, 750, 900 11. 10 12. 12. 13. 18 14. 35 15. 24 16. 30 17. 6 18. 24 19. 30 20 Yes 21. No 22. No 23. No 24. No
Challenge: Answers will vary

Page 49 1. Factors of 4: 1, 2, 4 Factors of 8: 1, 2, 4, 8 Common Factors: 1, 2, 4 GCF: 4 2. Factors of 16: 1, 2, 4, 8, 16 Factors of 20: 1, 2, 4, 5, 10, 20 Common Factors: 1, 2, 4 GCF: 4 3. 5 4. 12 5. 2 6. 3 7. 1 8. 4 9. 3 10. 5 11. 1 12. 6 players 13. 1, 2, 4, 8, 16, 31, 62, 124, 248

Page 50 Prime Factors:
```
2. 60            3.   54          4. 24
   / \                / \            / \
  2 x 30            6 x 9         2 x 12
    / \            / \   / \          / \
   2 x 15       2 x 3  3 x 3       3 x 4
     / \                              / \
    3 x 5                           2 x 2
 2 x 2 x 3 x 5    2 x 3 x 3 x 3   2 x 3 x 2 x 2
```
5. 72=2x2x2x3x3 6. 55=5x11 7. 44=2x2x11 8. 54=2x3x3x3 9. 19x5 10. 2x2x2x5x5 11. 5 12. 17 13. 29&31, 41&43 14. 3,5,7; 37,39,41; 39,41,43 15. 5x5x7

Page 51 1. 1/3 2. 2/7 3. 1/7 4. 6/7 5. 1/6 6. 1/2 From left to right: Tibbitt, Toto, Toosh, Tondo, Tutu

Page 52 1. 1/6 2. 3/4 3. 3/10 4. 6/6=1
5. What's 1/3 of 12? 6. What's 1/5 of 20? 7.What's 1/3 of 9?

■□□□	●○○○○	★☆☆
■□□□	●○○○○	★☆☆
■□□□	●○○○○	★☆☆
	●○○○○	

From left to right: Baby Gavin, Cathy, Ernie, Agatha, Barbara, Freda, Dennis

Page 53 1. 3/36 2. 1/3 3. 9/12 4. 4/4 5. 4/4 6. 8/36 7. 7/14 8. 1/9 9. 14/24 10. 39/45 11. 4/32 12. 4/20 13. 8/12 14. 2/3 15. 35/105 16. 6/10=3/5 17. 3/12=1/4 18. 7/8=28/32 19. 13/26=1/2 20. 11/20-22/40 21. 3/8=18/48 22. 2/9=4/18 23. 13/14=26/28 24. 11/15=33/45

Page 54 1. 36/36, equivalent 2. 105/60, not equivalent 3. 12/18, not equivalent 4. 180/180, equivalent 5. 315/280, not equivalent 6. 360/360, equivalent 7. 6 8. 12 9. 24 10. 40 11. 24 12. 10

Page 55 1. $\frac{10}{12}, \frac{11}{12}$ 2. $\frac{5}{15}, \frac{6}{15}$ 3. $\frac{5}{20}, \frac{6}{20}$ 4. $\frac{12}{33}, \frac{3}{33}$ 5. $\frac{3}{30}, \frac{8}{30}$ 6. $\frac{3}{9}, \frac{2}{9}$ 7. $\frac{27}{45}, \frac{20}{45}$ 8. $\frac{9}{63}, \frac{35}{63}$ 9. $\frac{1}{7} < \frac{4}{7}, \frac{4}{7} < \frac{3}{7}, \frac{3}{7} < \frac{4}{7}$ 10. $\frac{3}{8} < \frac{3}{4}, \frac{5}{8} < \frac{3}{4}, \frac{6}{8} > \frac{3}{4}$ 11. $\frac{1}{3} > \frac{1}{12}, \frac{1}{3} < \frac{5}{12}, \frac{1}{3} < \frac{7}{12}$ 12. $\frac{1}{2} > \frac{1}{8}, \frac{1}{2} > \frac{3}{8}, \frac{1}{2} < \frac{5}{8}$ 13. 16/24 on Internet, 21/24 watching TV 14. 3/12 Wednesday, 4/12 Friday 15. 14/35 Friday, 15/35 Saturday 16. 3/8 Madison, 4/8 Ashton

Page 56 1. 2/3 2. 3/4 3. 1/5 4. 1/4 5. 5/9 6. 7/9 7. GCF=3 8. GCF=4 9. GCF=3 10. 1/3 11. 1/5 12. 1/4 13. 1/4 14. 1/2 15. 2/3 16. 2/3 17. 1/3 18. 1/3 19. 7/10 20. 5/8 21. 2/5 Waterfront Story: 22. 9/10 23. 29/36 24. 1/19

Page 57 1. 5/2 2. 24/5 3. 19/8 4. 21/5 5. 17/5 6. 8/3 7. 19/3 8. 61/9 9. 61/8 10. 23/3 11. 17/2 12. 7/4 13. 4/3 14. 13/8 15. 16/7 16. 91/15 17. $1\frac{5}{6}$ 18. $1\frac{6}{11}$ 19. $2\frac{1}{7}$ 20. $4\frac{1}{8}$ 21. $5\frac{1}{5}$ 22. 5 23. $8\frac{1}{3}$ 24. $8\frac{8}{9}$ 25. 8 26. $5\frac{6}{7}$ 27. $15\frac{1}{2}$ 28. $9\frac{7}{9}$

Page 58 1. $15\frac{3}{4}$ 2. $4\frac{1}{3}$ 3. $2\frac{2}{5}$ 4. $9\frac{1}{3}$ 5. $4\frac{1}{3}$ 6. $3\frac{1}{3}$ 7. $4\frac{3}{4}$ 8. $6\frac{1}{2}$ 9. 3 Boxes 10. 12 Recipes 11. $1\frac{7}{8}$ 12. $5\frac{1}{3}$
Faces and Shapes:
a. □₆ ⬡₂ b. ▽₂ □₃ c. △₂ □₃ d. ▭₄ □₂ □₁

Page 59 1. .4 2. .225 3. .0875 4. .55 5. .318 6. 4.07 7. 9.125 8. 4.625 9. .18 10. .025 11. .3 12. .58 13. .09 14. 8.67 15. 1.375 16. 5.68 17. .02 18. .375 19. .45 20. .06 21. .568 22. 7.87 23. 7.4 24. 3.625 25. .75 26. .64 27. .82 28. .83 29. 5.3 30. 7.201 31. 8.8 32. 9.6. Time Out: The steak cost 86¢ more per pound.

Page 60 1. $\frac{3}{4}$ 2. $1\frac{1}{9}$ 3. $\frac{1}{2}$ 4. $\frac{3}{10}$ 5. $\frac{9}{16}$ 6. $\frac{3}{4}$ 7. $1\frac{2}{15}$ 8. $\frac{2}{5}$ 9. $\frac{2}{9}$ 10. $\frac{15}{19}$ 11. $\frac{9}{11}$ 12. 1 13. $\frac{1}{3}$ 14. $\frac{1}{8}$ 15. $1\frac{2}{5}$ 16. $\frac{11}{12}$ 17. $\frac{3}{10}$ 18. $1\frac{13}{28}$ 19. $1\frac{5}{12}$ 20. $\frac{1}{18}$ 21. $\frac{5}{8}$ 22. $1\frac{1}{30}$ 23. $\frac{1}{3}$ 24. $\frac{1}{20}$

Page 61 1. $8\frac{3}{20}$ 2. $11\frac{1}{8}$ 3. $4\frac{1}{15}$ 4. $8\frac{2}{5}$ 5. $8\frac{3}{5}$ 6. $16\frac{1}{10}$

Page 62 1. 7/24 2. 3/8 3. 5/18 4. 1/3 5. 1/2 6. 8/45 7. 5/28 8. 2/3 9. 3/16 10. 1/5 11. 3/10 12. 5/24 13. 1/12 14. 1/2 15. 28/33 16. 5/13 17. 7/39 18. 9/104

Page 63 1. $12\frac{1}{4}$ 2. $15\frac{1}{2}$ 3. $17\frac{19}{24}$ 4. $15\frac{41}{42}$ 5. 19 6. $10\frac{2}{5}$ 7. $\frac{5}{3}$ 8. $\frac{8}{4}$ 9. $\frac{11}{7}$ 10. $\frac{12}{6}$ 11. $\frac{9}{5}$ 12. $\frac{4}{3}$ 13. $\frac{1}{8}$ 14. $\frac{11}{8}$ 15. $\frac{21}{18}$ 16. $\frac{1}{25}$ 17. $\frac{1}{142}$ 18. $\frac{7}{4}$ 19. $\frac{14}{13}$ 20. $\frac{25}{6}$ 21. $\frac{1}{32}$ 22. $\frac{1}{16}$

Page 64 1. $1\frac{1}{2}$ 2. $1\frac{3}{7}$ 3. $6\frac{2}{9}$ 4. $1\frac{1}{8}$ 5. $\frac{12}{19}$ 6. $1\frac{3}{5}$ 7. $\frac{15}{16}$ 8. $\frac{2}{3}$ 9. $1\frac{29}{75}$ 10. $1\frac{19}{392}$ 11. $\frac{3}{20}$ 12. $\frac{3}{4}$ 13. $1\frac{43}{56} < 4\frac{2}{15}$ 14. $5\frac{5}{8} > 1\frac{13}{24}$ 15. $12\frac{15}{32} > 9\frac{7}{12}$ 16. $6\frac{13}{34} < 51\frac{1}{3}$

Page 65 1. P= 1 2/3 yards 2. $2.25 3. $3.90 4.a) 1.5 gallons b) no c) 2 gallons d) 10.5 gallons 5. 5/12 6. 1/8 7. 1/4

Page 66 1. $\frac{154}{167}$ 2. $1\frac{21}{37}$ 3. $1\frac{13}{154}$ 4. $\frac{29}{77}$ 5. $\frac{37}{416}$ 6. $\frac{29}{208}$ 7. $19\frac{8}{43}$ 8. $\frac{43}{825}$ 9. $\frac{5}{42}$ 10. $\frac{1}{6}$ 11. $\frac{7}{100}$ 12. 20

Page 67 A. 3, B. 4 C. 20 D. 37 1. 75¢ each 2. 10¢ 3. $7.50 4. 40 /box 5. $320.00 /camera 6. 50 /minute 7. 24 /row 8. 2 /student 9. 4 /ride 10 $.29 /print Part-time Earnings: 2 days=$97.00 5 days=$242.50 10 days=$485.00 Time Out: 10 minutes/section

Page 68 1. yes 2. no 3. no 4. no 5. yes 6. no 7. 7:12 or $\frac{7}{12}$ 8. 12:20 or $\frac{3}{5}$ 9. 60:2 or $\frac{60}{2}$ 10. 8:2 or $\frac{8}{2}$ 11. 20:3 or $\frac{20}{3}$ 12. 13:12 or $\frac{13}{12} = 1\frac{1}{12}$ 13. p=2 14. a=60 15. x=10 16. x=6 17. k=4.5 18. x=14

Page 69 1. n=20 2. a=2 3. n=18 4. a=15 5. a=90 6. a=9 7. x=8 8. x=30 9. x=51 10. n=9 11. y=23 12. p=52

13. 18 players 14. $3.73 15. no 16. yes 17. yes

Page 70 1. $\frac{13}{100}$ 2. $\frac{27}{100}$ 3. $\frac{9}{100}$ 4. $\frac{2}{5}$ 5. $\frac{1}{2}$ 6. $\frac{9}{10}$ 7. **$\frac{17}{20}$** 8. **$\frac{3}{25}$** 9. $\frac{1}{25}$ 10. 67% 11. 7% 12. 90%

Page 71 1. 65% 2. 7% 3. 3% 4. 12% 5. 72% 6. 41% 7. 29% 8. 50% 9. 84% 10. 0.34 11. 0.58 12. 0.13 13. 0.91 14. 0.08 15. 0.16

Page 72 1. 1/12 2. 1/6 3. 1/4 4. 1/2 5. 3/8 6. 1/4 7. 1/2 8. 1/2 9. 2/9 10. 5/9 11. 1/9 12. can't tell 13. 1/4 14. 7/12 15. 1/6 16. 0

Page 73 1. 4000 + 6000 + 800 + 70 + 6 2. 1,000 3. 7,000 4. 6,000 5. 9,000 6. 15 7. 36 8. 100 9. 24 10. $\frac{13}{14}, \frac{26}{28}$ 11. $\frac{11}{20}, \frac{22}{40}$ 12. $\frac{7}{8}, \frac{28}{32}$ 13. $\frac{2}{9}, \frac{4}{18}$ 14. $\frac{2}{3}$ 15. $\frac{1}{2}$ 16. $\frac{3}{7}$ 17. $\frac{2}{3}$ 18. $\frac{4}{9}$ 19. $\frac{8}{11}$ 20. $\frac{1}{3}$ 21. $\frac{5}{8}$ 22. $\frac{4}{9}$ 23. $\frac{5}{12}$ 24. $14\frac{1}{6}$ 25. 16 26. $3\frac{1}{5}$ 27. $2\frac{1}{7}$ 28. $\frac{1}{12}$ 29. 5 30. 65 31. $3\frac{3}{17}$ 32. $\frac{4}{81}$ 33. 79% 34. 83% 35. 15% 36. 5% 37. 52%

Page 76 The color gray

Page 77 1. No 2. yes 3. yes 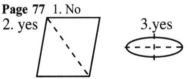 4. No 5. Yes 6. No 7. Yes 8. No 9. No 10. Yes 11. No

Page 78 1. V=1134 cm³ 2. V=720 cm³ 3. V=264 m³ 4. V=50.4 cm³ 5. V=180 m³ 6. V=197.392 cm³

Page 79 1. C 2. CBD 3. CDB 4. DC 5. MQ 6. ML 7. MN 8. MQN 9. NMQ 10. MNQ

Page 80 1. Median=18 Mean=18 Mode=no mode Range=13 2. Median=62 Mean=58.8 Mode=no mode Range=39 3. Median=38 Mean=39.83 Mode=no mode Range=29 4. Median=139.5 Mean=146.75 Mode=no mode Range=52 5. Yes 6. No 7. No 8. Yes 9. No 10. Yes 11. Yes 12. 1 13. –3 14. 5 15. 3 16. –5 17. 1 18. –7 19. 0 20. 6 21. –8 22. –6 23. 7 24. 8 25. 10 26. 30 27. –45 28. –72 29. 17 30. –100 31. 200 32. –160 33. –240 34. –9999 35. 1000 36. 873 37. –342 38. –16 39. 72 40. –249 41. –21 42. –199 43. –467 44. –81 45. 81 46. 240 47. 342 48. –61 49. 100 50. –91 51. –82

Page 81 1. -4 2. -11 3. -4 4. -2 5. 19 6. -21 7. -25 8. 10 9. 2 10. 7 11. 0 12. -26 13. -9 14. 57 15. -8 16. 6 17. -2 18. 0 19. 72 20. -4 21. -20 22. 80 23. -45 24. 51 25. -36 26. -24 27. -45 28. 0 29. 77 30. -60 31. 78 32. -72 33. 12 34. 35 35. 40 36. -12 37. -26 38. 60 39. -60 40. 0 41. 40 42. 1 43. 25 44. 48 45. 63 46. 60 47. -21 48. 18 49. -2 50. 6 51. -9 52. -13 53. -8 54. -8 55. -7 56. -21 57. 6 58. 7 59. 0 60. 23 61. -8 62. -2 63. -4 64. -16 65. 8 66. -9 67. 3 68. -2 69. 2 70. 6 71. -6 72. 3

Page 82 1. $-9\frac{1}{2}$ 2. -9.8 3. 5.33 4. -9.3 5. $1\frac{1}{8}$ 6.
-1.128 7. $\frac{1}{10}$ 8. -11 9. 5 10. $-1\frac{2}{3}$ 11. 19 12. -11.54 13.
$-10\frac{9}{10}$ 14. 5.95 15. 0 16. -6.049 17. $-2\frac{1}{2}$

Page 83 1. n=-4 2. x=-15 3. b=-15 4. p=1 5. z=-2
6. t=2 7. b=-43 8. t=-1 9. y=-45 10. n=19 11. d=-9 12.
k=-7 equations: 1. 57-9 2. (q+8) 3. s=43 4. w=98 5. 7x
6. b=55 7. a/15 8. r=61 9. y=59 10. c=40 11. t=26 12.
m=336

Page 84 1. A=4 2. B=5 3. C=15563 4. E=17 5. F=10.91
6. G=9.8432718

Page 88 1. D 2. G 3. K 4. C 5. M 6. B 7. J 8. N 9. H
10. A 11. F 12. L 13. I 14. E 15. O

Page 90 ACROSS 1. plateau 3. desert 5. cape 7. isthmus
8. prairie 9. lagoon 10. tundra 11. glacier 12. volcano 16.
jungle 18. fjord DOWN 2. archipelago 4. swamp 6. mesa
14. atoll 15. butte 17. gulf

Page 91 Canada: 1. Arctic Ocean 2. Banks Island 3. Victoria
Island 4. Queen Elizabeth Islands 5. Ellesmere Island 6. Baffin
Island 7. Newfoundland 8. Labrador 9. Labrador Sea 10. *St.
Johns 11. Prince Edward Island 12. Gulf of St. Lawrence 13.
Lle d'Anticosti 14. Charlottetown 15. Nova Scotia 16.
*Halifax 17. New Brunswick 18. *Fredericton 19. Atlantic
Ocean 20. *Ottawa 21.*Toronto 22. Lake Hurron 23. St.
Lawrence River 24. *Quebec City 25. Appalachian Mnts. 26.
Quebec 27.James Bay 28. Hudson Bay 29. Ontario 30. Lake
Winnipeg 31. Manitoba 32. *Winnipeg 33. Saskatchewan
34.*Regina 35. *Edmonton 36. Alberta 37. Great Slave Lake
38. *Yellowknife 39. Northwest Territories 40. Great Bear
Lake 41. Mackenzie River 42. Yukon Territory 43.
Whitehorse 44. British Columbia 45. Fraser River 46. Coast
Mnts. 47. *Victoria 48. Vancouver Island 49. Pacific Ocean
50. Rocky Mnts. 51. Laurentian Mnts.

Page 92 ACROSS 1. coastline 4. Eskimo 6. dominion 8.
Antarctica 10. Prime Minister 11. bagpipes 14.
parliamentary 16. second 17. kilts DOWN 2.
Auroraborealis 3. O Canada 5. Klondike 7. Intuit 9.
independence 12. French 13. Britain 15. Montreal

Page 93 1. Macdonald 2. Lampton 3. English, French 4.
dollar 5. Maple 6. Ottawa, Ontario 7. Quebec 8. Arctic,
tundra 9. bilingual 10. mosaic, ethnic 11. Mounties, beaver

Page 94 1. Wyoming, Cheyenne 2. Hawaii, Honolulu 3.
Texas, Austin 4. Pennsylvania, Harrisburg 5. Alaska, Juneau
6. Oregon, Salem 7. Iowa, Des Moines 8. Vermont,
Montpelier 9. Maryland, Annapolis 10. Virginia, Richmond
11. Kansas, Topeka 12. Minnesota, St. Paul 13. California,
Sacramento 14. Georgia, Atlanta 15. Montana, Helena 16.
South Carolina, Columbia 17. New Hampshire, Concord 18.
Maine, Augusta 19. Idaho, Boise 20. Nebraska, Lincoln 21.
New Mexico, Santa Fe 22. Ohio, Columbus 23. Wisconsin,
Madison 24. Delaware, Dover 25. Nevada, Carson City 26.
New Jersey, Trenton 27. Michigan, Lansing 28. Rhode

Island, Providence 29. Illinois, Springfield 30. Connecticut,
Hartford 31. Arkansas, Little Rock 32. Utah, Salt Lake City
33. Mississippi, Jackson 34. Massachusettes, Boston 35.
Florida, Tallahassee 36. North Carolina, Raleigh 37.
Colorado, Denver 38. Tennessee, Nashville 39. North
Dakota, Bismarck 40. Indiana, Indianapolis 41. South
Dakota, Pierre 42. Arizona, Phoenix 43. Oklahoma,
Oklahoma City 44. New York, Albany 45. Kentucky,
Frankfort 46. Missouri, Jefferson City 47. Washington,
Olympia 48. Louisiana, Baton Rouge 49. Alabama,
Montgomery 50. West Virginia, Charleston

Page 95 1. Maine 2. Maryland 3. Rhode Island 4. New
York 5. Pennsylvania 6. Vermont 7. Delaware 8.
Massachusetts 9. Connecticut 10. New Hampshire 11. New
Jersey NEW ENGLAND - Vermont, New Hampshire,
Maine, Massachusetts, Rhode Island, Connecticut MID-
ATLANTIC - New York, New Jersey, Pennsylvania,
Maryland,Delaware

Word Search Answers:

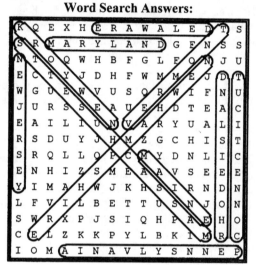

Page 96 Southern Region 1. Texas, *Austin 2. Arkansas,
*Little Rock 3. Louisiana, *Baton Rouge 4. Tennessee,
*Nashville 5. Mississippi, *Jackson 6. Alabama,
*Montgomery 7. Georgia, *Atlanta 8. Florida, *Tallahassee
9. South Carolina, *Columbia 10. North Carolina, *Charlotte
11. Kentucky, *Frankfort 12. Virginia, *Richmond 13. West
Virginia, *Charleston (From top to bottom) Mississippi,
West Virginia, Georgia, Alabama, Virginia, Tennessee, South
Carolina, North Carolina, Louisiana, Tennessee

Page 97 Midwest Region 1. OK 2. IA 3. MI 4. KS 5. WI
6. SD 7. MN 8. OK 9. ND 10. MO 11. NE
1. North Dakota, *Bismarck 2. South Dakota, *Pierre
3. Nebraska, *Lincoln 4. Kansas, *Topeka 5. Oklahoma,
*Oklahoma City 6. Minnesota, *St. Paul 7. Iowa, *Des
Moines 8. Missouri, *Jefferson City 9. Wisconsin, *Madison
10. Illinois, *Springfield 11. Indiana, *Indianapolis 12. Ohio,
*Columbus 13. Michigan, *Lansings

Page 98 Capitals (from top to bottom) 11, 7, 5, 13, 12, 3, 8,
2, 4, 1, 9, 6, 10 Cities (from top to bottom) 13, 10, 1, 5, 2,
3, 6, 7, 8, 12, 4, 9, 11

Page 99 Branch-Executive, Who? President, What? Carry out and enforce laws, How? Commander in Chief of Armed Forces, Cabinet and Executive Staff. Branch-Legislative, Who? Congress (Senate & House of Representatives), What? Make the Laws, How? Laws passed by majority vote. Branch-Judicial, Who? Supreme Court and Lower Courts, What? To interpret or explain laws, How? Hears and makes decisions about cases involving questions about the Constitution, Federal Laws, treaties and shipping.

Page 100 The three sections of the flag are (from left to right) green, white and red. The emblem in the middle is brown.

The Aztecs were looking for a place to settle. Their Gods told them to look for the place where an Eagle stood on a cactus with a snake in it's mouth. They saw this in the middle of a lake, and founded their capital, Tenochtitan (later Mexico City) on the spot.

Page 101 Central America 1. Belmopan, *Belize 2. Guatemala, *Guatemala City 3. Honduras, *Tegucigalpa 4. El Salvador, *San Salvador 5. Nicaragua, *Managua 6. Costa Rica, *San Jose 7. Panama, *Panama City

Page 102 1. Bahamas Islands 2. Windward 3. Caribbean 4. Straight of Florida 5. Hispanola 6. Caribbean 7. European 8. Dutch 9. Rimland 10 Poverty

Page 103 South America 1. Venezuela, *Caracas 2. Columbia, *Bogota 3. Ecuador,*Quito 4. Peru, *Lima 5. Guyana,*Georgetown 6. Suriname, *Paramaribo 7. French Guiana, *Cayenne 8. Brazil, *Brasilia 9. Bolivia, *La Paz and Sucre 10. Chile, *Santiago 11. Argentina, *Buenos Aires 12. Paraguay, *Asuncion 13. Uruguay, Montevideo

Page 104 "What hath God Wrought!"

Page 105 Answers will vary

Page 106 Western & Eastern Europe - **Western** - 1.Malta, *Valletta 2. Italy, *Rome 3. San Marino, *San Marino 4. Vatican, *Vatican 5. France, *Paris 6. Monaco, *Monaco 7. Spain, *Madrid 8. Andorra, *Andorra La Vella 9. Portugal, *Lisbon 10. Switzerland, *Bern 11. Austria, *Vienna 12. Liechtenstein, *Vaduz 13. Montenegro, *Belgrade 14. Belgium, *Brussels 15. Netherlands, *Amsterdam 16. Germany, *Berlin 17. Denmark, *Copenhagen 18. Iceland, *Reykjavik 19. Finland, *Helsinki 20. Sweden, *Stockholm 21. Norway, *Oslo 22. Greece, *Athens 23. Ireland, *Dublin 24. England, *London 25. Cardiff 26. Scotland, *Edinburgh 27. N. Ireland, *Belfast 28. Gibraltar (UK), *Gibraltar **Eastern** 29 Russia, *Moscow 30. Poland, *Warsaw 31. Ukraine,*Kiev 32. Belarus, *Minsk 33. Romania, *Bucharest 34. Hungary, *Budapest 35. Lithuania, *Vilnius 36. Latvia, *Riga 37. Estonia, *Tallinn 38. Bulgaria, *Sofia 39. Albania, *Tirana 40. Czech Republic, *Prague 41. Slovak Republic, *Bratislava 42. Bosnia / Herzegovina, *Sarajevo 43. Croatia, *Zagreb 44. Slovenia, *Ljubljana 45. Moldova, *Kishinev 46. Macedonia, *Skopje 47. Serbia, *Belgrade 48. Turkey, *Estanbul 49. Kaliningrad, Russia 50. Wales

Page 107 Answers will vary

Page 108 ACROSS 3. Hera 5. Ares 6. Cronus 7. Aphrodite 12. Hebe 13. Poseidon 15. Persephone 16. Hades 17. Artemis 18. Erinyes DOWN 1. Zeus 2. Thetis 4. Athena 5. Apollo 8. Hephaestus 9. Iris 10. Eros 11. Hermes 14. Demeter

Page 109 241BC-H, 218BC-C, 206BC-J, 202BC-M, 60BC-E, 44BC-A, 31BC-AD14-G, AD98-117-B, AD117-138-L, AD138-161-I, AD193-D, AD293-K, AD306-337-N, AD391-F

Page 110 Answers will vary. Some Examples: Page-Began in household of lord at age 7, learned to ride a horse, received religious training and instruction on table manners, hunting and dancing. Squire-Became assistant to a knight at age 12-13, looked after knight's weapons and armor, became skilled in their use, served knight his meals, followed him into battle (only one squire was allowed to assist in tournaments), older squires began entering tournaments, went through "ordeal" right before becoming an accolade. Knight-sworn to uphold code of chivalry, fought on horseback, owned expensive armor, weapons and horses, owned land and castles, fought in the Crusades.

Page 111 KUSH Where? South of Egypt, When? 750BC-AD150 History? Dominated by Egypt, learned much of their culture, Resources? Iron tools, gold objects, Accomplishments? Defeated Egypt, was a center of culture ETHIOPIA Where? between the Nile River and the Red Sea, When? about AD325 to present, History? rich and powerful trade center, King Ezana became a Christian in AD324, Resources? Location between the Red Sea and the African Interior, Accomplishments? Destroyed Meroe, it's major trade city Axum remained Christian and undefeated MALI Where? West Africa on Senegal and West Niger rivers, When? AD1235-1468, History? emerged after fall of Ghana trade and learning center Timbuktu, Resources? Gold, salt for trade, Accomplishments? a learned, rich and generous city, they were great traders. SONGHAI Where? West African Niger river, When? About 1464-1591, History? Controlled West Africa after conquering Mali, Resources? Salt, Trading center at Timbuktu, Accomplishments? Great trade center, center of commerce, Tarhaza where houses were built of salt slabs

Page 112 1. L 2. F 3. N 4. B 5. R 6. J 7. D 8. S 9. P 10. C 11. M 12. G 13. Q 14. A 15. I 16. T 17. O 18. E 19. K 20. H Time Out: Answers will vary

Page 113 1. Artists 2. Scientists 3. Writers 4. Religious Reformers 5. Queens 6. Italian City-States 7. Inventors 8. Kings/Absolute Monarchs 9. Poets 10. Composers 11. Vocal Composers

Page 114 ACROSS 3. Vespucci 5. Hudson 9. Cabral 10. Daverrazano 11. Pizarro 12. Drake DOWN 1. De Balboa 2. Cabot 4. Ponce De Leon 6. Dechamplain 7. Cortes 8. Magellan 9. Columbus 10. Dagama 12. Dias

Page 115 Sample Answers: 1. Effect: Improved technology, caused growth of the working middle class, growth of cities 2. Effect: French Revolution 3. Cause: Peter the Great traveled incognito through Europe and became convinced that Russia was backward in technical and social development. 4. Effect: Rise of Lenin and the Communist Revolution 5. Cause: Stalin began a series of "5 Year Plans" to modernize Russia 6. Effect: World War I 7. Cause: Germans blame the Treaty of Versailles and economic depression for their troubles 8. Effect: Germany and the Axis Powers loose World War II 9. Cause: Allied leaders met at Yalta to plan Europe's future

Page 116 From left to right: 17. 2590BC, 1. 1500BC, 9. 1200BC, 6. 776BC, 11. 753BC, 5. 202BC, 18. 0, 10. AD641, 2. AD750, 19. AD790, 8. AD1175, 12. AD1200, 7. AD1614, 20. AD1760, 3. AD1761, 14. AD1776, 13. AD1789, 16. AD1863, 4. AD1917, 15. AD1989

Page 118 1. H 2. A 3. V 4. E 5. A 6. G 7. O 8. O 9. D 10. S 11. U 12. M 13. M 14. E 15. R 16. ! The message is "HAVE A GOOD SUMMER!"

Page 119 North America 1. United States of America, *Washington D.C. 2. Greenland, *Godthab 3. Canada, *Ottawa 4. Mexico, *Mexico City 5. Guatemala, *Guatemala 6. Belize, *Belmopan 7. Honduras, *Tegucigalpa 8. El Salvador, *San Salvador 9. Nicaragua, Managua 10. Costa Rica, *San Jose 11. Panama, *Panama City 12. Grenada, *St. George's 13. Barbados, *Bridgetown 14. St. Vincent & The Grenadines 15. St. Lucia, *Castries 16. Dominica, *Roseau 17. Antigua, *St. Johns 18. St. Kitts-Nevis 19. Puerto Rico, *San Juan 20. Dominican Republic, *Santo Domingo 21. Haiti, *Port-au-Prince 22. Jamaica, *Kingston 23. Cuba, *Havana 24. Bahamas, *Nassau 25. Gulf Of Mexico 26. Caribbean Sea 27. Atlantic Ocean 28. Arctic Ocean 29. Pacific Ocean 30. Hudson Bay 31. Mississippi River 32. Colorado River 33. Mackenzie River 34. Rocky Mnts.

Page 120 Caribbean 1. Atlantic Ocean 2. Gulf Of Mexico 3. Caribbean Sea 4. Pacific Ocean 5. Tropic Of Cancer 6. Greater Antilles 7. Lesser Antilles 8. Netherland Antilles 9. Leeward Islands 10. Windward Islands 11. Island Of Hispaniola 12. Puerto Rico, *San Juan (USA) 13. Dominican Republic * Santo Domingo 14. Cuba, *Havana 15. Jamaica, *Kingston 16. Bahamas Islands 16b. *Nassau 17. USA Virgin Islands 18. British Virgin Islands 19. Barbuda & Antigua, *St. Johns 20. Guadeloupe, *Basse-Terre (Fr.) 21. St. Kitts-Nevis 22. Montserrat (UK) 23. Dominica, *Roseau 24. Martinique, *Fort-de-France 25. St. Lucia, *Castries 26. St. Vincent & The Grenadines, *Kingstown 27. Barbados, *Bridgetown 28. St. George's, *Grenada 29. Tobago 30. Trinidad, *Port Of Spain 31. Bonaire 32. Curacao 33. Aruba 34. South America 35. Central America 36. Mexico 37. Yucatan Channel 38. Cayman Islands 39. Florida 40.Straits Of Florida 41. Turks & Caicos Islands (UK) 42 Islands known as-West Indies. 43. Haiti, *Port-au-Prince

Page 121 South America 1. Argentina, *Buenos Aires 2. Bolivia, *La Paz 3. Brazil, *Brasilia 4. Chile, *Santiago 5. Peru, *Lima 6. Ecuador, *Quito 7. Columbia, * Bogota 8. Venezuela, *Caracas 9. Guyana, *Georgetown 10.Suriname, *Paramaribo 11. French Guiana, *Cayenne 12. Paraguay,

*Asuncion 13. Uruguay, *Montevido 14. Trinidad & Tobago, *Port Of Spain 15. Equator 16. Atlantic Ocean 17. Pacific Ocean 18. Andes Mnts. 19. Amazon River 20. Tapajos River 21. Branco River. 22. Negro River 23. Orinoco River

Page 123 1. 24 One zone for each hour in the day. The amount of time it takes the earth to rotate on its axis. 2. longitude 15° 3. 0° 4. A. 4am B. 3pm C. 2am D. 6am E. 10pm F. 7am 5. west, east 6. 24, 1 day, lose 7. 4, 5 8. Answers will vary 9. 360°

Page 124 Africa 1. Somalia, *Mogadishu 2. Ethiopia, *Addis Ababa 3. Djibouti, *Djibouti 4. Eriteria, *Asmera 5. Uganda, *Kampala 6. Rwanda, *Kigali 7. Burundi, *Bujumbura 8.Tanzania, *Dar-es-Salaam 9. Kenya, *Nairobi 10. Gabon, *Libreville 11. Congo, *Brazzaville 12.Central African Republic, *Bangui 13. Sudan, *Khartoum 14. Zaire, *Kinshasa 15. Equatorial Guinea, *Malabo 16. Cameroon, *Yaounde 17. Chad, *N'Djamena 18. Sao Tome & Principe, * Sao Tome 19. Mali, *Bamako 20. Mauritania, *Nouakchott 21. Burkina Faso, *Ouagadougou 22. Benin, * Porto-Novo 23. Senegal, *Dakar 24. Niger, *Niamey 25. Ivory Coast, *Abidjan 26. Guinea, *Conakry 27. Liberia, *Monrovia 28. Sierra Leone, *Freetown 29. Gambia, * Banjul 30.Guinea-Bissau, *Bissau 31. Nigeria, *Abuja 32. Ghana, *Accra 33. Togo, *Lome 34. Namibia, *Windhoek 35. Lesotho, *Maseru 36. Zimbabwe, *Harare 37. Swaziland, *Mbabane 38. *Mozambique, *Maputo 39. South Africa, *Cape Town 40. Botswana, *Gaborone 41. Angola, *Luanda 42. Zambia, *Lusaka 43. Malawi, *Lilongwe 44. Madagascar, *Antananarivo 45. Comoros, *Maroni 46. Seychelles, *Victoria 47. Cape Verde, *Praia 48. Mauritius, *Reunion 49. Western Sahara, *El Aajun 50. Egypt, *Cairo 51.Tunisia, *Tunis 52. Morocco, *Rabat 53. Libya, *Tripoli 54. Algeria, *Algiers. 55. Lake Victoria 56. Indian 57. Red Sea 58. Mediterranean 59. Atlantic Ocean

P 125 Asia 1. Russia, *Moscow 2. Mongolia, *Ulaanbaatar 3. China, *Beijing 4. North Korea, *Pyongyang 5. South Korea, *Seoul 6. Japan, *Tokyo 7. Taiwan, *Taipei 8. Philippines, *Manila 9. Brunei, *Bandar Seri 10.Malaysia, *Kuala Lumpur 11. Indonesia, *Jakarta 12. Singapore, *Singapore 13. Vietnam *Hanoi 14. Cambodia, *Phnom Penh 15. Laos, *Vientiane 16. Thailand, *Bangkok 17. Myanmar, Yangon 18. Bangladesh, *Dhaka 19. Bhutan, *Thimphu 20. Nepal, *Kathmandu 21. India, *New Delai 22. Sri Lanka, *Colombo 23. Maldives, *Male 24. Pakistan, *Islamabad 25. Afghanistan, *Kabul 26. Iran, *Tehran 27. Iraq, *Baghdad 28. Kuwait, Kuwait City 29. Saudi Arabia, *Riyadh 30. Quatar, *Doha 31. Bahrain, *Manama 32. United Arab Emirates, *Abu Dhabi 33. Oman, *Muacat 34. Yemen, *Sana'a 35. Cyprus, *Nicosia 36. Israel *Jerusalem 37. Jordan, *Amman 38. Lebanon, *Beirut 39. Syria, *Damascus 40. Turkey, *Ankara 41. Kazakhstan, *Alma Ata 42. Kyrgyzstan, *Bishkek 43. Tajikistan, *Dushanbe 44. Uzbekistan, *Tashkent 45. Turkmenistan, *Ashkhabad 46. Azerbaijan, *Baku 47. Armenia, *Yerevan 48. Georgia, *Tebilisi 49. Black Sea 50. Caspian Sea 51. Mediterranean Sea 52. Red Sea 53. Persian Gulf 54. Arabian Sea 55. Indian Ocean 56. Bay Of Bengal 57. South China Sea 58. East China Sea 59. Sea Of Japan 60. Pacific Ocean 61. Sea Of Okhotsk 62. Bering Sea 63. Arctic Ocean

Page 126 Oceania 1. Western Australia, *Perth
2. Northern Australia, * Darwin 3. South Australia, Adelaide
4. Queensland, *Brisbane 5. New South Wales, *Sydney
6. Victoria, *Melbourne 7. Australian Capital Territory,
*Canberra 8. Tasmania, *Hobart 9. Papua New Guinea, *Port
Moresby 10. New Zealand 11. South Island 12. North Island,
*Wellington 13. New Caledonia (Fr.), *Noumea 14. Solomon
Islands 15. Vanuatu, *Vila 16. Fiji, *Suva 17. Hawaiian
Islands 18. Tahiti, *Papeete 19. Tonga, *Nuku'alofa
20. French Polynesia 21. Tropic of Capricorn 22. International
Date Line 23. Cook Islands 24. North Pacific Ocean 25. South
Pacific Ocean

Page 130 ACROSS 3. evolution 4. botanist 8. extinct 9.
key 11. adaptation 14. species **DOWN** 1. Moneran 2.
classifying 5. natural 6. kingdom 7. plant 10. fungus 12.
Protist 13. animal

Page 131 1. Pluto 2. Equal Night and Day 3. A deciduous
tree sheds its leaves annually, while a non-deciduous tree is
evergreen. 4. It is warm blooded, breathes air, bears its young
alive, and feeds them milk. 5. They are all crystals. 6. Eight
7. Galileo 8. Vasco Nunez de Balboa 9. No 10. Thomas
Alva Edison 11. Neil Armstrong 12. Each has a hexagonal
pattern and no two are alike. 13. Opossum 14. Water from
the earth evaporates into the atmosphere where it is condensed
and falls back to earth as rain. 15. 3 Months (or 90 days) 16.
They don't have eye lids. 17. Neptune

Page 132 1. ocean 2. water 3. necessary 4. frozen 5. cycle
6. clouds 7. underneath 8. absorbs 9. sun 10. daylight 11.
precipitation

Page 136 ACROSS 5. lava 10. continental drift 12. core
13. Pangea 14. tension 15. mantle 16. waves **DOWN** 1.
fault 2. compression 3. synclines 4. magnitude 6. plate
tectonics 7. Richter Scale 8. seismograph 9. fracture 11.
anticlines

Page 138 1. crust 2. Mohorovicic discontinuity 3.
lithosphere 4. mantle 5. asthenosphere 6. mesosphere 7.
core 8. outer core 9. inner core 10. Gutenberg discontinuity

Page 141 Answer will vary based upon your body weight.

Page 147 First Drawing: Euglena, Second Drawing:
Amoeba, Third Drawing: Trypanosoma, Fourth Drawing:
Paramecium, Fifth Drawing: Stentor

Page 151 ACROSS 2. Arachnids 5. Aves 6. Crustacia 8.
Regenerate 9. Arthropods 10. Reptiles 11. Amphibians
DOWN 1. Thorax 3. Invertebrates 4. Mammals 7.
Annelids

Page 153 1. kidney 2. ovary 3. scale 4. anus 5. intestine
6. stomach 7. fin 8. liver 9. heart 10. mouth 11. eye 12.
dorsal aorta

Page 154 In Order: Geologists, plates, trench, mantle,
magma, volcanoes, mountain. cinder, shield, composite,(in
any order) reservoir, conduit, craters, fissures, Pacific, Igneous,
molten, lava.

Page 155

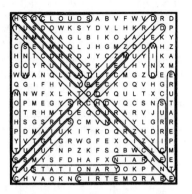

Page 156 1. seismograph 2. earthquake 3. focus 4. fault 5.
Tsunami 6. epicenter 7. landslide 8. after shocks

Page 160 Examples:

SYSTEM	MAJOR ORGAN	FUNCTION
Circulatory	Heart	Pumps blood to all parts of the body
Muscular	Skeletal Muscles	Are used to contract or relax skeletal muscles
Respiratory	Lungs	The exchange of oxygen and carbon dioxide takes place

Page 161 Eye: candle flame, illumination, lens, optic, pupil,
fluorescent, retina, convex, photoelectric, mirror, prism,
hologram, laser, photon, incandescent, farsightedness,
concave, X-rays, iris, violet rays, luminous, infrared rays,
cone, spectrum, ultraviolet, intensity **Ear:** thunder, music,
ultrasonic, listen, harp, sonar, Hz, anvil, cochlea, vibration,
timbre, pitch, auditory nerve, tone, percussion, decibel,
stirrup, intensity

Page 162 ACROSS 1. Aids 2. Goiter 4. Impetigo 10.
Multiplesclerosis 13. Cholera 15. Diabetes 16. Hepatitis
DOWN 1. Arthritis 3. Rheumatic Fever 5. Tuberculosis 6.
Influenza 7. Dysentery 8. Glaucoma 9. Osteoporosis 11.
Leukemia 12. Shingles 14. Colitis

Page 163 1. Cell Membrane 2. Nucleus 3. Vacuole 4.
Cytoplast 5. Nucleus 6. Chloroplast 7. Cell Wall

Page 164 Answers will vary.

Page 165 1. Because the image is reverted and shines back on
the screen 2. Upside down 3. Yes. It will work just like the
process that one sees through one's own eyes.

Page 166 / Page 167 Answers will vary.

TODAY

A Great Time To Be a Kid!

People from throughout the world continue to celebrate the beginning of a new decade and millennium. It is a time of great wonder and excitement as nations look toward a new beginning and future filled with the promise of peace and opportunity. Today's technology breaks down barriers and allows people from different backgrounds the opportunity to explore and learn about things that never before were within their grasp. The Internet gives children in China the chance to learn how families live in Canada. Satellites spinning thousands of miles above the Earth broadcast movies and telephone conversations to people all over the planet.

On a separate sheet of paper, write about how the technology of global communication is changing our world. Discuss in detail the possibilities for greater peace and understanding that may result between people and groups

Welcome to the New

MILLENNIUM

 Summer Bridge Activities • TIME & TECHNOLOGY SECTION
© Rainbow Bridge Publishing • Reproduction Prohibited

TOMORROW

What Will the World be Like in. . .

What will the world be like in 50, 500 or even 1,000 years? Will everyone have a jet-pack instead of a car? Will robots do all of our chores? Will cereal still be around? Nobody really knows, but it sure is fun imagining what it will be like.

In the space below, draw a picture of how you think you will look in 50 years. Include 5 things that you don't have today. Example: flying skateboards, a robot to do your chores, clothes that change on their own.

Place this picture into the time capsule which you will create on the following page.

You......in fifty years!

TIME CAPSULE

Your Very Own!

Fill in the information on the following pages. Once you are finished, fold, roll, or place it into a shoebox, coffee can, or an envelope — this container will be your very own time capsule. Give the capsule to your parents or grandparents to hide for five years. In five summers, open your time capsule to see how much you have changed! People normally hide a time capsule for many years and, maybe even one hundred years! Can you imagine how much they change from the time they made the time capsule until it is opened?

TIME CAPSULE

Information About Myself

Fill in the information below.

Date _____

Name _____

Age _____

Address _____

Grade _____

My school name _____

My friends' names _____

My favorite teacher _____

My favorite subject _____

My favorite pet _____

My favorite sport _____

My favorite TV show _____

My favorite games _____

My favorite Internet site _____

My favorite instrument _____

My favorite car _____

My favorite color _____

My favorite hobbies or interests _____

When I graduate from high school I want to: _____

_____

_____

TIME CAPSULE

Information About Myself

Write a descriptive paragraph about yourself below.

_____

_____

_____

_____

_____

_____

_____

_____

_____

_____

_____

_____

TIME CAPSULE

A Picture of Me

Draw a picture or paste a photo of yourself below.